Good Housekeeping

grilling

More than **275** Perfect
Year-Round Recipes

Tex-Mex Burgers, page 76

Good Housekeeping

grilling

**More than 275 Perfect
Year-Round Recipes**

HEARST BOOKS
A division of Sterling Publishing Co., Inc.

New York / London
www.sterlingpublishing.com

GOOD HOUSEKEEPING
Rosemary Ellis, *Editor in Chief*
Sara Lyle, *Lifestyle Director*
Susan Westmoreland, *Food Director*
Samantha Cassetty, M.S., R.D., *Nutrition Director*
Sharon Franke, *Kitchen Appliances and Technology Director*

Book Design: Anna Christian
Project Editor: Pamela Hoenig
Production Editor: Sarah Scheffel
Photography Credits on page 295

Library of Congress Cataloging-in-Publication Data

Good housekeeping grilling : more than 275 perfect year-round recipes.
    p. cm.
 ISBN 978-1-58816-714-9
1. Barbecuing. I. Good housekeeping (New York, N.Y.)
II. Title: Grilling.
  TX840.B3G66 2011
  641.7'6—dc22
                                      2010028170

10 9 8 7 6 5 4 3 2 1

The Good Housekeeping Cookbook Seal guarantees that the recipes in this cookbook meet the strict standards of the Good Housekeeping Research Institute. The Institute has been a source of reliable information and a consumer advocate since 1900, and established its seal of approval in 1909. Every recipe has been triple-tested for ease, reliability, and great taste.

Published by Hearst Books
A division of Sterling Publishing Co., Inc.
387 Park Avenue South, New York, NY 10016

Good Housekeeping is a registered trademark of Hearst Communications, Inc.
www.goodhousekeeping.com

For information about custom editions, special sales, premium and corporate purchases, please contact Sterling Special Sales Department at 800-805-5489 or specialsales@sterlingpublishing.com.

Distributed in Canada by Sterling Publishing
c/o Canadian Manda Group, 165 Dufferin Street
Toronto, Ontario, Canada M6K 3H6

Distributed in Australia by
Capricorn Link (Australia) Pty. Ltd.
P.O. Box 704, Windsor, NSW 2756 Australia

Manufactured in China

ISBN 978-1-58816-714-9

Tomato, Portobello, and Mozzarella Melts, page 40

Lemon Chicken with Grilled Summer Squash, page 105

Contents

Foreword

For Americans, grilling is not just a cooking method, it's an event. We savor the enticing aromas and incomparable flavors of a backyard barbecue and have extended the grilling season long beyond those summer events. In recent years, grilling has become a bit of a phenomenon, being touted as a great way to cook by everyone from chefs to dieticians. Though they may endorse grilled food for different reasons, there is no denying that juicy steaks and burgers, fresh vegetables, chicken, seafood, panini, pizzas, and even desserts, all taste better when enhanced by the intense heat and savory smoke of the grill. Couple that with amazing ease and versatility and it's clear why grilling is everyone's favorite cooking method. But the best news is you can enjoy luscious grilled food year round. Whether you grill in a hat and gloves (or under an umbrella!) in inclement weather, or prepare one of our outstanding grill pan

recipes from the comfort of your kitchen, we provide the know-how—and more than 275 delectable, triple-tested recipes.

But before you start your grill, bone up on essential tools, techniques, and safety procedures by reviewing "The Way to Great Grilling" on page 10. We discuss the different types of grills—the foolproof gas grill (the favorite of most backyard griller's today), the traditional charcoal grill, and the latest thing in grilling, the electric grill, which allows you to cook without an open flame, so it's perfect for a small deck or patio. An overview of grilling baskets and skewers, instant-read thermometers and a variety of fire starters will help you pick the right gear, and our tips on lighting and maintaining proper heat will help ensure great results. If you want to imbue your food with even more aroma, check out our tips on flavoring the fire. The grill pan is so fast and easy to use, it has become a favorite tool in the weeknight (and dieters') repertoire. Follow our advice on getting the most from your grill pan to enjoy equally delicious grilled meals on those days when you want grilled flavor without stepping outside.

Recipes start with crowd-pleasing appetizers—from quesadillas to bruschetta to wings— you'll be delighted to serve these at any soirée. Pesto and Mozzarella Pizzas and Salmon BLTs are proof that the grill is ideal for preparing pizzas and panini. Our grilled salads offerings will tempt you to fill your salad bowl with healthy options like Grilled Chicken and Mango Salad (and even a grilled Caesar salad) every night. And, of course, because burgers are everyone's favorite grilled food, we offer twenty-five juicy takes, from beef to black bean, many of which can be made in a grill pan.

But the meat of this cookbook is the entrées: Some, like Garden Fresh Chicken Parmesan and Hoisin-Glazed Pork Tenderloin, are ideal for easy weeknight suppers. Plum-Good Baby Back Ribs, Sweet and Tangy BBQ Chicken, and Jamaican Jerk Catfish with Grilled Pineapple require a bit more time, which makes them just right for a leisurely weekend barbecue. Our chapter on rubs, sauces, salsas, and more

will add mouthwatering flavor to even a simple chicken breast. Vegetables and sides are stars on the grill, too: Whether you want to grill a platter of veggies, pop on a packet of potatoes, or serve up Hot Buttered Chili-Lime Corn, we've got you covered.

Desserts on Fire moves beyond classic s'mores to Chocolate, Hazelnut, and Banana Pizza, Toasted Angel Cake with Summer Berries, and Fire-Roasted Nectarines—grand finales! So fire up your grill (or grill pan) and enjoy our triple-tested recipes year round!

—Susan Westmoreland
Food Director, *Good Housekeeping*

The Way to Great Grilling–Outdoors and In

Whether you cook on a shoebox-size hibachi or in a state-of-the-art gas grill with side burners and an infrared rotisserie, you know that grilling imparts an incomparable flavor that no other cooking method can. The intense heat, the savory smoke, and the pleasure of cooking (and eating) outdoors all enhance the natural flavor of top-grade steaks, plump chicken breasts, sparkling seafood, and garden-fresh vegetables.

Before you fire up your grill, spend a few minutes with these pages to assess your grill and utensils, bone up on techniques and flavor-enhancing tricks, and review safety procedures.

TYPES OF GRILLS

Whether you prefer to cook on a gas, charcoal, or electric grill (and some avid grillers own more than one type of grill), manufacturers are now offering consumers an enticing array of options to choose from.

Gas Grills

Offering speed and ease of operation, the gas grill has become America's favorite type of grill. And what's not to like? Open the gas valve, turn on the controls, preheat for about 10 minutes, and you're ready to go. With gas grills—fueled by either liquid propane or natural gas—you've got a world of features to choose from, including:

■ a wide range of BTU capacities, up to almost 50,000 BTUs, depending on the manufacturer

■ stainless steel, cast-iron (holds the heat better for a superior sear), or porcelain-coated cooking grates (makes for easy clean-up)

■ stainless steel or porcelain-coated

flavor bars (V-shaped bars that catch dripping fat and return it to the cooking food in the form of tasty smoke)

- infrared burners for searing
- side burners that allow you to do stovetop cooking while you grill
- a special lower-BTU smoker burner, as well as a smoker box for wood chips
- a rotisserie burner and attachment
- a warming rack, which allows you to stop food from cooking as soon as it's done
- built-in grill thermometers, grill lights, and storage

In terms of size, you can find a gas grill to fit your needs, whether you're cooking for one or the entire neighborhood.

Charcoal Grills

Fueled by charcoal briquettes or natural hardwood charcoal chunks, charcoal grills are, on the whole, less expensive than their gas-powered brethren. Look for a charcoal grill made of heavy-gauge steel; a porcelain-enamel coating will give you better protection from rust. Look for sturdy legs positioned to keep the grill steady. Other features you can look for in a charcoal grill include:

- plated steel, preseasoned cast-iron, or porcelain-enameled cooking grates
- adjustable-height fire grates
- side shelves and bottom storage
- warming rack
- temperature gauge
- removable ash trays for easy cleaning

As with gas grills, you can find a charcoal grill to fit your needs. If you're cooking for one or two, consider the hibachi, a small cast-iron grill that's just right for a pocket-sized patio.

Electric Grill

The electric grill offers an alternative to messing around with propane tanks and charcoal. Plug it in and you're good to go. Or, if you live where charcoal or gas is not allowed on the terrace, patio, or deck, there are tabletop versions as well as full-size electric grills available; just be sure to position your grill within reach of a grounded outlet.

OTHER EQUIPMENT

Cooking over fire calls for some specialized tools, and there are also optional gadgets to consider for easier grilling of fish, kabobs, and so on. Here are the basics, plus some extras:

GRILL TOPPER: If you often grill delicate foods such as seafood and vegetables, you'll want a grill topper, a perforated metal sheet or tray that provides a nearly smooth surface for grilling. Food is less likely to break up or fall through, and you can virtually "stir-fry" cut-up foods over the flames.

GRILLING BASKETS: This is another option for delicate or small foods. There are classic fish-shaped baskets (which hold whole fish) as well as square and oblong baskets with long handles to hold kabobs, baby vegetables, or fish fillets. Once the food is inside and the basket is clamped shut, you can turn the entire thing at once—easy!

TONGS: Better than a fork for turning foods, because they don't pierce the surface and release juices. Barbecue tongs should have heatproof handles and rounded ends that won't cut into the food.

SPATULA: Use one with a long, heatproof handle for flipping burgers and moving food around on a grill topper.

SKEWERS: Long metal skewers are a must for kabobs. Choose skewers with flat shafts rather than round ones; food will be less likely to slip or spin around as you turn the skewers.

BASTING BRUSH: A heatproof handle and a long shaft are two definite brush requirements. As for bristles, silicone is the way to go—it's nearly indestructible and has the added benefit of being nonstick, making cleanup a snap. Your next best bet is a brush with natural bristles, which will stand up to heat better than synthetic bristles other than silicone.

THERMOMETERS: Consider two different types of thermometers for grilling ease. The first measures the internal temperature of the food you're cooking (see "Is It Done?," page 15). You

can do this with an instant-read thermometer (available as a dial or a battery-powered digital probe), which is inserted into the center of the food when you think it's getting close to done. Another alternative is a thermometer that consists of a probe that is inserted into the food as it goes onto the grill, which is attached to a digital readout that sits outside the grill.

The other kind of thermometer is a grill surface thermometer, which measures the heat of the fire. When you're cooking with charcoal, it takes the guesswork out of determining whether you've got a hot or medium fire (see "How Hot Is Your Fire?," opposite). It's especially useful when you're cooking "low and slow," which requires maintaining an even temperature over many hours.

GRILLING MITTS: A more serious version of oven mitts, these are longer and better insulated, to protect more of your arm from higher heat. Heavy suede mitts are excellent.

BRASS-BRISTLED SCRUB BRUSH: Use this to clean the grill rack. The best time for this? While the grill is still hot.

FOR THE FIRE

Gas and electric grills are easy to light; just follow the manufacturer's directions. A charcoal fire requires a little more finesse. Be sure to leave enough time after starting the fire for the coals to develop a light layer of ash before you start cooking. Allow 20 minutes to be on the safe side.

Getting Started on Your Charcoal Grill

You don't want to run out of heat before your food is cooked, so start with enough briquettes. Estimate the right amount by spreading an even layer over the bottom of the firebox. Before lighting, stack them into a pyramid to allow air to circulate among them. The following are options to help you get the fire going:

CHIMNEY STARTER: This is an open-ended metal cylinder with a handle. Stuff crumpled newspaper in the bottom of it, fill the top portion with briquettes, then light the paper through an opening in the bottom. The briquettes will burn to ash-covered readiness.

ELECTRIC STARTER: A loop-shaped heating element with a handle, this device is placed in a bed of briquettes; plug it in and the briquettes will ignite.

LIQUID FIRE STARTER: Saturate briquettes with the liquid, then wait for a minute before lighting. By the time the coals are ready for proper cooking, the fluid will have burned off and will not affect the flavor of the food. Never add liquid starter to a fire that's already burning or to hot coals; a spark could ignite the whole can.

SOLID FIRE STARTER: Place these waxy-looking cubes in the firebox, pile briquettes on top, and light. They're safer to handle than liquid starter.

SELF-STARTING BRIQUETTES: These are impregnated with starter fluid. A match will ignite them immediately. Don't add them to a fire that's already lit.

HOW HOT IS YOUR FIRE?

You'll know the coals are ready when they are about 80 percent ashy gray (at night, you'll see them glow red). To test the level of heat, hold your palm above the coals at cooking height (about 6 inches): If you can keep your palm over the fire for just 2 to 3 seconds, the fire is hot (above 375°F); 4 to 5 seconds, the fire is medium (above 300°F); 5 to 6 seconds, the fire is low (above 200°F).

Tapping the coals will remove their ash cover and make the fire hotter. Pushing the coals together intensifies the heat; spreading them apart decreases it. Opening the vents on a covered grill increases the temperature, and partially closing them lowers the heat.

8 Safety Rules for the Backyard Chef

1. Make sure the grill is on a level surface and not too close to the house, trees, fences, or even deck railings—all can catch fire from flare-ups or flying sparks.

2. Don't line the bottom of a gas or charcoal grill with aluminum foil; it will obstruct airflow, and the fire will die out faster.

3. Use lighter fluid only to start a fire; don't squirt it onto hot coals to get a dying fire going again, because it can ignite in the can as you pour it.

4. We can't say it too often: Reduce the risk of cross contamination and food poisoning by transferring cooked food from the grill to a clean plate, not one that held raw meat, fish, or poultry.

5. Boil used marinades and glazes for 1 minute if you want to serve them with cooked meat. Or reserve some in a separate dish before it comes in contact with the meat, fish, or poultry.

6. Use long-handled barbecue utensils (not your regular kitchen set) for good reach and control. And watch out for dangling sleeves.

7. Be careful not to serve undercooked meat, poultry, or fish. (See "Is It Done?," opposite, for guidelines.)

8. Don't throw water on flare-ups; it produces steam vapors, which can cause severe burns. Instead, remove the food from the grill until the fire subsides or cover the grill for a few minutes. To prevent flare-ups, trim excess fat from meats.

Choose Your Cooking Method

One of the keys to successful grilling is cooking over the right kind of heat—direct or indirect—over the right level heat for the food you're preparing. Here's a primer to get you started.

DIRECT COOKING: The gas grill is preheated with all the burners on or, in a charcoal grill, the prepared coals are spread evenly. Food is placed on the grill rack directly over the heat source. This method works best with foods that take less than 25 minutes, such as steaks, chops, and vegetables. Direct heat is necessary for searing, which gives meats that nice crusty surface.

INDIRECT COOKING: Place your food on the grill rack of a gas grill, over the drip pan. Preheat the burners on the two outer sides for a three-burner grill (or on one side for a two-burner grill). Set the food over the unheated burner. For a charcoal grill, push the briquettes to the edges of the kettle and place a drip pan in the middle before placing your food on the rack. Indirect cooking is best for longer-cooking meats such as roasts and whole chickens or turkeys, or for delicate foods like fish fillets that might be scorched or dried out by direct heat. Consider placing the food in a pan rather than directly on the grill rack.

TO COVER OR NOT TO COVER? Most grill manufacturers—both gas and charcoal—recommend closing the cover for all grilling. It reduces flare-ups, helps prevent charring, and greatly shortens cooking time.

HIGH VERSUS MEDIUM HEAT: Use high or medium-high heat for thin cuts of meat that cook quickly: skirt steak, thin pork or lamb chops, frankfurters, or shrimp and other shellfish. Use medium heat for $3/4$- to 1-inch-thick rib-eye, tenderloin, or flank steaks; hamburgers; chicken parts; vegetables; fruit; or whole fish. It's a good idea to sear thick steaks over high heat first, then reduce the heat so the meat can cook through. In all of our recipes, we indicate what level of heat to use.

MAINTAINING PROPER HEAT: For long, slow cooking, you may need to adjust the controls on your gas grill. It's a bit trickier with a charcoal model. If the fire is too hot, close or partially close vents (top, bottom, or both); if it's not hot enough, open the vents fully or add more briquettes after each additional hour as the manufacturer recommends. Most gas and some charcoal grills have thermometers that permit you to monitor the interior temperature without lifting the lid (uncovering causes the temperature to drop very quickly).

FLAVORING THE FIRE

It's the delicious taste of food cooked over flames that makes grilling such a popular cooking method. You can enhance the effect by adding flavor to the fire itself, or, more specifically, the smoke that rises from it. This works best in a covered grill, which holds the smoke in. Aromatic woods, such as mesquite or hickory, are well known for the tang they add to grilled meats. Herbs, spices, and other cooking ingredients add their own flavors.

Grilling woods are sold in chunks or chips to be tossed onto a charcoal fire or into foil packets or the smoker box of a gas grill. You want the wood to smoke slowly, not burn quickly, so soak it in water before adding it. Chips require about half an hour of soaking; larger chunks should be soaked for up to two hours. Here's how to suit the wood to the food:

■ Use oak and mesquite, which are strongly flavored, for cooking beef and pork; their smoke can overpower poultry and seafood.

■ Hickory's sweetness is well suited to turkey, chicken, and pork.

■ Fruitwoods, such as apple and cherry, are mild enough to use with chicken and seafood.

If you've got a gas grill, use wood chips, not chunks. If your gas grill doesn't have a smoker box, wrap the chips up in heavy-duty foil, punch a few holes in it, and place it over the flavor bars.

If you're using a charcoal grill, add chunks of wood to the fire from the start; place chips on the coals later in the cooking process.

Dried grapevines give off a subtle wine flavor, and corncobs (dried for a few days after you've cut the kernels off) produce a hickory-like smoke. Partially cracked nuts in the shell, soaked for 15 minutes or so, release their flavors when heated.

Whole spices or fresh or dried herbs can be placed in the smoker box or on the fire to complement the seasonings in a marinade, glaze, or rub (see pages 266–271). Soak them for about 30 minutes before using. Fennel is traditional for grilling fish, while rosemary, thyme, bay leaves, and cilantro are other options. Experiment with other smoke flavorings, such as whole cinnamon sticks or cloves, strips of orange or lemon peel, and whole garlic cloves.

ENTERTAINING OUTDOORS

For many of us, grilling is a year-round proposition, but grilling really comes into its own when you can enjoy the fire-roasted fruits of your labors outdoors. And when you're planning a patio party or barbecue bash, there's no reason not to approach it as you would an indoor shindig and let your personal style shine through. Here are some pointers for your next outdoor soiree from our own *Good Housekeeping* staff:

■ Plant an old wooden tool caddy with potted herbs for a centerpiece.

■ Fill antique bottles with field flowers—arrange five in the middle of the table or put a bottle at each place setting.

■ Press rosemary, basil, or wildflowers such as Queen Anne's lace under the glass of a large picture frame to make a serving tray.

Mediterranean Swordfish Salad, page 70

■ If it's really buggy out, stow everything from barbeque chicken to potato salad to pie in picnic baskets on the table and keep them closed while everyone's eating.

■ Make a colorful, edible centerpiece: peaches, nectarines, and plums, with a sprinkle of berries, arranged in a footed glass bowl.

■ Chill water, soda, seltzer, wine, and beer in old galvanized-steel tubs filled with ice.

■ Arrange long flatbread crackers in an enamel pail or child's beach pail.

■ Offer bread and cheese on a tray covered with pretty leaves. Just make sure they aren't poisonous (mint and basil are good choices)!

■ For dessert, fill a rustic wooden box with four kinds of cookies, and serve with vanilla ice cream. Or tuck a homemade pound cake with sliced fruit into the box.

■ Use colorful cotton dish towels for napkins. Slide cookie cutters (such as butterflies or flowers) over the rolled towels for napkin rings.

■ Place forks, knives, and spoons in small, clean terra-cotta flowerpots.

■ Use miniature pepper or cherry tomato plants as centerpieces.

■ Pour lemonade into old mason jars or retro soda-fountain glasses. To frost glasses, pop them in the freezer for a few hours.

■ Arrange grilled meat on platters lined with banana leaves (sold fresh or frozen in Asian and Hispanic markets) or green-onion tops.

■ Serve dips in a hollowed-out cabbage or radicchio head, or a scooped-out crusty bread round. Cut the top off to make it level, then spoon out the insides, leaving a 3/4-inch-thick border all around so the dip doesn't soak through. (Don't fill bread more than 1 hour ahead of time.)

NOT GUILTY!

Concerned about taking salads or sandwiches made with mayonnaise on a picnic because the mayo might spoil? You're blaming the wrong ingredient: Mayo has a clean record. The rumors began decades ago with homemade mayonnaise, which contains raw eggs; commercial brands, made with pasteurized eggs, have a high acid content (they contain vinegar and lemon juice) that actually prevents the growth of food-poisoning bacteria. The real culprits? Low-acid salad ingredients and sandwich fillings, such as tuna, ham, chicken, eggs, potatoes, and macaroni. When mishandled (left unrefrigerated too long or prepared with hands or utensils that have not been washed properly), they can encourage bacterial growth, even if dressed with mayo.

GOING MOBILE

Want to take your grilling on the road for a picnic at a park? Here are some tips for efficient packing and food safety when you have to leave your refrigerator behind.

■ Gingham-trimmed baskets are romantic, but they won't keep food cold. You need a cooler—and it should be the right size. A full cooler keeps food cold longer than a partially empty one. (If necessary, pack empty space with ice or frozen juice boxes.)

■ For the ultimate in cool, prechill carriers (especially beverage holders) by filling them with ice water and pouring it out just before packing.

■ A cooler can't chill foods that aren't already cold. To be sure foods and drinks are completely cold before stowing, refrigerate them until the last minute. Make dressed salads and cooked meats the night before.

■ To keep things neat and clean at the picnic, do as much prep as possible at home. Wash fruit and lettuce, and pat dry. Shape burgers, cut tomato and onion rounds, slice cheese. Remove chicken or steak from store wrappings, pat dry, and season as desired.

■ Double-bag raw meat, poultry, and seafood—whether it's marinated or not—in zip-tight plastic bags to prevent juices from contaminating other food.

■ Put ice packs next to perishables like chicken and cold cuts, but don't place them directly on top of fragile greens, vegetables, or fruits, which can freeze and then wilt, even through their wrappings.

■ At the grill, have a clean plate on hand for cooked foods. Discard any unused marinade or glaze that's touched raw meat or poultry.

■ Once you've finished eating, pack up the buffet. Discard foods left outdoors for more than two hours. Cold cuts, which are especially sensitive to heat, shouldn't be left out longer than thirty minutes. Refrigerate leftovers as soon as you get home.

GRILLING INDOORS

Even if you're an intrepid, all-weather sort of grillmeister, sometimes grilling outdoors just isn't an option—or you'd simply prefer to get your grill on indoors. But that doesn't mean you can't still enjoy the great taste of grilled food. When you think indoors, think grill pan.

A grill pan is a essentially a skillet with ridges in the bottom. Grill pans come in a wide range of sizes, including griddle-style pans without sides built for cooking over two stovetop burners at once—very useful when you're cooking food for more than two people. You've also got your choice of materials, from the classic cast iron and enameled cast iron to stainless steel and hard-anodized aluminum. One thing to consider when purchasing a grill pan is whether you want a stay-cool handle. If you opt for one without that feature, please remember that the handle will get just as hot as the rest of the pan, so don't absentmindedly grab it. If you do, you'll end up with a nasty burn on the palm of your hand.

We do not recommend buying a grill pan with a nonstick coating; these should not be preheated empty and if they are heated over more than medium heat, the coating can begin to degrade, releasing harmful chemicals. Seasoned cast iron pans are naturally nonstick. Whether you've seasoned your pan or you've bought it preseasoned from the factory, all you need to clean it after each use is a rinse in hot water and a good scrubbing with a stiff brush—no detergent, as that can remove the seasoning. Immediately dry your pan to keep it from rusting. And if it does develop rust, just tackle it with a scouring pad, rinse well, towel dry, and reseason it.

So, can you prepare anything you cook on an outdoor grill in a grill pan? No, but there's an awful lot you can do—all manner of steaks, burgers, lamb, veal, and pork chops, fish steaks and fillets, scallops and shrimp, boneless chicken breasts, and turkey cutlets. Vegetables and greens work too—try whole endive, radicchio, and romaine, as well as asparagus, strips or rings of bell peppers, and thick slices of veggies like squash, eggplant, and fennel. You can also pan-grill slices of pineapple, or peach, plum, or nectarine halves. And try using your grill pan to toast bread for bruschetta.

Grilled Salmon with Herb-Caper Cream, page 220

You can also use your grill pan to make grilled sandwiches or panini. Usually you see people making these on a contact grill or panini press, but a grill pan works just fine. To weight the sandwiches down, you can either set another, smaller, cast-iron pan on top of the sandwiches, or invest in a device that is also, confusingly, called a panini press, a heavy, flat piece of cast iron with a handle.

We've sprinkled an assortment of grill pan recipes throughout the book, and whenever possible, we offer grill pan variations—including lots of great burgers you can grill up on your stovetop. From Sizzling Shrimp Quesadillas and Croque Monsieur to Pan-Grilled Pork Cutlets and Coriander Steak with Warm Corn Salad, these easy-to-execute recipes all boast great grilled flavor.

Whether you're inside or outdoors, happy grilling!

Appetizers

Nothing says "patio party" like finger foods and tasty tidbits hot off the grill. We've supplied you with a baker's dozen (plus one) of easy-to-put-together starters with oh-so-big flavors.

If you've got a package of pita or tortillas, try Grilled Pitas with Caramelized Onions and Goat Cheese or one of our deliciously cheesy quesadillas, cut into smaller appetizer-sized wedges. Or make the most of juicy, summer-ripe tomatoes and serve them as part of one of our crispy grilled bruschettas. Serve up a platter of personal-sized skewers—choose one of our Asian satés or opt for Skewered Shrimp, with its bright, refreshing flavors of lemon and dill. Or serve your guests the ultimate finger food—wings. Pick from our grilled interpretation of Buffalo wings, with its traditional blue-cheese dipping sauce, or enjoy the deep, satisfying flavor of Hoisin-Glazed Chicken Wings. You could even forget the main course and make it a party of starters!

Grilled Corn and Jack Quesadillas, page 23

Grilled Pitas with Caramelized Onions and Goat Cheese

Long, slow cooking makes onions very sweet. The onions can be cooked up to three days ahead—just bring them to room temperature before spooning the goat cheese on top.

PREP: 45 minutes   **GRILL:** about 3 minutes
MAKES: 8 appetizer servings

4   tablespoons olive oil
2   jumbo (1 pound each) onions, coarsely chopped
1   teaspoon sugar
¼   teaspoon salt
¼   teaspoon dried tarragon
¼   teaspoon dried thyme
4   (6-inch) pitas, split horizontally in half
6 to 7 ounces soft goat cheese, crumbled
1   tablespoon chopped fresh parsley

1. In nonstick 12-inch skillet, heat 2 tablespoons oil over medium heat. Add onions, sugar, and salt. Cook, stirring frequently, until very soft, about 15 minutes. Reduce heat to medium-low and cook, stirring frequently, until onions are golden brown, about 20 minutes longer.

2. Prepare outdoor grill for direct grilling over low heat.

3. In cup, stir together remaining 2 tablespoons oil, tarragon, and thyme. Brush cut sides of pitas with herb mixture. Spread with goat cheese, then top with caramelized onions.

4. Place pitas, topping side up, on grill rack and grill until bottoms are crisp and topping is heated through, about 3 minutes.

5. To serve, sprinkle with parsley and cut each pita into 4 wedges.

EACH SERVING: About 245 calories, 8g protein, 27g carbohydrate, 12g total fat (4g saturated), 10mg cholesterol, 310mg sodium

> **TIP:** For a tasty variation, try this with whole-wheat pitas, crumbled feta cheese, and fresh snipped dill.

Grilled Corn and Jack Quesadillas

These quesadillas make a fun and simple summer appetizer. To save time, grate the cheese for the quesadillas while the corn is grilling. For photo, see page 20.

PREP: 15 minutes plus cooling
GRILL: about 12 minutes
MAKES: 8 appetizer servings

3   large ears corn, husks and silk removed
4   (8- to 10-inch) low-fat flour tortillas
1   cup shredded reduced-fat Monterey Jack cheese (4 ounces)
½   cup mild or medium-hot salsa
2   green onions, thinly sliced

1. Prepare outdoor grill for covered direct grilling over medium-high heat.

2. Place corn on hot grill rack. Cover grill and cook corn, turning frequently, until brown in spots, 10 to 15 minutes.

3. Transfer corn to plate; set aside until cool enough to handle. When cool, with sharp knife, cut kernels from cobs.

4. Place tortillas on work surface. Evenly divide Monterey Jack, salsa, green onions, and corn on half of each tortilla. Fold tortilla over filling to make 4 quesadillas.

5. Place quesadillas on hot grill rack. Grill, turning once, until browned on both sides, 1 to 2 minutes. Transfer to cutting board; cut each quesadilla into 4 pieces.

EACH SERVING: About 165 calories, 8g protein, 16g carbohydrate, 5g total fat (2.5g saturated), 10mg cholesterol, 470mg sodium

Cubano Quesadillas

The delicious flavors of a Cuban sandwich in a quesadilla!

PREP: 15 minutes   **GRILL:** 2 to 3 minutes
MAKES: 8 appetizer servings

8   (6-inch) low-fat flour tortillas
¼   cup yellow mustard
4   ounces thinly sliced Black Forest ham
8   sandwich-cut dill pickle slices
4   ounces thinly sliced roast pork from the deli
4   ounces thinly sliced part-skim Swiss cheese

1. Prepare outdoor grill for direct grilling over medium heat.

2. Brush 1 side of each tortilla with mustard. Evenly divide ham, pickles, pork, and Swiss cheese on 4 tortillas. Cover with remaining tortillas, pressing firmly.

3. With large metal spatula, place quesadillas on hot grill rack and cook until tortillas are browned and cheese melts, 2 to 3 minutes, carefully turning over once.

4. Transfer quesadillas to large cutting board; let stand 1 minute. To serve, cut each quesadilla into 4 wedges.

EACH SERVING: About 190 calories, 15g protein, 18g carbohydrate, 6g total fat (2g saturated), 27mg cholesterol, 640mg sodium

Sizzling Shrimp Quesadillas

Say adios to skimpy seafood portions. These fully loaded, fiery quesadillas are packed with a pound of spicy shrimp and garnished with fresh guacamole that can be prepared in minutes.

PREP TIME: 38 minutes
GRILL: 2 to 4 minutes per quesadilla
MAKES: 8 appetizer servings

1	pound shelled and deveined large shrimp
¼	teaspoon ground chipotle chile
3	teaspoons olive oil
2	limes
1	large red pepper (6 to 8 ounces), sliced
1	medium onion (6 to 8 ounces), sliced
1	ripe avocado, mashed
½	cup loosely packed fresh cilantro leaves, chopped
½	teaspoon freshly ground black pepper
2	ripe medium tomatoes, chopped
½	serrano chile, seeded and finely chopped
8	soft-taco-size (8-inch) flour tortillas
8	ounces shredded reduced-fat Mexican cheese blend
2	cups shredded romaine lettuce

1. In small bowl, toss shrimp with chipotle chile and 1 teaspoon oil. From limes, squeeze 4 tablespoons juice; set aside.

2. Heat large ridged grill pan on medium-high heat until hot. In large bowl, toss red pepper and onion with remaining 2 teaspoons oil. Place on grill pan and cook until tender and charred, 10 to 12 minutes, turning occasionally. Transfer to large cutting board.

3. Place shrimp on grill pan and cook until shrimp just turn opaque throughout, 5 to 6 minutes, turning once. Transfer shrimp to cutting board. Remove pan from heat and wipe with paper towel. Chop pepper, onion, and shrimp.

4. Meanwhile, prepare guacamole: In small bowl, combine avocado with 2 tablespoons lime juice, half of cilantro, and ¼ teaspoon pepper. Prepare tomato salsa: In another small bowl, combine tomatoes, serrano chile, remaining ¼ teaspoon pepper, and remaining 2 tablespoons lime juice. Set aside.

5. Heat same grill pan on medium. Place 1 tortilla in pan. Sprinkle with one-fourth of shrimp mixture, one-fourth of cheese, and one-fourth of remaining cilantro; top with second tortilla, pressing lightly. Repeat on other side of pan. Cook quesadillas until lightly toasted, about 3 minutes. Carefully turn quesadillas and cook until cheese melts, 1 to 2 minutes longer. Repeat with remaining tortillas to make 4 quesadillas.

6. Cut quesadillas into wedges; serve with guacamole, tomato salsa, and shredded romaine.

EACH SERVING: About 350 calories, 24g protein, 35g carbohydrate, 13g total fat (4g saturated), 101mg cholesterol, 665mg sodium

Tuscan White-Bean Bruschetta

A first course made with slices of grilled bread and the flavors of sunny Tuscany is the perfect way to begin an outdoor dinner cooked on the grill. For an attractive presentation, serve a tray of assorted bruschetta—we provide a trio of additional recipes here—plus a bowl of olives and extra olive oil for drizzling.

PREP: 15 minutes   **GRILL:** 6 to 10 minutes
MAKES: about 24 bruschetta
or 8 appetizer servings

1	long loaf (8 ounces) Italian bread
1	can (15½ to 19 ounces) white kidney beans (cannellini), rinsed and drained
1	tablespoon fresh lemon juice
1	teaspoon minced fresh sage
¼	teaspoon salt
⅛	teaspoon coarsely ground black pepper
3	tablespoons olive oil (see Tip)
3	teaspoons minced fresh parsley
2	garlic cloves, each cut in half

1. Prepare outdoor grill for direct grilling over medium heat, or lightly spray a ridged grill pan with nonstick cooking spray, then heat on medium until hot.

2. Cut off ends from loaf of bread; reserve for another use. Cut loaf on diagonal into ¹/₂-inch-thick slices.

3. In medium bowl, with fork, lightly mash beans with lemon juice, sage, salt, pepper, 1 tablespoon oil, and 2 teaspoons parsley.

4. Place bread slices on hot grill rack or pan and grill until lightly toasted, 3 to 5 minutes on each side. Transfer toast to wire racks to cool slightly. When cool enough to handle, rub 1 side of each toast slice with cut side of garlic. Discard garlic. Brush garlic-rubbed side of each toast with remaining 2 tablespoons olive oil.

5. Just before serving, spoon bean mixture over garlic-rubbed side of toast and sprinkle with remaining 1 teaspoon parsley.

EACH SERVING: about 170 calories, 6g protein, 21g carbohydrate, 6g total fat (1g saturated), 0mg cholesterol, 315mg sodium

> **TIP:** To add more flavor to the beans, use a fruity, full-bodied extra-virgin olive oil.

Tomato and Ricotta Salata Bruschetta

Ricotta salata is a white, firm, lightly salted cheese made from sheep's milk. Look for it in supermarkets, cheese shops, and Italian groceries. If you can't locate it, substitute feta cheese.

PREP: 25 minutes   **GRILL:** 6 to 10 minutes
MAKES: 16 bruschetta or 8 appetizer servings

1   pound (about 5 medium) ripe plum tomatoes, seeded and cut into ½-inch pieces

4   ounces ricotta salata or feta cheese, cut into ½-inch pieces

2   tablespoons extra-virgin olive oil

1   tablespoon finely chopped red onion

1   tablespoon chopped fresh basil

2   teaspoons balsamic vinegar

¼   teaspoon salt

¼   teaspoon coarsely ground black pepper

8   slices (each about 4" by 3" by ½" thick) country-style bread

1   garlic clove, cut in half

1. Prepare outdoor grill for direct grilling over medium heat, or lightly spray a ridged grill pan with nonstick cooking spray, then heat on medium until hot.

2. In medium bowl, gently toss tomatoes with ricotta salata, oil, onion, basil, vinegar, salt, and pepper. If not serving right away, cover tomato mixture and let stand at room temperature for up to 2 hours.

3. Place bread slices on hot grill rack or pan and grill until lightly toasted, 3 to 5 minutes on each side. Rub 1 side of each toast slice with cut side of garlic and cut the toast in half. Discard garlic.

4. Just before serving, spoon tomato mixture over garlic-rubbed side of toast slices.

EACH SERVING: About 140 calories, 4g protein, 14g carbohydrate, 7g total fat, (3g saturated), 13mg cholesterol, 355mg sodium

Goat Cheese and Tomato Bruschetta

You can make the goat-cheese mixture a day ahead, but bring it to room temperature before using; assemble the bruschetta at the last minute. For an even lovelier presentation, use a mix of red and yellow tomatoes and sprinkle with snipped chives.

PREP: 15 minutes   GRILL: 6 to 10 minutes
MAKES: about 24 bruschetta or 8 appetizer servings

1	long loaf (8 ounces) Italian bread
1	package (5½ ounces) soft mild goat cheese, such as Montrachet
1	teaspoon finely chopped fresh oregano
¼	teaspoon coarsely ground black pepper
2	ripe medium tomatoes, seeded and chopped
⅛	teaspoon salt
3	tablespoons olive oil
2	teaspoons finely chopped fresh parsley
2	garlic cloves, each cut in half

1. Prepare outdoor grill for direct grilling over medium heat, or lightly spray a ridged grill pan with nonstick cooking spray, then heat on medium until hot.

2. Cut off ends from loaf of bread; reserve for another use. Cut loaf on diagonal into ½-inch-thick slices.

3. In small bowl, with fork, stir goat cheese, oregano, and pepper until blended. In medium bowl, stir tomatoes, salt, 1 tablespoon oil, and 1 teaspoon parsley.

4. Place bread slices on hot grill rack or pan and grill until lightly toasted, 3 to 5 minutes on each side. Transfer toast to wire racks to cool slightly. When cool enough to handle, rub 1 side of each toast slice with cut side of garlic. Discard garlic. Brush garlic-rubbed side of each toast with remaining 2 tablespoons oil.

5. Just before serving, spread goat-cheese mixture over garlic-rubbed side of toast and top with tomato mixture. Sprinkle with remaining 1 teaspoon parsley.

EACH SERVING: About 180 calories, 6g protein, 16g carbohydrate, 10g total fat (4g saturated), 9mg cholesterol, 280mg sodium

Bruschetta with Tomatoes and Basil

The taste of summer—crunchy grilled bread topped with garden-fresh tomatoes and basil.

PREP: 15 minutes   GRILL: 6 to 10 minutes
MAKES: about 24 bruschetta
or 8 appetizer servings

1   long loaf (8 ounces) Italian bread
1   large garlic clove, cut in half
1¼   pounds plum tomatoes (8 medium), seeded and cut into ¼-inch pieces
2   tablespoons thinly sliced fresh basil
2   tablespoons extra-virgin olive oil
¼   teaspoon salt
⅛   teaspoon ground black pepper

1. Prepare outdoor grill for direct grilling over medium heat, or lightly spray a ridged grill pan with nonstick cooking spray, then heat on medium until hot.

2. Cut off ends from loaf of bread; reserve for another use. Cut loaf on diagonal into ½-inch-thick slices.

3. Place bread slices on hot grill rack or pan and grill until lightly toasted, 3 to 5 minutes on each side. Transfer toast to wire racks to cool slightly. When cool enough to handle, rub 1 side of each toast slice with cut side of garlic. Discard garlic.

4. In small bowl, gently toss tomatoes, basil, oil, salt, and pepper until combined.

5. Just before serving, spoon 1 heaping tablespoon tomato mixture on garlic-rubbed side of each toast slice.

EACH SERVING: About 115 calories, 3g protein, 17g carbohydrate, 5g total fat (1g saturated), 0mg cholesterol, 235mg sodium

---

FRESH TIPS FOR TOMATOES

How to select: Tomatoes should be plump, firm, and unblemished, with a vibrant hue. They'll give slightly to gentle pressure when touched and should have a faint sweet aroma. You can recognize a tomato that's fully vine ripened if the red is darker on the bottom and paler toward the stem. Skip tomatoes that have been refrigerated (check with your produce manager)—chilling below 55°F absolutely kills the flavor.

How to ripen: You have a choice. You can slip tomatoes into a brown paper bag, closed to trap ethylene gas (a natural ripening agent); place them in a bowl and surround them with other fruits (limes, apples, pears, or bananas) to speed up the process; or keep them on the kitchen counter out of direct sunlight. Always stand tomatoes stem side up to protect the delicate "shoulders."

Fired-up Green-Onion Pancakes

These tempting appetizers are cooked right on the grill for a rustic look and great flavor. If you like, the dough can be prepared through step 4 up to 24 hours ahead, covered loosely with greased plastic wrap, and refrigerated. When you're ready, proceed as directed.

PREP: **20 minutes plus dough rising**
GRILL: **4 to 6 minutes per batch**
MAKES: **18 appetizer servings**

1¼ cups warm water (105° to 115°F)
1   package active dry yeast
1   teaspoon sugar
4   cups all-purpose flour, plus more if needed
12   green onions, chopped (about 1⅓ cups)
1   tablespoon olive oil
1   tablespoon Asian sesame oil
2   teaspoons salt
1   teaspoon coarsely ground black pepper

1. Prepare outdoor grill for direct grilling over medium heat.

2. In small bowl, combine warm water, yeast, and sugar; stir to dissolve. Let stand until foamy, about 5 minutes.

3. In large bowl, combine 1¹⁄₂ cups flour, green onions, olive oil, sesame oil, salt, pepper, and yeast mixture. With wooden spoon, stir until blended. Gradually stir in 2¹⁄₂ cups flour. With floured hand, knead mixture until combined.

4. Turn dough onto lightly floured surface and knead 10 minutes, until smooth and elastic, working in more flour (about ¹⁄₄ cup) if needed.

5. Shape dough into ball; place in greased large bowl, turning dough to grease top. Cover with plastic wrap and let stand in warm place (80° to 85°F) until doubled in volume, about 1 hour.

6. Punch down dough. Turn onto lightly floured surface; cover and let rest 15 minutes.

7. Shape dough into 6 balls. With hand, firmly press each ball into an 8-inch round. Place 3 rounds on hot grill rack and grill until grill marks appear on underside and dough stiffens, 2 to 3 minutes. With tongs, turn rounds over and grill until grill marks appear on underside and pancakes are cooked through, 2 to 3 minutes longer. Repeat with remaining dough.

8. To serve, cut each pancake into 6 wedges.

EACH SERVING (2 WEDGES): About 130 calories, 4g protein, 25g carbohydrate, 2g total fat (0g saturated), 0mg cholesterol, 240mg sodium

Gingered Beef and Chicken Saté

No doubt about it, saté makes for a fun outdoor party appetizer. Skewers are served up hot from the grill, with peanut sauce for dipping and our Cucumber Relish to cool the fire.

PREP: 45 minutes plus marinating
GRILL: 3 to 7 minutes per batch
MAKES: 12 appetizer servings

1	pound skinless, boneless chicken breast halves
1	boneless beef top sirloin steak, 1 inch thick (about 1¼ pounds; see Tip)
2	limes
¼	cup plus 1 tablespoon soy sauce
1	tablespoon grated, peeled fresh ginger
2	teaspoons sugar
2	garlic cloves, crushed with garlic press
¼	cup creamy peanut butter
¼	cup very hot tap water
4	teaspoons seasoned rice vinegar
1	tablespoon light (mild) molasses
⅛	teaspoon crushed red pepper
1	recipe Cucumber Relish (page 283)
24	(12-inch) metal skewers

1. Cut chicken breasts lengthwise into ¾-inch-wide strips; place in bowl. Holding knife almost parallel to work surface, slice steak crosswise into thin strips; place in separate bowl.

2. From limes, grate 2 teaspoons peel and squeeze 2 tablespoons juice. In small bowl, with fork, mix lime peel and juice, ¼ cup soy sauce, ginger, sugar, and garlic. Stir half of soy-sauce mixture into chicken and remaining half into beef. Cover both bowls and let stand 30 minutes in the refrigerator.

3. Prepare outdoor grill for direct grilling over medium heat, or lightly spray a ridged grill pan with nonstick cooking spray, then heat on medium until hot.

4. Meanwhile, in medium bowl, with wire whisk, mix peanut butter, hot water, vinegar, remaining 1 tablespoon soy sauce, molasses, and crushed red pepper until smooth.

5. Prepare Cucumber Relish.

6. Separately thread chicken strips and beef strips, accordion-style, onto metal skewers.

7. Place 12 skewers on hot grill rack and grill, turning once, until just cooked through, 3 to 7 minutes. Repeat with remaining skewers. Serve with peanut sauce and relish.

EACH SERVING: About 185 calories, 20g protein, 6g carbohydrate, 10g total fat (2g saturated), 50mg cholesterol, 460mg sodium

TIP: For variety, try strips of boneless pork loin instead of beef. Grill pork satés, turning once, until cooked through, about 8 minutes.

Thai Chicken Saté

Here's another take on saté, this time with chicken marinated in curried coconut milk and teamed with pickled cucumbers. The creamy peanut sauce is kicked up with jalapeño.

**PREP: 45 minutes   GRILL: 5 to 8 minutes
MAKES: 6 appetizer servings**

1	English (seedless) cucumber, thinly sliced crosswise
1½	teaspoons salt
1	tablespoon Thai green curry paste
¼	cup plus ⅓ cup well-stirred unsweetened coconut milk (not cream of coconut)
4	medium skinless, boneless chicken breast halves (about 1¼ pounds total), each cut diagonally into 6 strips
¼	cup creamy peanut butter
2	teaspoons soy sauce
1	teaspoon packed dark brown sugar
⅛	teaspoon ground red pepper (cayenne)
1	tablespoon hot water
¼	cup rice vinegar
3	tablespoons granulated sugar
2	medium shallots, thinly sliced
1	jalapeño chile, seeded and minced
12	(12-inch) metal skewers

1. In medium bowl, toss cucumber with salt; let stand 30 minutes at room temperature.

2. In another bowl, stir together curry paste and ¼ cup coconut milk until blended. Add chicken and turn to coat. Let stand 15 minutes at room temperature, stirring occasionally.

3. Prepare outdoor grill for direct grilling over medium heat.

4. Meanwhile, prepare peanut sauce: In small bowl, with wire whisk, mix peanut butter, soy sauce, brown sugar, ground red pepper, remaining ⅓ cup coconut milk, and hot water until blended and smooth. Transfer sauce to serving bowl. Makes about ⅔ cup.

5. Drain cucumber, discarding liquid in bowl. Pat cucumber dry with paper towels. Return cucumber to bowl; stir in vinegar, granulated sugar, shallots, and jalapeño; cover and refrigerate until ready to serve.

6. Thread 2 chicken strips, accordion-style, on each of 12 metal skewers; discard marinade. Place skewers on hot grill rack. Cover grill and cook, turning skewers once, just until chicken loses its pink color throughout, 5 to 8 minutes.

7. Arrange skewers on platter. Serve with peanut sauce and cucumbers.

EACH SERVING CHICKEN: About 175 calories, 23g protein, 10g carbohydrate, 4g total fat (2g saturated), 60mg cholesterol, 350mg sodium

EACH 1 TABLESPOON PEANUT SAUCE: About 50 calories, 2g protein, 2g carbohydrate, 5g total fat (2g saturated), 0mg cholesterol, 90mg sodium

Grilled Buffalo Wings

Here's a crowd-pleaser. We made the tangy blue-cheese dipping sauce with reduced-fat mayonnaise, cutting calories but not the great taste.

PREP: 20 minutes   **GRILL:** 25 to 27 minutes
MAKES: 8 appetizer servings

BLUE-CHEESE DIPPING SAUCE

1   small container (8 ounces) sour cream (about 15 tablespoons)
4   ounces blue cheese, crumbled (about 1 cup)
¾   cup reduced-fat mayonnaise
1   green onion, finely chopped
2   tablespoons cider vinegar
1   teaspoon Worcestershire sauce
¼   teaspoon salt

BUFFALO WINGS

4   pounds medium chicken wings (about 24)
¾   cup cayenne pepper sauce (see Tip)

celery and carrot sticks

1. Prepare dipping sauce: In small bowl, with wire whisk, mix sour cream, blue cheese, mayonnaise, green onion, vinegar, Worcestershire sauce, and salt until well combined. Cover and refrigerate until ready to use or up to 3 days. Makes about 2 cups.

2. Prepare outdoor grill for covered direct grilling over medium heat.

3. Meanwhile, prepare wings: Separate wings at joints; refrigerate tips for another use. Place wings on hot grill rack over medium heat. Cover grill and cook wings, turning occasionally, until browned, about 20 minutes. Brush wings generously with cayenne pepper sauce and grill, brushing with remaining sauce and turning frequently, until glazed and juices run clear when thickest part of wing is pierced with tip of knife, 5 to 7 minutes longer.

4. Serve wings with dipping sauce and celery and carrot sticks.

EACH SERVING WINGS: About 300 calories, 27g protein, 1g carbohydrate, 20g total fat (6g saturated), 86mg cholesterol, 675mg sodium

EACH 1 TABLESPOON SAUCE: About 45 calories, 1g protein, 1g carbohydrate, 4g total fat (2g saturated), 8mg cholesterol, 105mg sodium

> **TIP:** Cayenne pepper sauce is a milder variety of hot pepper sauce that adds tang and flavor, not just heat. It can be found in the condiment section of the supermarket, near the ketchup.

Hoisin-Glazed Chicken Wings

These wings will make the perfect start to a barbecue featuring Asian flavors.

PREP: 5 minutes **GRILL:** 25 to 27 minutes
MAKES: 8 appetizer servings

¼   cup hoisin sauce
1   tablespoon soy sauce
3   pounds medium chicken wings
    (12 to 16 wings)

1. Prepare outdoor grill for covered direct grilling over medium heat.

2. In cup, combine hoisin sauce and soy sauce.

3. Separate wings at joints; refrigerate tips for another use. Place wings on hot grill rack. Cover grill and cook wings, turning occasionally, until browned, about 20 minutes. Brush wings generously with hoisin glaze and grill, brushing with remaining sauce and turning frequently, until wings are glazed and juices run clear when thickest part of wing is pierced with tip of knife, 5 to 7 minutes longer.

EACH SERVING: About 260 calories, 22g protein, 7g carbohydrate, 16g total fat (4g saturated), 65mg cholesterol, 565mg sodium

Skewered Shrimp

Seafood doesn't get any speedier than these crowd-pleasing kabobs.

ACTIVE TIME: 25 minutes   **TOTAL TIME:** 35 minutes
MAKES: 16 appetizer servings

16 (10-inch) metal or bamboo skewers
2   lemons plus lemon wedges for garnish
2   tablespoons olive oil
1   large clove garlic, crushed with press
4   tablespoons chopped fresh dill plus
    additional sprigs
½   teaspoon salt
¼   teaspoon ground black pepper
2¼ pounds peeled and deveined large shrimp
1   pint grape tomatoes

1. Soak bamboo skewers in hot water at least 20 minutes. Prepare outdoor grill for direct grilling over medium heat.

2. From 2 lemons, grate 4 teaspoons peel and squeeze 2 tablespoons juice. In bowl, with wire whisk or fork, whisk lemon peel and juice, olive oil, garlic, 3 tablespoons chopped dill, salt, and pepper until blended. Add shrimp; toss to coat.

3. Thread shrimp and tomatoes alternately on skewers. Place on grill and cook 4 to 5 minutes or until shrimp are opaque and tomatoes are slightly charred, turning skewers occasionally.

4. To serve, transfer skewers to platter; sprinkle with remaining 1 tablespoon chopped dill. Garnish platter with lemon wedges and dill sprigs.

EACH SERVING: About 85 calories, 13g protein, 2g carbohydrate, 3g total fat (1g saturated), 97mg cholesterol, 170mg sodium

Pizza, Panini, and Other Sandwiches

If you haven't tried pizza on the grill yet, you are in for a crispy, crunchy, gooey, salty, savory, cheesy surprise. Making use of store-bought pizza dough, these recipes take about 20 minutes to put together and require only five minutes on the grill to yield wood-fired flavor you'll never forget. Serve to your family for dinner, or cut them into small pieces and offer them up as appetizers at your next get-together.

How can you make a tasty sandwich even better? Put it on a grill or in a panini press and watch foccacia or sourdough or country-style bread turn golden brown, while your choice of cheese gets all melty and mingles with the other ingredients between the two slices. From Classic Croque Monsieur to Salmon BLTs with Lemon-Dill Mayonnaise or Tuna Melt with Carrot-Raisin Salad, we've got a recipe to satisfy your hunger.

Pesto and Mozzarella Pizzas, page 38

Pesto and Mozzarella Pizzas

Garden tomatoes and basil make wonderful toppings for pizza cooked over the coals. Serve as a main course or cut into wedges for appetizers. For photo, see page 36.

PREP: 25 minutes   GRILL: about 4 minutes
MAKES: 4 pizzas or 4 main-dish servings

nonstick cooking spray

1   pound refrigerated fresh pizza dough from supermarket or pizzeria, at room temperature (see Tip, opposite)
¼   cup refrigerated pesto sauce
3   plum tomatoes, seeded and chopped
8   ounces fresh mozzarella cheese, thinly sliced
½   teaspoon coarsely ground black pepper

1. Prepare outdoor grill for covered direct grilling over medium heat.

2. Spray 2 large cookie sheets with cooking spray. On work surface, divide dough into quarters; spray with cooking spray. Press each piece of dough into a round about ⅛ inch thick. Transfer 2 rounds to each cookie sheet; cover loosely with plastic wrap. (Bring dough and topping ingredients to grill for pizza assembly.)

3. Place dough rounds on hot grill rack. Cover grill and cook until grill marks appear on underside and dough stiffens (dough may puff slightly), 2 to 3 minutes. With tongs, carefully return dough to cookie sheets, grilled side up.

4. Spread pesto on grilled side of dough rounds; top with tomatoes, mozzarella, and pepper.

5. Return pizzas to grill, toppings side up. Cover grill and cook until bottom of dough stiffens and mozzarella begins to melt, 2 to 3 minutes. Cut into wedges to serve.

EACH SERVING: About 530 calories, 19g protein, 59g carbohydrate, 24g total fat (9g saturated), 47mg cholesterol, 275mg sodium

MONTEREY JACK PIZZAS: Prepare recipe as in steps 1, 2, and 3. In step 4, spread *1 cup prepared black-bean dip* on grilled side of dough rounds; top with *1 cup shredded Monterey Jack or pepper jack cheese (4 ounces)*. Finish as in step 5. Transfer pizzas to board; top with *2 cups thinly sliced iceberg lettuce* and *½ cup of your favorite salsa.*

EACH SERVING MONTEREY JACK PIZZA: About 440 calories, 17g protein, 64g carbohydrate, 12g total fat (5g saturated), 25mg cholesterol, 1,080mg sodium

ARUGULA AND TOMATO PIZZAS: In cup, mix *1 tablespoon extra-virgin olive oil* and *1 tablespoon balsamic vinegar*. Prepare recipe as in steps 1, 2, and 3. In step 4, sprinkle *3 cups loosely packed baby arugula or spinach leaves* on grilled side of dough; top with *6 plum tomatoes (about 1 pound)*, thinly sliced, and *2 ounces Parmesan cheese*, thinly shaved with vegetable peeler (about *½ cup*). Finish as in step 5. Transfer pizzas to cutting board; drizzle with balsamic mixture and sprinkle with *¼ teaspoon salt* and *⅛ teaspoon ground black pepper.*

EACH SERVING ARUGULA AND TOMATO PIZZA: About 400 calories, 15g protein, 60g carbohydrate, 12g total fat (4g saturated), 11mg cholesterol, 545mg sodium

Fontina and Pepper Pizza

Impress your guests with individual grilled pizzas topped with Fontina, roasted peppers, and a sprinkle of fresh marjoram.

PREP: 20 minutes   **GRILL:** 5 to 7 minutes
MAKES: 4 pizzas or 4 main-dish servings

1	pound refrigerated fresh pizza dough from supermarket or pizzeria, at room temperature (see Tip)
6	ounces Italian Fontina or Provolone cheese, shredded
2	jarred roasted red and/or yellow peppers, thinly sliced (1 cup)
1	tablespoon chopped fresh marjoram or thyme

1. Prepare outdoor grill for covered, direct grilling over medium-low heat.

2. Cut dough into 4 equal pieces. On one end of oiled cookie sheet, with fingertips, spread and flatten 1 piece of dough to about ⅛-inch thickness. (Edge does not need to be even.) On same cookie sheet, repeat with another piece of dough. Repeat with a second oiled cookie sheet and remaining dough.

3. Place all 4 pieces of dough, oiled side down, on hot grill rack. Cook until grill marks appear on underside (dough will stiffen and puff), 2 to 3 minutes.

4. With tongs, turn crusts over. Working quickly, arrange equal amounts Fontina and peppers on each crust. Cover grill and cook pizzas until undersides are evenly browned and cooked through, 3 to 4 minutes longer.

5. Transfer to cutting board; sprinkle with marjoram. Cut into wedges.

EACH SERVING: About 465 calories, 18g protein, 57g carbohydrate, 18g total fat (9g saturated), 49mg cholesterol, 640mg sodium

THREE-CHEESE PIZZA: Prepare pizza recipe as directed through step 3. In step 4, top crusts with *4 ounces fresh mozzarella cheese,* coarsely shredded; then dollop with *½ cup part-skim ricotta cheese,* and sprinkle with *⅓ cup freshly grated Pecorino Romano cheese* and *½ teaspoon coarsely ground black pepper.* In step 5, sprinkle *1 tablespoon chopped fresh parsley* over pizzas.

EACH SERVING THREE-CHEESE PIZZA: About 435 calories, 18g protein, 56g carbohydrate, 15g total fat (7g saturated), 38mg cholesterol, 260mg sodium

> **TIP:** Look for fresh pizza dough in the dairy section of your supermarket, usually near the tortillas. (Frozen pizza dough is also available. Allow several hours for it to thaw before using.) Or you can purchase dough from a local pizzeria; they'll usually sell it to you in 1-pound balls if you ask.

Tomato, Portobello, and Mozzarella Melts

To clean portobello mushrooms, wipe the caps with a damp paper towel to remove any dirt— never soak them in water.

PREP: 10 minutes   GRILL: 7 to 10 minutes
MAKES: 2 sandwiches or 4 servings

2	cups loosely packed arugula or watercress, trimmed
2	tablespoons balsamic vinegar
1	loaf (about 1 inch thick) focaccia or ciabatta bread
4	large portobello mushrooms (about 1 pound total), stems removed and each cut in half
2	ripe medium tomatoes (6 to 8 ounces each), cut into ¾-inch-thick slices
2	tablespoons extra-virgin olive oil
¼	teaspoon salt
¼	teaspoon coarsely ground black pepper
4	ounces fresh mozzarella cheese, thinly sliced

1. Prepare outdoor grill for direct grilling over medium-high heat.

2. In small bowl, toss arugula and vinegar until evenly coated. From loaf of focaccia, with serrated knife, cut two 8" by 2" pieces. Cut each piece horizontally in half to make a total of four 8" by 2" pieces.

3. Brush mushrooms and tomatoes on both sides with oil; sprinkle with salt and pepper. Place mushrooms, stem-sides up, and tomatoes on hot grill rack and cook until tender and charred, 6 to 8 minutes, turning over once. Transfer tomatoes to plate. Arrange mozzarella on mushrooms; cover and cook until cheese melts, 1 to 2 minutes longer.

4. Place bread, cut-sides up, on work surface; top with arugula mixture, grilled tomatoes, and cheese-topped mushrooms. Cut each sandwich in half and serve immediately.

EACH SERVING: About 355 calories, 14g protein, 43g carbohydrate, 15g total fat (5g saturated), 22mg cholesterol, 595mg sodium

A KINDER CUT

Unless you have a razor-sharp edge on a chef's knife, you're better off using a serrated knife on a tomato, which will glide effortlessly through the skin and flesh instead of crushing it into a pulpy mess. Tip: To retain the juice inside the tomato, not on the cutting board, slice tomatoes from stem to blossom end instead of crosswise.

Croque Monsieur

A delicious take on a French classic.

PREP: **15 minutes**   GRILL: **10 minutes**
MAKES: **4 servings**

2   tablespoons butter or margarine
1   tablespoon all-purpose flour
½   cup whole milk
salt and ground black pepper
ground nutmeg
8   slices firm white or country-style bread
2   ounces Gruyère, shredded (½ cup)
8   ounces sliced deli baked ham

1. In 1-quart saucepan, melt 1 tablespoon butter over medium heat. With wire whisk, stir in flour and cook until mixture browns slightly, 1 to 2 minutes, stirring constantly. Add milk and a pinch each of salt, pepper, and nutmeg. Heat to boiling, stirring 1 to 2 minutes longer or until sauce thickens. Remove from heat.

2. Spread remaining 1 tablespoon butter on one side of each slice of bread. Place 4 slices bread on work surface, buttered sides down; top with Gruyère. Arrange ham over cheese, folding slices to fit. Spread about 2 tablespoons sauce on 1 unbuttered side of each remaining bread slice. Top sandwiches with bread, sauce side down.

3. Heat large ridged grill pan on medium heat until hot. Arrange sandwiches in skillet with cheese layer on bottom. Cook sandwiches until bread is golden brown, about 6 minutes. Turn sandwiches over and cook until bread is brown and cheese melts, 3 to 4 minutes longer.

EACH SERVING: About 320 calories, 19g protein, 30g carbohydrate, 14g total fat (5g saturated), 47mg cholesterol, 1,115mg sodium

Grilled Three-Cheese Sandwiches

Upgrade the traditional pairing of a grilled-cheese sandwich and tomato soup and serve these outdoor-grilled sandwiches with a cold fresh tomato soup.

PREP: **10 minutes**   GRILL: **about 8 minutes**
MAKES: **3 sandwiches or 6 servings**

6   large slices sourdough bread, each about ½ inch thick
½   cup coarsely shredded Asiago cheese
6   ounces fresh mozzarella cheese, sliced
4   ounces Fontina cheese, sliced

1. Prepare outdoor grill for covered direct grilling over medium heat.

2. Place 3 slices bread on clean work surface. Sprinkle bread with Asiago, then top with mozzarella and Fontina. Top with remaining bread.

3. Place sandwiches on hot grill rack. Cover grill and cook until bread is toasted and cheese melts, 8 to 10 minutes, turning over once. Cut each sandwich in half to serve.

EACH SERVING: About 285 calories, 16g protein, 21g carbohydrate, 15g total fat (9g saturated), 49mg cholesterol, 525mg sodium

Caramelized Onion and Goat Cheese Panini

With savory seasonal fillings and a flame-charred crunch, these melty, satisfying sandwiches are grilled cheese for grown-ups. A heavy skillet does the work of a panini maker to hot-press the ingredients together.

PREP: 15 minutes   **GRILL:** 7 to 8 minutes
MAKES: 4 panini or 8 servings

2	tablespoons olive oil
2	jumbo sweet onions (1 pound each), thinly sliced
1/2	teaspoon salt
1/4	teaspoon ground black pepper
1/2	teaspoon chopped fresh thyme leaves
8	center slices (1/2-inch-thick) country-style bread
4	ounces soft fresh goat cheese

1. In nonstick 12-inch skillet, heat oil on medium. Stir in onions, salt, and pepper; cover and cook 15 minutes or until very soft, stirring occasionally. Uncover and cook 15 to 25 minutes longer or until onions are golden brown, stirring often. Stir in thyme; set aside.

2. Prepare outdoor grill for direct grilling over medium heat, or heat ridged grill pan on medium until hot.

3. Place 4 slices bread on work surface. Spread 1 ounce goat cheese on each and top with onion mixture. Top with remaining bread slices.

4. Place 2 panini on hot grill grate or pan. Place heavy skillet on top, press, and cook 6 to 8 minutes or until bread is toasted on both sides, turning over once. Repeat with remaining panini. Cut in halves or quarters to serve.

EACH SERVING: About 190 calories, 7g protein, 24g carbohydrate, 8g total fat (3g saturated), 7mg cholesterol, 375mg sodium

RED PEPPER AND PROVOLONE PANINI: Prepare panini as above, but omit step 1. In step 3, in small bowl, combine *1 jar (7 ounces) roasted red peppers*, drained and sliced; *1/4 cup white wine vinegar*; *1 clove garlic, crushed with press*; and *1/4 teaspoon ground black pepper*. Set aside 10 minutes; drain. Divide *6 ounces sliced provolone, 4 ounces sliced Genoa salami*, and *marinated red peppers* among 4 bread slices; top with remaining bread. Complete as in step 4.

EACH SERVING: About 215 calories, 11g protein, 17g carbohydrate, 11g total fat (5g saturated fat), 28mg cholesterol, 675mg sodium

MOZZARELLA, TOMATO, AND BASIL PANINI: Prepare panini as above but omit step 1. In step 3, divide *2 ripe plum tomatoes*, cored and sliced; *6 ounces fresh mozzarella*, sliced; *1/2 cup loosely packed fresh basil leaves*; *1/8 teaspoon salt*; and *1/4 teaspoon ground black pepper* among 4 bread slices. Top with remaining bread. Complete as in step 4.

EACH SERVING: About 145 calories, 7g protein, 17g carbohydrate, 6g total fat (3g saturated fat), 17mg cholesterol, 230mg sodium

Peking Chicken Roll-Ups

The traditional Chinese recipe for duck is labor-intensive and takes several days to make. Our version, prepared in minutes, is made with grilled boneless chicken thighs and served in flour tortillas with hoisin sauce.

PREP: 25 minutes   GRILL: 10 to 12 minutes
MAKES: 4 servings

8	(8-inch) flour tortillas
2	tablespoons honey
2	tablespoons soy sauce
1	tablespoon grated, peeled fresh ginger
⅛	teaspoon ground red pepper (cayenne)
2	garlic cloves, crushed with garlic press
6	skinless, boneless chicken thighs (about 1¼ pounds total)
1	teaspoon vegetable oil
¼	cup hoisin sauce
½	English (seedless) cucumber, cut into 2 by ¼-inch matchsticks
2	green onions, thinly sliced

1. Prepare outdoor grill for direct grilling over medium-high heat.

2. Stack tortillas and wrap in foil. In small bowl, mix honey, soy sauce, ginger, ground red pepper, and garlic until blended. Set aside tortillas and honey mixture.

3. Coat chicken with oil and place on hot grill rack. Grill, turning once, 5 minutes. Brush chicken all over with honey mixture and grill until juices run clear when thickest part of thigh is pierced with tip of knife, 5 to 7 minutes longer, turning over once.

4. While chicken is cooking, place foil-wrapped tortillas on same grill rack and heat until warm, 3 to 5 minutes.

5. Transfer chicken to cutting board and thinly slice. Spread hoisin sauce on one side of tortillas. Top with chicken, cucumber, and green onions; roll up to serve.

EACH SERVING: About 400 calories, 27g protein, 50g carbohydrate, 10g total fat (3g saturated), 75mg cholesterol, 1,255mg sodium

Mediterranean Chicken Sandwiches

Kalamata olives, tomatoes, fennel seeds, and thyme give this sandwich its Mediterranean flavor profile. For double the grilled flavor, slice the bread as directed, then grill it alongside the chicken breasts for about 1 1/2 minutes per side.

PREP: 25 minutes   **GRILL: 10 to 12 minutes**
MAKES: 4 servings

- 1   teaspoon fennel seeds
- 1/2   teaspoon dried thyme
- 1/2   teaspoon salt
- 1/4   teaspoon coarsely ground black pepper
- 4   medium skinless, boneless chicken breast halves (about 1 1/4 pounds total)
- 1/4   cup Kalamata olives, pitted and minced
- 2   tablespoons mayonnaise
- 1   loaf (8 ounces) Italian bread
- 2   ripe small tomatoes (4 ounces each), each cut into 4 slices

1. Prepare outdoor grill for direct grilling over medium heat.

2. In mortar with pestle, crush fennel seeds with thyme, salt, and pepper. Rub both sides of chicken breasts with fennel-seed mixture; set aside.

3. In small bowl, mix olives and mayonnaise. Cut bread crosswise into 4 equal pieces, then cut each piece horizontally in half. Spread olive mixture evenly on cut sides of bread; set aside.

4. Place chicken on hot grill rack and grill until juices run clear when thickest part of breast is pierced with tip of knife, 10 to 12 minutes, turning over once. Transfer chicken to cutting board.

5. To assemble sandwiches, cut chicken breasts crosswise into 1/4-inch-thick slices. On bottom halves of bread, layer sliced chicken and tomatoes. Replace top halves of bread.

EACH SERVING: About 400 calories, 38g protein, 32g carbohydrate, 12g total fat (2g saturated), 86mg cholesterol, 910mg sodium

Steak Sandwiches with Grilled Onions

Marinating the steak with a delicious blend of Asian flavors and grilling it takes this classic sandwich to a new level.

PREP: 15 minutes plus marinating
GRILL: 12 to 15 minutes

MAKES: 4 servings

¼ cup soy sauce

¼ cup balsamic vinegar

1 tablespoon brown sugar

1 tablespoon fresh thyme leaves

¼ teaspoon ground black pepper

1 beef flank steak (about 1¼ pounds)

1 (12-inch) metal skewer

1 medium red onion (about 8 ounces), cut into 4 thick slices

8 slices sourdough bread, toasted on grill, if you like

2 ripe medium tomatoes (6 to 8 ounces each), sliced

1 bunch (5 ounces) arugula, trimmed

1. In large zip-tight plastic bag, mix soy sauce, vinegar, brown sugar, thyme, and pepper. Add steak, turning to coat. Seal bag, pressing out excess air. Place bag on plate; let marinate 15 minutes at room temperature or 1 hour in the refrigerator, turning several times.

2. Prepare outdoor grill for covered direct grilling over medium heat.

3. Meanwhile, for easier handling, insert skewer horizontally through onion slices; set aside.

4. Remove steak from marinade; pour marinade into 1-quart saucepan. Heat marinade over high heat to boiling; boil 1 minute.

5. Place steak and onion slices on hot grill rack. Cover grill and cook steak and onions, brushing both with marinade occasionally and turning over once, until onions are browned and tender and meat is medium-rare, 12 to 15 minutes. Transfer steak to cutting board; let stand 10 minutes to allow juices to set for easier slicing. Separate onion into rings.

6. Thinly slice steak diagonally across grain. Arrange onion rings and steak on 4 slices of bread; spoon any meat juices from board over onion and steak. Top with tomatoes, arugula, and remaining 4 slices of bread.

EACH SERVING: About 210 calories, 9g protein, 38g carbohydrate, 3g total fat (1g saturated), 5mg cholesterol, 815mg sodium

Grilled Green Tomato Focaccia Sandwiches

Instead of frying up green tomatoes, put slices on the grill for an elegant low-fat version of the Southern summer specialty. The smoke mellows yet brings out the tart taste of the not-quite-ripe tomato, balancing the salty Canadian bacon.

PREP: 20 minutes   **GRILL:** 11 to 13 minutes
MAKES: 4 servings

1	large lemon
½	cup light mayonnaise
½	teaspoon coarsely ground black pepper
3	medium (1 pound) green (unripe) tomatoes, cut into ½-inch-thick slices
¼	teaspoon salt
1	tablespoon olive oil
8	slices Canadian bacon
1	loaf focaccia bread, about 10" by 6" (1 pound), cut horizontally in half

1. Prepare outdoor grill for direct grilling over medium heat.

2. From lemon, grate 1 teaspoon peel and squeeze 2 tablespoons juice. In cup, combine lemon peel and juice, mayonnaise, and pepper.

3. Sprinkle tomato slices with salt; brush lightly with oil. Place tomatoes on hot grill rack and cook until browned and slightly softened, 6 to 7 minutes, turning over once. On same grill rack, cook Canadian bacon until heated through, 2 minutes, turning over once. Transfer tomatoes and bacon to platter. Place focaccia, cut sides down, on grill rack and grill until lightly toasted, 3 to 4 minutes.

4. Assemble sandwiches: Spread mayonnaise mixture on cut sides of focaccia. On bottom half of focaccia, layer tomatoes, then Canadian bacon. Replace top half of focaccia. To serve, cut sandwich into 4 pieces.

EACH SERVING: About 510 calories, 22g protein, 59g carbohydrate, 22g total fat (4g saturated), 40mg cholesterol, 1,565mg sodium

Backyard BLTs

Our piquant lemon-herb mayonnaise makes this classic sandwich even better than ever!

PREP: **15 minutes**   GRILL: **5 minutes**

MAKES: **4 servings**

1	lemon
⅓	cup light mayonnaise
1	tablespoon chopped fresh parsley
½	teaspoon chopped fresh thyme
⅛	teaspoon coarsely ground black pepper
3	ripe medium tomatoes (6 to 8 ounces each), cut into ¼-inch-thick slices
⅛	teaspoon salt
8	slices (½-inch-thick) sourdough bread
8	ounces thinly sliced Canadian bacon (about 24 slices)
8	small romaine lettuce leaves

1. Prepare outdoor grill for direct grilling over medium heat.

2. From lemon, grate ¼ teaspoon peel and squeeze 1 teaspoon juice. In small bowl, mix lemon peel and lemon juice with mayonnaise, parsley, thyme, and pepper until blended; set aside. Place tomato slices on sheet of waxed paper and sprinkle with salt.

3. With tongs, place bread slices on hot grill rack and grill just until grill marks appear on bottom side of bread. Set aside.

4. With tongs, place bacon slices on grill rack and grill just until grill marks appear on bacon, about 2 minutes (do not overcook; bacon will dry out and toughen).

5. To assemble sandwiches, spread mayonnaise mixture on ungrilled side of bread slices. Top 4 bread slices with half of bacon, all tomato, remaining bacon, then lettuce leaves. Place remaining 4 bread slices, grilled side up, on top. Cut each sandwich in half to serve.

EACH SERVING: About 315 calories, 17g protein, 32g carbohydrate, 14g total fat (2g saturated), 35mg cholesterol, 1,195mg sodium

Salmon BLTs with Lemon-Dill Mayonnaise

Keep the skin on salmon fillets for grilling to prevent them from falling apart.

PREP: 15 minutes   GRILL: 11 to 13 minutes
MAKES: 4 servings

⅓ cup light mayonnaise

2 teaspoons chopped fresh dill

1 teaspoon freshly grated lemon peel

4 pieces salmon fillet with skin on, 1 inch thick (about 6 ounces each)

¼ teaspoon salt

⅛ teaspoon coarsely ground black pepper

8 center slices (½-inch-thick) country-style bread

4 romaine lettuce leaves

2 ripe medium tomatoes (6 to 8 ounces each), sliced

6 slices bacon, cooked until crisp and each broken in half

1. Lightly grease grill rack. Prepare outdoor grill for covered direct grilling over medium heat.

2. In small bowl, stir mayonnaise, dill, and lemon peel until mixed; set aside. Sprinkle salmon with salt and pepper.

3. Place salmon, skin side down, on hot grill rack. Cover grill and cook until salmon is opaque throughout, 10 to 12 minutes, without turning over. Slide thin metal spatula between salmon flesh and skin. Lift salmon from skin and transfer to plate; discard skin. Meanwhile, place bread on grill rack and cook about 1 minute on each side, until lightly toasted.

4. Spread lemon-dill mayonnaise on 1 side of toasted bread slices. Place 1 lettuce leaf, folding to fit, on each of 4 bread slices. Top each with 2 or 3 tomato slices, 1 salmon fillet, 3 pieces of bacon, and another bread slice.

EACH SERVING: About 570 calories, 44g protein, 41g carbohydrate, 24g total fat (5g saturated), 108mg cholesterol, 955mg sodium

Tuna Melt with Carrot-Raisin Salad

For a more traditional carrot salad, replace the cumin with cinnamon. You can also substitute dried cranberries, dates, or other dried fruits for the raisins.

PREP: 10 minutes   **GRILL:** 5 minutes
MAKES: 4 servings

TUNA MELT

1	tablespoon butter or margarine
1	can (12 ounces) solid white tuna in water, drained
1	stalk celery, thinly sliced
¼	cup reduced-fat mayonnaise
8	slices rye bread (about 8 ounces total)
4	ounces sliced Cheddar cheese or Swiss cheese (8 slices)

CARROT-RAISIN SALAD

1	container (8 ounces) plain low-fat yogurt
1	bag (10 ounces) shredded carrots
½	cup raisins
⅛	teaspoon ground cumin
⅛	teaspoon salt

1. Prepare tuna melt: In small bowl, with fork, combine tuna, celery, and mayonnaise. Spread butter on one side of each slice of bread.

2. Heat large ridged grill pan on medium heat until hot. Meanwhile, place 1 slice cheese on unbuttered sides of 4 bread slices. Spread tuna mixture evenly over cheese. Top each with 1 slice cheese and a second slice of bread, buttered side up.

3. Arrange sandwiches in pan. Cook until cheese melts and bread is toasted, 5 to 7 minutes, turning sandwiches over once.

4. Meanwhile, prepare salad: In small bowl, stir yogurt, carrots, raisins, cumin, and salt until combined. Makes about 4 cups.

5. Serve each tuna melt with a scoop of salad alongside.

EACH SERVING: About 440 calories, 31g protein, 33g carbohydrate, 20g total fat (7g saturated), 61mg cholesterol, 1,055mg sodium

Salads

An inspired mix of tastes and textures—sweet tomatoes, buttery ripe avocado, crisp and refreshing romaine, peppery arugula, charry onion slices, tender steak, plump shrimp, and don't forget the fresh herbs!—grilled salads are the perfect summer food.

We've included side salads like Grilled Eggplant Caponata Salad or Portobello and Prosciutto Salad, with big flavors that can stand up to your grilled main course. Or forgo the main course and make your protein part of the salad! You've got a world of flavors to choose from— Vietnamese Chicken Salad, Thai Beef Salad, Shrimp and Pineapple Salad with Basil and Baby Greens, Mediterranean Swordfish Salad. Or try our grilled twists on everybody's favorite salads like Caesar, taco, and panzanella (here we supplement the tomatoes and croutons with grilled chicken). Start grilling your salad tonight!

Greek Steak Salad, page 58

Grilled Caesar Salad

Grilling romaine, or other sturdy greens that grow in a head (like endive, radicchio, or chicory), transforms it into a seemingly different vegetable with a rich "meaty" taste that can add instant flavor to any salad.

PREP: **8 minutes**   GRILL: **6 minutes**
MAKES: **4 side-dish servings**

2	tablespoons olive oil
4	ounces Italian bread, cut into ½-inch-thick slices
¼	cup light mayonnaise
¼	cup freshly grated Parmesan cheese
3	tablespoons fresh lemon juice (from 1 lemon)
1	teaspoon anchovy paste or 2 anchovy fillets, mashed
¼	teaspoon coarsely ground black pepper
1	garlic clove, cut in half
1	package (18 to 22 ounces) hearts of romaine, each head cut lengthwise in half

1. Prepare outdoor grill for direct grilling over medium heat.

2. Prepare croutons: Use 1 tablespoon oil to lightly brush bread slices on both sides. Place bread on hot grill rack over medium heat and cook until toasted, 2 to 3 minutes, turning over once. Transfer to plate to cool.

3. Meanwhile, prepare dressing: In small bowl, whisk together mayonnaise, Parmesan, lemon juice, anchovy paste, $^1/_4$ teaspoon coarsely ground black pepper, and remaining 1 tablespoon oil.

4. When bread is cool, lightly rub both sides of each slice with cut garlic clove. Cut bread into $^1/_2$-inch cubes.

5. Place romaine halves on hot grill rack and cook until lightly browned and wilted, 4 to 5 minutes, turning over once. Transfer romaine to 4 salad plates; drizzle with dressing and sprinkle with croutons to serve.

EACH SERVING: About 245 calories, 7g protein, 20g carbohydrate, 14g total fat (3g saturated), 10mg cholesterol, 420mg sodium

SPRINKLE TO YOUR GOOD HEALTH

Sprinkle on oregano, basil, parsley, or cilantro, and you'll boost the health value of your dish. In a recent study by the Department of Agriculture, researchers found that, gram for gram, herbs pack more disease-fighting antioxidant wallop than fruits and vegetables, with fresh oregano leading the group. (One tablespoon has more antioxidants than a whole apple, the researchers found.) So instead of sprinkling just a teaspoon of chopped basil over your salad, use a handful of whole leaves to replace your customary lettuce.

Charred Corn and Bean Salad

A fresh mix of sweet corn, red onion, and pinto beans is tossed with a zesty south-of-the-border vinaigrette.

PREP: **25 minutes**　GRILL: **10 to 15 minutes**
MAKES: **6 side-dish servings**

3　medium ears corn, husks and silk removed

1　small red onion, cut into 4 slices

1　can (15 to 19 ounces) pinto or small pink beans, rinsed and drained

1　jalapeño chile, seeded and minced

1/2　cup loosely packed fresh cilantro leaves, chopped

3　tablespoons fresh lime juice

1　tablespoon olive oil

3/4　teaspoon salt

1/4　teaspoon coarsely ground black pepper

1. Prepare outdoor grill for direct grilling over medium-high heat.

2. Place corn and onion slices on hot grill rack. Grill corn, turning occasionally, until golden, 10 to 15 minutes. Grill onion, turning once, until tender and golden, 10 minutes.

3. Transfer vegetables to cutting board. Cut corn kernels from cobs and chop onion. In large bowl, mix corn and onion with beans, jalapeño pepper, cilantro, lime juice, oil, salt, and pepper. Cover and refrigerate up to 4 hours if not serving right away.

EACH SERVING: About 140 calories, 6g protein, 25g carbohydrate, 3g total fat (0g saturated), 0mg cholesterol, 500mg sodium

Grilled Pepper and Onion Salad

To keep last-minute work to a minimum, grill the peppers and onions ahead.

PREP: **20 minutes**　GRILL: **10 to 15 minutes**
MAKES: **10 side-dish servings**

6　red, yellow, and/or orange peppers, halved lengthwise and seeded

2　medium red onions, each cut into 6 wedges

4　tablespoons olive oil

3　tablespoons balsamic vinegar

1　teaspoon Dijon mustard

1/2　teaspoon salt

1/2　teaspoon sugar

1/4　teaspoon coarsely ground black pepper

2　bunches arugula (4 ounces each), trimmed

1. With hand, flatten each pepper half. In bowl, toss onion wedges with 1 tablespoon oil.

2. Prepare outdoor grill for direct grilling over medium heat. Place peppers, skin side down, with onion wedges on hot grill rack and cook until pepper skins are blistered and onions are tender and golden, 10 to 15 minutes, turning onions once halfway through grilling. Transfer onions to plate. Cover peppers to allow them to steam, about 15 minutes. Uncover peppers. Peel off and discard skins. Cut peppers into 1/2-inch-wide strips. Transfer to plate with onions.

3. In small bowl, whisk 3 tablespoons oil with vinegar, mustard, salt, sugar, and pepper. To serve, line platter with arugula; arrange vegetables on top; drizzle with dressing.

EACH SERVING: About 85 calories, 2g protein, 8g carbohydrate, 6g total fat (1 saturated), 0mg cholesterol, 125mg sodium

Grilled Eggplant Caponata Salad

Eggplant simply absorbs the smoky goodness from the grill. This delicious salad of fresh tomatoes, sweet raisins, and briny capers, mixed with grilled onions, celery, and eggplant will become one of your go-to sides for almost any kind of meat, poultry, or oily-fleshed fish cooked over fire.

PREP: 25 minutes   **GRILL:** 8 to 10 minutes
MAKES: 14 side-dish servings

2	small red onions, cut into ½-inch-thick slices
2	small eggplants (1 to 1¼ pounds each), cut into ¾-inch-thick slices

nonstick cooking spray

4	medium stalks celery
½	teaspoon salt
2	tablespoons red wine vinegar
2	tablespoons extra-virgin olive oil
1	teaspoon sugar
¼	teaspoon coarsely ground pepper
6	medium plum tomatoes (about 1½ pounds total), cut into ½-inch chunks
1	cup Kalamata, Gaeta, or green Sicilian olives, pitted and chopped
¼	cup golden raisins
3	tablespoons drained capers
½	cup loosely packed fresh Italian parsley leaves

1. Prepare outdoor grill for covered direct grilling over medium heat.

2. Meanwhile, if you like, for easier handling, insert metal skewers through onion slices. Lightly spray both sides of eggplant slices with cooking spray. Sprinkle onions, eggplants, and celery with salt.

3. Place onions, eggplants, and celery on hot grill rack. Cover grill and cook vegetables until tender and lightly browned, 8 to 10 minutes, turning over once and transferring to plate as they are done. Cool slightly until easy to handle.

4. Cut eggplants and celery into ¾-inch chunks; coarsely chop onions. In large bowl, mix vinegar, oil, sugar, and pepper until blended. Stir in tomatoes, olives, raisins, capers, and parsley. Add eggplant, onions, and celery, and gently toss to coat.

5. Serve salad at room temperature or cover and refrigerate up to 1 day to serve later.

EACH SERVING: About 75 calories, 1g protein, 11g carbohydrate, 3g total fat (1g saturated), 0mg cholesterol, 240mg sodium

Portobello and Prosciutto Salad

Thick and meaty portobello mushrooms have a natural affinity for the grill. They're great in a salad or served alongside a thick, juicy steak. The stems, which are woody, may be saved and used in soups or stocks, where they'll lend an earthy flavor.

PREP: 30 minutes   **GRILL:** about 9 minutes
MAKES: 4 side-dish servings

- 2   bunches arugula (4 ounces each), trimmed
- 2   tablespoons balsamic vinegar
- 2   tablespoons olive oil
- 2   tablespoons minced shallots
- 2   tablespoons chopped fresh parsley
- ¼   teaspoon salt
- ¼   teaspoon coarsely ground black pepper
- 4   portobello mushrooms (about 1½ pounds total), stems removed
- 8   ounces thinly sliced prosciutto
- ½   cup shaved Parmesan cheese curls (1 ounce; see Tip)

1. Prepare outdoor grill for direct grilling over medium heat. Arrange arugula on platter.

2. In small bowl, with wire whisk, mix vinegar, oil, shallots, parsley, salt, and pepper until blended.

3. Place mushrooms, stem side down, on hot grill rack. Brush mushrooms with 1 tablespoon dressing. Grill 4 minutes. Turn mushrooms and brush with 2 tablespoons dressing. Grill until tender, about 5 minutes longer.

4. Thinly slice mushrooms and arrange on arugula. Spoon remaining dressing over salad. Arrange prosciutto on platter with salad. Top with Parmesan curls.

EACH SERVING: About 270 calories, 23g protein, 9g carbohydrate, 17g total fat (4g saturated), 51mg cholesterol, 1,320mg sodium

TIP: Making Parmesan curls is a snap using a vegetable peeler.

PORTOBELLO PRIMER

Look for portobellos with a smooth, fresh appearance and dry surface; refrigerate and use within several days. To keep them longer, place in a brown paper bag in the refrigerator or, if packaged, leave them in their tray but remove the plastic wrap and rewrap them with paper towels. Before using whole portobellos, trim off the tough end of the stem.

Greek Steak Salad

This salad can be ready in just ten minutes! For photo, see page 52.

PREP: **10 minutes plus standing**
GRILL: **7 to 9 minutes**
MAKES: **4 main-dish servings**

1	beef top round steak, ¾ inch thick (about ¾ pound)
½	teaspoon salt
½	teaspoon ground black pepper
3	tablespoons fresh lemon juice
2	tablespoons extra-virgin olive oil
1	package (10 ounces) romaine salad mix (about 8 cups)
½	English (seedless) cucumber, unpeeled, thinly sliced
1	pint grape tomatoes
4	ounces feta cheese, crumbled (1 cup)
4	pieces pita bread, warmed, for serving

1. Heat ridged grill pan over high heat. (To grill steak outdoors, see instructions opposite.)

2. Add steak to pan; sprinkle with ¼ teaspoon salt and ¼ teaspoon pepper. Cook steak for medium-rare, 7 to 9 minutes, turning over once. Transfer to cutting board; let stand 10 minutes to allow juices to set for easier slicing.

3. Meanwhile, in large bowl, whisk lemon juice, oil, and remaining ¼ teaspoon salt and ¼ teaspoon pepper.

4. Add romaine, cucumber, tomatoes, and feta to dressing; toss to coat. Thinly slice steak on the diagonal across the grain. Serve on salad with pita on the side.

EACH SERVING: About 315 calories, 25g protein, 10g carbohydrate, 19g total fat (7g saturated), 79mg cholesterol, 660mg sodium

CUCUMBER PRIMER

English (or hothouse) cucumbers are more expensive than your classic cukes, but worth the price as they are virtually seedless. If you substitute a garden-variety cucumber with a waxed skin, peel it and cut it in half lengthwise. Then, using a teaspoon, scoop out the seeds in the center by scraping down the length. Slice or chop as directed in the recipe.

Thai Beef Salad

This is a perfect choice for a hot weeknight evening.

PREP: 20 minutes plus marinating
GRILL: 10 to 15 minutes
MAKES: 4 main-dish servings

2   tablespoons Asian fish sauce
2½ teaspoons sugar
1   beef top round steak, ¾ inch thick (about 1 pound)
2   limes
3   tablespoons vegetable oil
¼   teaspoon crushed red pepper
¼   teaspoon coarsely ground black pepper
2   bunches watercress (4 ounces each), tough stems trimmed
1   cup loosely packed fresh mint leaves
1   cup loosely packed fresh cilantro leaves
1   bunch radishes, each cut in half and thinly sliced
½   small red onion, thinly sliced

1. In 8-inch or 9-inch square glass baking dish, stir 1 tablespoon fish sauce and 1 teaspoon sugar. Add steak, turning to coat; marinate 15 minutes at room temperature or 1 hour in refrigerator, turning occasionally.

2. Prepare outdoor grill for covered direct grilling over medium heat. (To grill steak on stovetop grill pan, see instructions opposite.)

3. Meanwhile, from limes, with vegetable peeler, remove peel in 2″ by ³/₄″ strips. With sharp knife, cut enough peel crosswise into matchstick-thin strips to equal 1 tablespoon. Squeeze enough juice from limes to equal 3 tablespoons. In small bowl, whisk lime juice, oil, crushed red pepper, black pepper, and remaining 1 tablespoon fish sauce and 1½ teaspoons sugar until blended.

4. In large bowl, toss watercress, mint, cilantro, radishes, onion, and lime peel; cover and refrigerate until ready to serve.

5. Place steak on hot grill rack. Cover grill and cook steak 10 to 15 minutes for medium-rare or until desired doneness, turning over once. Transfer steak to cutting board; let stand 10 minutes to allow juices to set for easier slicing. Thinly slice steak on the diagonal across the grain.

6. Add steak and dressing to watercress mixture and toss until well coated. To serve, divide among 4 dinner plates.

EACH SERVING: About 310 calories, 28g protein, 7g carbohydrate, 23g total fat (4g saturated), 73mg cholesterol, 295mg sodium

Grilled Thai Chicken Salad

Add zest to boneless chicken with a spicy Thai seasoning blend, then grill it and slice for a delicious main-course salad.

PREP: **30 minutes**   GRILL: **10 to 12 minutes**
MAKES: **4 main-dish servings**

THAI DRESSING

2   tablespoons fresh lime juice

4   teaspoons Asian fish sauce

1   tablespoon reduced-sodium soy sauce

1   teaspoon sugar

CHICKEN SALAD

4   large skinless, boneless chicken thighs (about 1½ pounds total)

2   tablespoons Thai seasoning (see Tip)

2   bags (10 ounces each) torn romaine lettuce leaves

2   cups loosely packed fresh mint leaves

2   papayas and/or mangoes, each, peeled, seeded, and thinly sliced

2   green onions, thinly sliced

1. Prepare outdoor grill for direct grilling over medium heat.

2. Prepare dressing: In cup, combine lime juice, fish and soy sauces, and sugar; set aside.

3. Prepare chicken salad: In medium bowl, toss chicken with Thai seasoning. Place chicken on hot grill rack; grill, turning once, until juices run clear when thickest part of thigh is pierced with tip of knife, 10 to 12 minutes. Transfer chicken to cutting board.

4. In large bowl, toss lettuce, mint, papaya, and green onions with dressing. Thinly slice chicken. Divide salad among 4 dinner plates. Top with chicken slices.

EACH SERVING: About 375 calories, 38g protein, 24g carbohydrate, 15g total fat (4g saturated), 121mg cholesterol, 1,215mg sodium

> **TIP:** Seasoning mixes vary among manufacturers, especially with regard to sodium content. Add salt to taste if necessary.

SOMETHING FISHY (IN A GOOD WAY)

Fish sauce is a pungent seasoning that's used in Southeast Asian cooking much the way we use salt. Many supermarkets now carry the sauce; you may have a choice of *nam pla* (from Thailand), *nuoc mam* (Vietnam), or *patis* (the Philippines). Country of origin doesn't matter, but color does—the lighter the sauce, the milder the flavor. In Asia, the darker liquid (almost like soy sauce) is used for cooking, while the lightest (a clear amber) is saved for table use. Fish sauce can be stored indefinitely in a cool dark place; the color will deepen over time.

Vietnamese Chicken Salad

One of the wonderful qualities of Vietnamese cooking is the interplay of textures and flavors. Here the dressing brings together the sweetness of brown sugar, the complex saltiness of fish sauce, the pleasing tartness of lime, and the bite of garlic. Combine that with a refreshing noodle salad of grilled chicken, crunchy iceberg lettuce and cucumbers, and cool fresh mint, and you've got a winner of a meal for a hot summer night.

PREP: 20 minutes   GRILL: 5 to 6 minutes

MAKES: 4 main-dish servings

½ (7 to 9 ounce) package vermicelli rice noodles

⅓ cup Asian fish sauce

3 tablespoons brown sugar

2 tablespoons fresh lime juice

1 small garlic clove, crushed with garlic press

1 pound chicken-breast tenders

¼ cup water

½ head iceberg lettuce, thinly sliced

2 medium carrots, shredded

2 small Kirby cucumbers, shredded

½ cup loosely packed fresh mint leaves, chopped

½ cup unsalted dry-roasted peanuts, chopped (optional)

1. Prepare outdoor grill for direct grilling over medium heat.

2. Heat medium saucepan of water to boiling over high heat. Add rice noodles and cook as label directs; drain and set aside.

3. In small bowl, combine fish sauce, brown sugar, lime juice, and garlic. Transfer 3 tablespoons fish-sauce mixture to medium bowl; add chicken and toss to coat. Stir water into remaining fish-sauce mixture.

4. Place chicken on hot grill rack and cook just until chicken loses its pink color throughout, 5 to 6 minutes, turning over once. Transfer chicken to cutting board; cut into 1-inch chunks.

5. Divide noodles among 4 large dinner plates. Top with lettuce, carrots, cucumber, mint, chicken, and, if using, peanuts; drizzle with remaining fish-sauce mixture.

EACH SERVING: About 330 calories, 30g protein, 44g carbohydrate, 4g total fat (1g saturated), 72mg cholesterol, 1,985mg sodium

Grilled Chicken Panzanella Salad

Show off the fresh flavors of tomato and basil with this effortless salad.

PREP: 5 minutes **GRILL:** 10 to 12 minutes
MAKES: 4 main-dish servings

1	tablespoon red wine vinegar
1	clove garlic, crushed with press
¾	teaspoon salt
½	teaspoon ground black pepper
4	tablespoons olive oil
4	ounces country-style bread (¼ small loaf), cut into ¾-inch-thick slices
2	medium red peppers, each cut lengthwise into quarters
1	medium red onion, cut into ½-inch-thick slices
1	pound skinless, boneless chicken breast halves
2	pounds plum tomatoes (12 medium), cut into 1-inch chunks
¼	cup loosely packed small fresh basil leaves or 2 tablespoons chopped leaves

1. Prepare outdoor grill for covered direct grilling over medium heat.

2. Meanwhile prepare vinaigrette: In large bowl, whisk together wine vinegar, garlic, ½ teaspoon salt, ¼ teaspoon pepper, and 2 tablespoons olive oil until blended; set aside.

3. In jelly-roll pan, brush bread, red peppers, and onion slices with remaining 2 tablespoons olive oil to lightly coat both sides; sprinkle with remaining ¼ teaspoon salt and pepper. With tongs, place bread slices, red peppers, onion slices, and chicken on hot grill grate. Cover grill and cook bread about 3 minutes or until lightly toasted, turning over once. Cook peppers and onion about 8 minutes or until lightly browned and tender, turning over once. Cook chicken 10 to 12 minutes or until chicken loses its pink color throughout, turning over once. As bread, vegetables, and chicken are done, transfer to cutting board. Cut bread slices, chicken, peppers, and onions into ½-inch pieces.

4. Into vinaigrette in bowl, stir chopped tomatoes, basil, bread, peppers, onions, and chicken; toss to combine. Scoop into bowls to serve.

EACH SERVING: About 405 calories, 32g protein, 33g carbohydrate, 17g total fat (3g saturated), 66mg cholesterol, 690mg sodium

Grilled Chicken and Mango Salad

If mangoes are not available, try firm, ripe nectarines, plums, peaches, or a combination of all three.

PREP: 30 minutes plus marinating
GRILL: 10 to 12 minutes
MAKES: 4 main-dish servings

¼   cup olive oil
¼   cup seasoned rice vinegar
¾   teaspoon salt
¼   teaspoon ground red pepper (cayenne)
4   skinless, boneless chicken breasts (about 1½ pounds total)
1   large shallot, minced
¼   cup loosely packed fresh cilantro leaves, chopped
1   tablespoon chopped fresh mint
1   tablespoon minced, peeled fresh ginger
½   teaspoon freshly grated lemon peel
1   mango, peeled, pitted, and cut into ¼-inch pieces
1   Kirby cucumber (about 5 ounces), cut into ¼-inch pieces
4   medium ears corn, husks and silk removed
10   cups mixed baby greens (5 ounces)

1. In medium bowl, with wire whisk or fork, mix oil, vinegar, salt, and ground red pepper. Spoon 3 tablespoons oil mixture into pie plate. Add chicken to pie plate; turn to coat. Let stand, turning once, 15 minutes at room temperature or 30 minutes in the refrigerator.

2. Prepare outdoor grill for direct grilling over medium heat.

3. Meanwhile, stir shallot, cilantro, mint, ginger, and lemon peel into oil mixture remaining in bowl. Stir in mango and cucumber; set aside.

4. Place chicken on hot grill rack; discard marinade in pie plate. Grill chicken until juices run clear when thickest part is pierced with tip of knife, 10 to 12 minutes, turning over once. At the same time, grill corn, turning often, until lightly browned, 10 to 15 minutes. Transfer chicken and corn to plate; set aside until cool enough to handle.

5. When chicken is cool, with fingers, pull meat into shreds. With sharp knife, cut corn kernels from cobs. Toss chicken and corn with mango mixture.

6. To serve, divide greens among 4 plates; top with chicken mixture.

EACH SERVING: About 385 calories, 23g protein, 37g carbohydrate, 18g total fat (4g saturated), 70mg cholesterol, 655mg sodium

Grilled Chicken Taco Salad

A great way to prepare this Mexican favorite during the summer: Spicy chicken breasts are first grilled and then served over black-bean salsa, shredded lettuce, and crisp corn tortillas.

PREP: 25 minutes   **GRILL: 10 to 12 minutes**
MAKES: 4 main-dish servings

1	can (15 to 19 ounces) black beans, rinsed and drained
¾	cup medium-hot salsa
1	tablespoon fresh lime juice
1	cup loosely packed fresh cilantro leaves, chopped
2	tablespoons chili powder
1	teaspoon ground cumin
1	teaspoon ground coriander
1	teaspoon brown sugar
½	teaspoon salt
¼	teaspoon ground red pepper (cayenne)
1	tablespoon olive oil
1	pound skinless, boneless chicken breast halves
4	(8-inch) corn tortillas
4	cups thinly sliced lettuce

lime wedges, avocado slices, and sour cream (optional)

1. Prepare outdoor grill for direct grilling over medium-high heat.

2. In medium bowl, mix beans, salsa, lime juice, and half of cilantro; set aside.

3. In cup, stir chili powder, cumin, coriander, brown sugar, salt, ground red pepper, and oil until evenly mixed (mixture will be dry).

4. If necessary, pound breast halves to uniform ¼-inch thickness. With hands, rub chicken with chili-powder mixture.

5. Place chicken on hot grill rack and grill until juices run clear when thickest part of breast is pierced with tip of knife, 10 to 12 minutes, turning over once. Place tortillas on grill rack with chicken and cook until lightly browned, 3 to 5 minutes, turning over once.

6. Transfer chicken to cutting board. Place tortillas on 4 dinner plates. Cut chicken into long thin strips. Top tortillas with lettuce, bean mixture, and chicken. Sprinkle with remaining cilantro. If you like, serve with lime wedges, avocado slices, and sour cream.

EACH SERVING: About 370 calories, 35g protein, 45g carbohydrate, 8g total fat (2g saturated), 72mg cholesterol, 1,075mg sodium

Grilled Chicken Salad with Baby Spinach and Nectarines

Prepare this colorful salad with any ripe summer fruit. Try substituting a soft, creamy goat cheese for the feta and add a topping of chopped toasted pecans for extra crunch.

PREP: 25 minutes   **GRILL:** 10 to 12 minutes
MAKES: 4 main-dish servings

4	small skinless, boneless chicken breast halves (about 1 pound total)
1	teaspoon chopped fresh thyme
¾	teaspoon salt
½	teaspoon coarsely ground black pepper
2	tablespoons olive oil
1	tablespoon balsamic vinegar
½	teaspoon Dijon mustard
1	shallot, minced
2	large ripe nectarines, pitted and sliced
½	English (seedless) cucumber, cut lengthwise in half, then thinly sliced crosswise
8	ounces baby spinach (see Tip)
2	ounces feta cheese, crumbled (about ½ cup)

1. Prepare outdoor grill for direct grilling over medium heat.

2. Rub chicken with thyme, ½ teaspoon salt, and ¼ teaspoon pepper. Place on hot grill rack and grill until juices run clear when thickest part of breast is pierced with tip of knife, 10 to 12 minutes, turning over once. Transfer chicken to cutting board; set aside until cool enough to handle.

3. Meanwhile, in large bowl, with wire whisk, mix oil, vinegar, mustard, shallot, remaining ¼ teaspoon each salt and pepper. Stir in nectarines and cucumber.

4. To serve, cut chicken into ½-inch-thick slices. Toss spinach with nectarine mixture. Divide salad among 4 plates; top with sliced chicken and feta.

EACH SERVING: About 290 calories, 31g protein, 15g carbohydrate, 12g total fat (3g saturated), 78mg cholesterol, 730mg sodium

> **TIP:** Baby spinach, with its soft, delicate leaves, is often sold in prepackaged bags. If you can't find baby spinach, look for spinach with smooth, rather than ruffled, leaves and tender stems. Or substitute a mix of baby greens.

Grilled Shrimp, Corn, and Tomato Salad

This salad is truly the taste of summer—grilled corn cut straight from the cob, August-ripe tomatoes, and the incredible flavor of shrimp.

PREP: 30 minutes plus steaming
GRILL: 13 to 16 minutes
MAKES: 4 main-dish servings

2	limes
4	tablespoons olive oil
3/4	teaspoon salt
2	pinches ground red pepper (cayenne)
1	teaspoon ground coriander
1/2	teaspoon ground cumin
1	pound large shrimp, shelled and deveined, with tail part of shell left on if you like
3	ears corn, husks and silk removed
4	ripe medium tomatoes to (6 to 8 ounces each), each cut in half and seeded
2	medium poblano chiles (about 4 ounces each)
1	head green or red leaf lettuce, thinly sliced

1. Prepare outdoor grill for covered direct grilling over medium heat.

2. Meanwhile, from limes, grate 1 teaspoon peel and squeeze 3 tablespoons juice. In cup, with fork, mix lime juice with 2 tablespoons oil, 1/2 teaspoon salt, 1/2 teaspoon lime peel, and pinch ground red pepper. Set dressing aside.

3. In medium bowl, with fork, mix coriander and cumin with remaining 2 tablespoons oil, 1/2 teaspoon lime peel, 1/4 teaspoon salt, and pinch ground red pepper. Brush corn and tomatoes with half of oil mixture. Toss shrimp in oil mixture remaining in bowl.

4. Place corn and whole poblanos on hot grill rack. Cover grill and cook until corn is browned in spots and skin on poblanos is charred and blistered on all sides, 10 to 12 minutes, turning over occasionally. Transfer corn to cutting board. Transfer poblanos to large sheet of foil. Wrap foil around poblanos and allow to steam at room temperature until cool enough to handle, about 15 minutes.

5. While poblanos steam, place shrimp and tomatoes on hot grill rack (or hot flat grill topper). Cover grill and cook shrimp just until opaque throughout, 3 to 4 minutes, turning over once. Cook tomatoes until lightly browned, 4 to 6 minutes, turning over once. Transfer shrimp to large bowl and tomatoes to cutting board.

6. Remove poblanos from foil. Peel off skins and discard. Cut each poblano lengthwise in half; remove seeds and membranes. Cut poblanos crosswise into thin strips; add to shrimp in bowl. Cut corn kernels from cobs; add to same bowl. Peel off and discard skin from tomatoes. Cut tomatoes into thin strips; add to same bowl. Add 2 tablespoons dressing to shrimp mixture; toss to coat.

7. In another large bowl, toss lettuce with remaining dressing.

8. To serve, place lettuce on platter; top with shrimp mixture.

EACH SERVING: About 340 calories, 25g protein, 28g carbohydrate, 16g total fat (2g saturated), 180mg cholesterol, 675mg sodium

Shrimp and Pineapple Salad with Basil and Baby Greens

No grill basket? Thread shrimp onto skewers instead. If using wooden skewers, presoak in hot water at least twenty minutes to prevent them from burning.

PREP: 10 minutes   GRILL: 12 to 13 minutes
MAKES: 6 main-dish servings

3 to 4 limes
3   tablespoons olive oil
1½ cup loosely packed fresh basil leaves
½   teaspoon salt
¼   teaspoon coarsely ground pepper
1½ pounds large shrimp, shelled and deveined
1   pineapple (3 pounds)
12   (6-inch) corn tortillas
      olive-oil cooking spray
1   bag (5 to 6 ounces) baby greens
2   medium heads Belgian endive, sliced (see box, opposite)

1. Prepare outdoor grill for direct grilling over medium heat.

2. From limes, grate ¹/₂ teaspoon peel and squeeze ¹/₄ cup juice. In blender, place lime peel and juice, oil, ¹/₂ cup basil leaves, salt, and pepper. Blend until pureed.

3. Spoon 2 tablespoons dressing from blender into medium bowl. Add shrimp to bowl and toss to coat with dressing.

4. Cut off crown and stem ends from pineapple. Stand pineapple upright and slice off rind and eyes. Cut pineapple lengthwise into 8 wedges, then cut off core from each wedge.

5. Place pineapple wedges on hot grill rack and cook until lightly charred and tender, about 10 minutes, turning over once. Place shrimp in grill basket on same grill rack with pineapple wedges and cook until opaque throughout, 3 to 4 minutes, turning over once. Transfer shrimp to large bowl. Transfer pineapple to cutting board and cut into ¹/₂-inch chunks.

6. Lightly spray both sides of tortillas with cooking spray and place on hot grill rack. Cook until toasted, 2 to 3 minutes, turning over once.

7. To bowl with shrimp, add greens, endive, pineapple, and remaining 1 cup basil and dressing; toss to coat. Place 2 tortillas on each of 6 plates; top with salad.

EACH SERVING: About 350 calories, 23g protein, 43g carbohydrate, 11g total fat (2g saturated), 140mg cholesterol, 420mg sodium

Grilled Shrimp and Black Bean Salad

Tex-Mex black bean salad turns into a great summer supper when you add grilled shrimp. Rinsing the black beans removes excess sodium.

PREP: 15 minutes   GRILL: 3 to 4 minutes
MAKES: 4 main-dish servings

1	lime
2	cans (15 to 19 ounces each) black beans, rinsed and drained
2	small ripe plum tomatoes (about 4 ounces each), chopped
2	green onions, thinly sliced
1	small yellow pepper, stem and seeds removed, chopped
1	jalapeño chile, seeded and finely chopped
1/2	cup loosely packed fresh cilantro leaves, chopped
1	tablespoon olive oil
3/4	teaspoon salt
1	pound large shrimp, shelled and deveined
1	lime, cut into wedges

1. Prepare outdoor grill for direct grilling over medium-high heat.

2. Meanwhile, from lime, grate 1/2 teaspoon peel and squeeze 2 tablespoons juice. In large bowl, stir lime juice, 1/4 teaspoon peel, beans, tomatoes, green onions, yellow pepper, jalapeño, cilantro, oil, and 1/2 teaspoon salt. Set aside at room temperature while you grill shrimp. Makes about 5 cups.

3. Rinse shrimp with cold running water; pat dry with paper towels. In medium bowl, toss shrimp with remaining 1/4 teaspoon each lime peel and salt.

4. Place shrimp on hot grill rack (or hot flat grill topper) and grill just until opaque throughout, 3 to 4 minutes, turning over once.

5. Stir half of shrimp into bean salad; top with remaining shrimp. Serve with lime wedges.

EACH SERVING: About 290 calories, 31g protein, 41g carbohydrate, 5g total fat (1g saturated), 180mg cholesterol, 890mg sodium

THE INS AND OUTS OF ENDIVE

Pay less attention to the size and shape of the head of Belgian endive, which can vary, than to the color of this mildly bitter vegetable. It should be ivory, with pretty pastel-yellow leaf tips. Also called *witloof* (white leaf), Belgian endive is cultivated in complete darkness to prevent it from turning green and very bitter; the labor-intensive growing process involves harvesting the plant, cutting off the outer leaves, and planting it again. The best heads are crisp, firmly packed, and shipped between layers of opaque waxed paper to keep out the light. At home, wrap the endive in a paper towel, place in a plastic bag, refrigerate, and use within a few days.

Mediterranean Swordfish Salad

This salad is a deliciously different combination of bold flavors and contrasting textures, with crisp cucumber, juicy grape tomatoes, salty feta cheese, and the meaty grilled goodness of swordfish.

PREP: **14 minutes**   GRILL: **10 minutes**
MAKES: **4 main-dish servings**

1	swordfish steak, 1 inch thick (about 1¼ pounds)
3	tablespoons olive oil
¼	teaspoon ground black pepper
¾	teaspoon salt
2	tablespoons fresh lemon juice
1½	teaspoons chopped fresh oregano or ½ teaspoon dried oregano
1	English (seedless) cucumber (about 12 ounces)
1	pint grape or cherry tomatoes, halved
⅓	cup crumbled feta cheese

1. Heat ridged grill pan on medium-high heat until hot. Pat swordfish dry with paper towels. Rub 1 tablespoon oil all over swordfish and sprinkle with pepper and ½ teaspoon salt. Place swordfish in pan and cook until swordfish is browned on both sides and just turns opaque throughout, 6 to 8 minutes, turning over once.

2. Meanwhile, in large bowl, combine lemon juice, oregano, and remaining 2 tablespoons oil and ¼ teaspoon salt. Cut unpeeled cucumber into ½-inch chunks.

3. When swordfish is done, transfer to cutting board; trim and discard skin. Cut swordfish into 1-inch cubes. Add swordfish, cucumber, and tomatoes to dressing in bowl; toss gently to coat. Sprinkle with feta to serve.

EACH SERVING: About 315 calories, 32g protein, 8g carbohydrate, 17g total fat (5g saturated), 68mg cholesterol, 720mg sodium

Burgers

The burger is the bedrock of backyard grilling—what are Memorial Day, July 4th, and Labor Day without a grill full of sizzling burgers? We've got the recipe for The Perfect Burger, plus our "7 Secrets for a Great Burger," guaranteed to tranform you into grillmeister extraordinaire. If you're looking for ideas to jazz up your basic beef burger, we've got you covered, with all sorts of fun twists, like Tex-Mex Burgers, Blue and Black Burgers, Inside-Out Burgers with Avocado and Sprouts—even Meatloaf Burgers with Sautéed Carrots.

But how about striking out for territories beyond beef? We've included a delicious selection of pork, lamb, poultry, and fish burgers, including Greek Lamb Burgers with Minted Yogurt Sauce, Chicken Caesar Burgers, Grilled Cilantro Pork Burgers, and Fresh Salmon Burgers with Capers and Dill. And for those times when you'd like to go entirely meatless, try one of our vegetarian burgers.

BLT Burgers, page 77

The Perfect Burger

One of the most important keys to a delicious, juicy burger is to handle the ground beef as little as possible. Shape your burgers without compacting them too much.

PREP: **10 minutes plus soaking skewers**
GRILL: **8 to 10 minutes**

MAKES: **4 burgers**

4   (12-inch) bamboo skewers

1¼   pounds ground beef chuck

½   teaspoon coarsely ground black pepper

1   teaspoon salt

1   large sweet onion (12 ounces), such as Vidalia or Maui, cut into ½-inch-thick rounds

4   hamburger buns, split

4   green-leaf lettuce leaves

2   ripe medium tomatoes (6 to 8 ounces each), thinly sliced

1. Soak skewers in *hot water* to cover at least 20 minutes. Meanwhile, prepare outdoor grill for covered direct grilling over medium heat, or preheat ridged grill pan over medium heat until very hot.

2. Shape ground beef into four ³/₄-inch-thick patties. Sprinkle pepper and ³/₄ teaspoon salt on both sides of patties. Thread 1 skewer through center of each onion slice. Sprinkle onion with remaining ¹/₄ teaspoon salt.

3. Place burgers and onion on hot grill; cook 8 to 10 minutes for medium or to desired doneness, turning over once. Onion should be browned and tender. About 1 minute before the burgers are done, add buns, cut sides down, to grill. Grill just until toasted. Serve burgers on buns with lettuce, tomato, and onion.

EACH BURGER: About 485 calories, 31g protein, 33g carbohydrate, 25g total fat (9g saturated), 96mg cholesterol, 920mg sodium

7 Secrets for a Great Burger

1. Ground chuck is a favorite for burgers. Its rich flavor is a perfect partner to just about any condiment you pair it with. Its juiciness is due to its fat content. Chuck is 81 to 85 percent lean. Be sure to get 1¼ pounds for 4 burgers, because 5 ounces raw cooks down to 4 ounces.

2. If not using meat right away, refrigerate it in its supermarket wrap for up to 2 days. (And don't let the meat or its juice touch other foods; the spread of *E. coli* and other bacteria is a real risk.) For longer storage, repackage it in freezer wrap or foil and freeze; use within 3 months.

3. Handle beef gently when shaping it, so you don't end up with a dense, dry burger. Start with a mound, flatten it slightly, and smooth around the edges.

4. Make sure the grill is hot before putting the burgers on. A hot grill sears the meat, so it won't stick.

5. Don't flatten patties with a spatula while grilling: Pressing squeezes out the flavorful juices and won't speed up cooking.

6. For safety's sake, cook thoroughly, until there's just a trace of pink in the center (medium doneness, 160°F). Burgers don't have to be well done to be safe to eat, just not rare. It's risky to eat undercooked burgers because bacteria on the surface of the meat before it's ground can be transferred to its interior during the grinding process. Cooking times vary, depending on the thickness of the burgers and the heat of the grill, so the only way to be sure they're done is to make them all the same size, then fork into one of them to check for doneness.

7. Cheese lovers, don't get more cheese on the grill slats than on the burgers. Once the patties are cooked to medium, blanket the top with Cheddar, Swiss, or another favorite, and cook with the grill lid down for about a minute.

Tex-Mex Burgers

For an all-out splurge, serve these burgers with shredded lettuce, sliced red onion, extra salsa, and a topping of guacamole (page 283). For a spicier burger, choose a medium to hot salsa and increase the chili powder to 2 teaspoons. You can also top the burger with sliced Monterey Jack. Just cover the grill to melt the cheese, and you've got a Tex-Mex cheeseburger.

PREP: 5 minutes   **GRILL:** 10 to 12 minutes
MAKES: 4 burgers

1	pound lean (90%) ground beef
2	tablespoons minced onion
2	tablespoons bottled salsa
½	teaspoon salt
1	teaspoon chili powder
4	seeded rolls, split

1. Prepare outdoor grill for direct grilling over medium heat, or lightly spray a ridged grill pan with nonstick cooking spray, then heat on medium until hot.

2. In medium bowl, combine ground beef, onion, salsa, salt, and chili powder just until well blended but not overmixed. Shape mixture into four ³/₄-inch-thick patties, each 1 inch thick, handling meat as gently as possible, for best texture.

3. Place burgers on hot grill rack or pan and grill, turning once, 10 to 12 minutes for medium or to desired doneness.

4. Place rolls, cut side down, on grill over medium heat and toast, without turning, just until grill marks appear on cut side of rolls. Serve burgers on rolls.

EACH BURGER: About 325 calories, 27g protein, 23g carbohydrate, 14g total fat (5g saturated), 70mg cholesterol, 670mg sodium

THE STEPS

1. Divide meat into 4 equal portions; shape each into a ³/₄-inch-thick patty. Handle as little as possible so burgers won't be tough.

2. Cook thoroughly.

BLT Burgers

Take a classic American sandwich and turn it into a burger—perfect. For photo, see page 72.

PREP: 15 minutes   **GRILL:** 10 to 12 minutes
MAKES: 4 burgers

¼   cup ketchup
¼   cup light mayonnaise
1   tablespoon yellow mustard
1¼ pounds ground beef chuck
8   slices bacon
4   sesame-seed buns, split
sliced sweet onion, tomato, and romaine
    lettuce leaves

1. Prepare outdoor grill for direct grilling over medium heat, or lightly spray a ridged grill pan with nonstick cooking spray, then heat on medium until hot.

2. In small bowl, stir ketchup, mayonnaise, and mustard until blended. Set aside. Makes about ½ cup.

3. Shape ground beef into four ³⁄₄-inch-thick burgers, handling beef as gently as possible. Wrap each with 2 strips bacon, perpendicular to each other.

4. Place burgers on hot grill rack or pan; cook 10 to 12 minutes for medium or desired doneness, turning over once.

5. During last 2 minutes of cooking burgers, place rolls, cut sides down, on grill rack and heat until lightly toasted. Serve burgers on buns with onion, tomato, lettuce, and sauce on the side.

EACH BURGER: About 575 calories, 34g protein, 27g carbohydrate, 36g total fat (12g saturated), 111mg cholesterol, 870mg sodium

Blue and Black Burgers

A rich blue cheese filling and a drizzle of basil olive oil set this gourmet burger apart.

PREP: 15 minutes   **GRILL:** 12 to 14 minutes
MAKES: 4 burgers

2   tablespoons olive oil
2   tablespoons chopped fresh basil
1¼ pounds ground beef chuck
4   ounces blue cheese, divided into four 1-inch
    chunks
¾   teaspoon salt
1   tablespoon coarsely ground black pepper
4   brioche rolls, split
4   thin slices sweet onion

1. Prepare outdoor grill for direct grilling over medium heat, or lightly spray a ridged grill pan with nonstick cooking spray, then heat on medium until hot. In cup, combine oil and basil; brush on 1 cut side of each roll. Set aside.

2. Hold one-fourth of beef in your hand; press a chunk of blue cheese into center, then lightly press meat around to enclose cheese. Burger will be about 1¼ inches thick. Repeat with remaining beef and blue cheese. Sprinkle burgers with salt and pepper to season both sides.

3. Place burgers on hot grill rack or pan; cook 12 to 14 minutes for medium or desired doneness, turning over once.

4. During last 2 minutes of cooking, place rolls, cut sides down, on grill rack and heat until lightly toasted. Serve burgers with rolls and onion.

EACH BURGER: About 745 calories, 40g protein, 39g carbohydrate, 47g total fat (17g saturated), 190mg cholesterol, 1,235mg sodium

Patty Melts

Here's a new twist—burger and Swiss on rye!

PREP: 10 minutes   **GRILL:** 8 to 10 minutes
MAKES: 4 burgers

1½ pounds ground beef chuck
½   teaspoon salt
½   teaspoon ground black pepper
5   (8-inch) metal skewers
1   large onion (10 to 12 ounces), cut crosswise into 5 thick slices
4   slices (1 ounce each) Swiss cheese
2   tablespoons stone-ground mustard
4   oval slices rye bread

1. Prepare outdoor grill for covered direct grilling over medium heat, or lightly spray a ridged grill pan with nonstick cooking spray, then heat on medium until hot.

2. Meanwhile, shape ground beef into four ½-inch-thick oval patties, handling beef as gently as possible. Sprinkle salt and pepper on both sides of patties. For easier handling, insert skewers horizontally through onion slices.

3. Place patties and onion slices on hot grill rack or pan. Cover grill and cook 8 to 10 minutes for medium and until onion is tender and browned, turning patties and onion slices over once. During the last 2 minutes of cooking, place cheese slices on burgers to melt.

4. To serve, spread mustard on 1 side of each bread slice. Top each slice with a patty and some grilled onion, separating onion slices into rings.

EACH SERVING: About 535 calories, 38g protein, 24g carbohydrate, 31g total fat (14g saturated), 121mg cholesterol, 770mg sodium

---

THE GROUND ROUNDUP

Supermarkets offer so many choices in ground meat and poultry. Here's some help with choosing.

MEAT	FLAVOR PROFILE	APPROXIMATE NUTRITIONAL VALUES*	COOK-TO INTERNAL TEMPERATURE
Ground beef chuck, 80% lean	Juicy, rich, bold, robust, hearty	307 calories, 20g fat (8g saturated), 103mg cholesterol	160°F (medium doneness)
Ground lamb	Unique, full flavored, firm texture, aromatic	321 calories, 22g fat (9g saturated), 102mg cholesterol	160°F (medium doneness)
Ground pork	Delicate, mild, good alternative to beef and poultry	336 calories, 24 g fat (9g saturated), 107mg cholesterol	160°F (medium doneness)
Ground chicken	Lean, light texture, tender, subtle flavor	172 calories, 11g fat (3g saturated), 65mg cholesterol	170°F (well-done)
Ground turkey	Moist, delicate flavor, denser than chicken	213 calories, 12g fat (3g saturated), 113mg cholesterol	170°F (well-done)

*Per 4-ounce cooked burger. Values vary among brands.

Inside-Out Burgers with Avocado and Sprouts

Creative condiments—guacamole and alfalfa sprouts—and cheddar in the center give lean beef patties extra zip.

PREP: 15 minutes **GRILL: about 12 minutes**
MAKES: 4 main-dish servings

1½ pounds lean (90%) ground beef
2   ounces shredded sharp Cheddar cheese (½ cup)
½   teaspoon plus ⅛ teaspoon salt
¼   teaspoon pepper
1   ripe avocado
1   tablespoon fresh lime juice
1   cup alfalfa or radish sprouts
¼   cup loosely packed fresh cilantro leaves, chopped
3   multigrain hamburger buns, split
2   small tomatoes, each cut into 4 wedges

1. Lightly spray a ridged grill pan with nonstick cooking spray, then heat on medium until hot, or prepare outdoor grill for covered direct grilling over medium heat.

2. Meanwhile, on work surface, shape ground beef into 3½-inch patties, handling meat as gently as possible for best texture. Place Cheddar in center of 4 patties, leaving ½-inch border around each patty's edge. Top with remaining 4 patties, and press edges together to seal. Lightly sprinkle burgers with ½ teaspoon salt and pepper to season both sides.

3. Place burgers in hot grill pan or on hot rack, and cook 12 minutes for medium or to desired doneness, turning burgers over once halfway through cooking.

4. Meanwhile, in small bowl, mash avocado with lime juice and remaining ⅛ teaspoon salt. In another small bowl, combine alfalfa sprouts and chopped cilantro.

5. Serve burgers on buns topped with sprout and avocado mixtures. Serve tomato wedges on the side.

EACH SERVING: About 480 calories, 36g protein, 25g carbohydrate, 27g total fat (9g saturated), 102mg cholesterol, 730mg sodium

Meat Loaf Burgers
with Sautéed Carrots

Here's a kid-pleasing meal: Meat loaf patties on a hamburger bun with sautéed baby carrots on the side.

PREP: 15 minutes   GRILL: 10 to 12 minutes
MAKES: 4 main-dish servings

½   cup water
1   tablespoon butter or margarine
1   bag (16 ounces) baby carrots
½   teaspoon salt
¼   teaspoon freshly ground black pepper
1   tablespoon brown sugar
¼   cup ketchup
1   tablespoon spicy brown mustard
1¼   pounds lean (90%) ground beef
1   stalk celery
½   small onion, finely chopped
¼   cup plain dried bread crumbs
1   clove garlic, crushed with press
2   teaspoons Worcestershire sauce
4   potato rolls, split and toasted
4   lettuce leaves

1. In 12-inch skillet, heat water and butter over medium heat until simmering. Add carrots, ¼ teaspoon salt, and pepper; cook, covered, 10 minutes or until carrots are tender. Uncover; stir in sugar and cook 3 minutes or until carrots are coated and liquid evaporates. Remove from heat; cover and keep warm.

2. Meanwhile, lightly spray ridged grill pan with nonstick cooking spray, then heat over medium until hot.

3. In cup, combine ketchup and mustard. In large bowl, mix 1 tablespoon ketchup mixture with beef, celery, onion, bread crumbs, garlic, Worcestershire, and remaining ¼ teaspoon salt until blended; do not overmix. Shape beef mixture into four ³/₄-inch-thick burgers, handling meat as gently as possible for best texture.

4. Place burgers in hot grill pan; cook 10 to 12 minutes for medium or to desired doneness, turning burgers over once halfway through cooking.

5. Serve burgers on rolls with lettuce and remaining ketchup mixture. Serve carrots on the side.

EACH SERVING: About 505 calories, 36g protein, 52g carbohydrate, 18g total fat (5g saturated), 87mg cholesterol, 975mg sodium

Gingered Burgers with Lime Slaw

Flavored with fresh ginger, cilantro, green onions, and seasoned oil, these juicy burgers end up tasting like a spicy Asian meatball.

PREP: **20 minutes**   GRILL: **10 to 12 minutes**
MAKES: **4 main-dish servings**

- ¼ cup light mayonnaise
- 1 tablespoon reduced-sodium soy sauce
- 2 limes
- 8 ounces (3 ½ cups) shredded cabbage for coleslaw
- ½ teaspoon salt
- 1¼ pounds lean (90%) ground beef (see Tip)
- ½ cup loosely packed fresh cilantro leaves, coarsely chopped
- 2 green onions, chopped
- 1 tablespoon finely chopped, peeled fresh ginger
- 1 teaspoon Asian sesame oil
- ¼ teaspoon crushed red pepper
- 4 sesame-seed hamburger buns, split and toasted

1. In cup, stir mayonnaise and soy sauce until blended; set aside. From limes, grate ½ teaspoon peel and squeeze 3 tablespoons juice. In large bowl, toss together lime peel and juice with cabbage and ¼ teaspoon salt; set aside.

2. Lightly spray ridged grill pan with nonstick cooking spray, then heat on medium until hot, or prepare outdoor grill for covered direct grilling over medium heat.

3. Meanwhile, in medium bowl, combine beef, cilantro, green onions, ginger, sesame oil, crushed red pepper, and remaining ¼ teaspoon salt until blended, but do not overmix. Shape beef mixture into four ¾-inch-thick burgers, handling meat as gently as possible.

4. Place burgers in hot grill pan or on hot rack; cook 10 to 12 minutes for medium or to desired doneness, turning burgers over once halfway through cooking.

5. Serve burgers on buns with slaw and soy mayonnaise. Serve with any additional slaw on the side.

EACH SERVING: About 430 calories, 32g protein, 28g cargohydrate, 21g total fat (7g saturated fat), 92mg cholesterol, 865mg sodium

Tip: The Asian flavors in this dish go well with ground chicken and turkey, too. Prepare burgers as directed, but cook chicken or turkey burgers 15 minutes to assure doneness.

Grilled Cilantro Pork Burgers

This is a wonderful Asian-style take on the pork burger—almost like a pork dumpling on a bun! You can also make these burgers using ground chicken or turkey.

PREP: 15 minutes   **GRILL:** 10 to 12 minutes
MAKES: 4 burgers

¼   cup light mayonnaise

1   tablespoon soy sauce

1¼   pounds ground pork or chicken

½   cup loosely packed fresh cilantro leaves, coarsely chopped

3   green onions, chopped

1   tablespoon dry sherry

1   tablespoon finely chopped, peeled fresh ginger

1   teaspoon Asian sesame oil

¼   teaspoon crushed red pepper

¾   teaspoon salt

4   sesame-seed hamburger buns, split and toasted

1. Prepare outdoor grill for covered direct grilling over medium heat, or lightly spray a ridged grill pan with nonstick cooking spray, then heat on medium until hot.

2. In cup, stir mayonnaise and soy sauce until blended. Set aside.

3. In medium bowl, combine pork, cilantro, green onions, sherry, ginger, sesame oil, crushed red pepper, and salt until blended, but do not overmix. Shape pork mixture into four ³/₄-inch-thick burgers, handling meat gently for best texture.

4. Place burgers on hot grill rack or pan; cook until entirely cooked through, 10 to 12 minutes, turning over once—an instant-read meat thermometer inserted horizontally into center should register 160°F. (If using chicken or turkey, spray burgers with nonstick cooking spray and cook 12 to 14 minutes, to an internal temperature of 170°F.)

5. Serve burgers on buns with soy mayonnaise.

EACH BURGER: About 475 calories, 32g protein, 25g carbohydrate, 26g total fat (8g saturated), 106mg cholesterol, 1,120mg sodium

Greek Lamb Burgers with Minted Yogurt Sauce

These burgers can also be made with beef or poultry. If you decide to use chicken, spray the burgers with nonstick cooking spray and cook 12 to 14 minutes, to an internal temperature of 170°F.

PREP: 20 minutes **GRILL:** 10 TO 12 minutes
MAKES: 4 burgers

1	ripe plum tomato, chopped
½	cup plain low-fat yogurt
2	tablespoons light mayonnaise
¾	cup loosely packed fresh mint leaves, coarsely chopped
1	teaspoon salt
¼	teaspoon ground black pepper
1¼	pounds ground lamb
¼	cup walnuts, finely chopped (optional)
1	garlic clove, crushed with garlic press
2	teaspoons ground cumin
4	(6-inch) pitas
1	medium Kirby cucumber, sliced

1. Prepare outdoor grill for covered direct grilling over medium heat, or lightly spray a ridged grill pan with nonstick cooking spray, then heat on medium until hot.

2. In small bowl, stir tomato, yogurt, mayonnaise, 2 tablespoons mint, ¼ teaspoon salt, and pepper until blended; set sauce aside. Makes about ¾ cup.

3. Prepare burgers: In medium bowl, combine lamb, walnuts, if using, garlic, cumin, ¾ teaspoon salt, and remaining mint until just blended. Shape lamb mixture into four ¾-inch-thick burgers, handling meat gently for best texture.

4. Place burgers on hot grill rack or pan; cook 10 to 12 minutes for medium or to desired doneness, turning over once. (An instant-read meat thermometer inserted horizontally into center should register 160°F.)

5. To serve, cut off one-third from side of each pita; save for another use. Place burgers in pitas with yogurt sauce and cucumber.

EACH BURGER: About 485 calories, 32g protein, 31g carbohydrate, 25g total fat (10g saturated), 105mg cholesterol, 985mg sodium

Your Basic Chicken Burger

Here's your chicken burger, straight up, plus three suggestions for jazzing it up.

PREP: 20 minutes   GRILL: 12 to 14 minutes
MAKES: 4 burgers

1 pound ground chicken breast
1 medium carrot, peeled and grated (½ cup)
2 green onions, finely chopped
1 garlic clove, crushed with garlic press
4 hamburger buns, split and toasted
sliced cucumber, lettuce leaves, and green onion (optional)

1. Prepare outdoor grill for direct grilling over medium heat, or lightly spray a ridged grill pan with nonstick cooking spray, then heat on medium until hot.

2. In medium bowl, combine ground chicken, carrot, green onions, and garlic (mixture will be very soft and moist). On waxed paper, shape mixture into four 3½-inch patties.

3. Place patties on hot grill rack or pan. If grill has widely spaced grates, place burgers on perforated grill topper to keep them intact. Grill, turning once, until juices run clear when center of burger is pierced with tip of knife, 12 to 14 minutes. (An instant-read thermometer inserted horizontally into center should register 170°F.)

4. Place burgers on buns. Serve with cucumber, lettuce, and green onions, if you like.

EACH BURGER: About 275 calories, 30g protein, 24g carbohydrate, 5g total fat (1g saturated), 72mg cholesterol, 310mg sodium

TERIYAKI CHICKEN BURGERS: Prepare basic burgers as directed, but add *2 tablespoons soy sauce, 1 tablespoon seasoned rice vinegar, 2 teaspoons grated, peeled fresh ginger*, and *2 teaspoons Asian sesame oil* to ground chicken mixture in step 2. (Prepare burger mixture just before cooking to prevent ginger from changing texture of meat.)

EACH TERIYAKI CHICKEN BURGER: About 305 calories, 31g protein, 26g carbohydrate, 8g total fat (2g saturated), 72mg cholesterol, 940mg sodium

BARBECUE CHICKEN BURGERS: Prepare basic burgers as directed, but add *2 tablespoons chili sauce, 1 tablespoon light (mild) molasses, 2 teaspoons cayenne pepper sauce, 2 teaspoons Worcestershire sauce*, and *¼ teaspoon salt* to ground chicken mixture in step 2.

EACH BARBECUE CHICKEN BURGER: About 295 calories, 31g protein, 30g carbohydrate, 5g total fat (1g saturated), 72mg cholesterol, 715mg sodium

HERB CHICKEN BURGERS: Prepare basic burgers as directed, but add *2 tablespoons finely chopped fresh dill, 1 tablespoon dried mint, 1 tablespoon fresh lemon juice, 1 teaspoon ground cumin, ½ teaspoon salt*, and *⅛ teaspoon ground red pepper (cayenne)* to ground chicken mixture in step 2.

EACH HERB CHICKEN BURGER: About 280 calories, 31g protein, 25g carbohydrate, 5g total fat (1g saturated), 72mg cholesterol, 605mg sodium

Buffalo Chicken Burgers

We paired the traditional Buffalo-wing flavors of pungent blue cheese and fiery hot sauce to create this exciting chicken burger.

PREP: 15 minutes   GRILL: 12 to 14 minutes
MAKES: 4 burgers

¼   cup light mayonnaise

¼   cup reduced-fat sour cream

2   ounces blue cheese, crumbled (about ½ cup)

2   teaspoons cider vinegar

½   teaspoon Worcestershire sauce

1¼   pounds ground chicken or turkey

1   stalk celery, finely chopped

3   tablespoons cayenne pepper sauce, plus more for serving

nonstick cooking spray

4   hamburger buns, split and toasted

lettuce leaves

carrot and celery sticks

1. Prepare outdoor grill for direct grilling over medium heat, or lightly spray a ridged grill pan with nonstick cooking spray, then heat on medium until hot.

2. In small bowl, stir mayonnaise, sour cream, blue cheese, vinegar, and Worcestershire until blended. Set blue cheese sauce aside. Makes about ³/₄ cup.

3. In medium bowl, combine chicken, celery, and cayenne pepper sauce just until blended. Shape mixture into four ³/₄-inch-thick burgers. Spray both sides of burgers with cooking spray.

4. Place burgers on hot grill rack or pan. If grill has widely spaced grates, place burgers on perforated grill topper to keep them intact. Grill, turning once, until juices run clear when center of burger is pierced with tip of knife, 12 to 14 minutes. (An instant-read meat thermometer inserted horizontally into center should register 170°F.)

5. Serve burgers on buns with lettuce and some blue cheese sauce. Serve remaining blue cheese sauce with carrot and celery sticks for dipping. Pass additional cayenne pepper sauce with burgers if you like.

EACH BURGER WITHOUT SAUCE: About 345 calories, 27g protein, 22g carbohydrate, 16g total fat (1g saturated), 0mg cholesterol, 785mg sodium

EACH 1 TABLESPOON BLUE CHEESE SAUCE: About 40 calories, 1g protein, 1g carbohydrate, 4g total fat (2g saturated), 7mg cholesterol, 110mg sodium

Chicken Caesar Burgers

Everything delicious about a Caesar salad—lemon, Parmesan, and anchovy—makes an appearance in this easy chicken burger.

PREP: 20 minutes   GRILL: 12 to 14 minutes
MAKES: 4 burgers

1	lemon
2	anchovy fillets, minced
1	small garlic clove, minced
1/3	cup light mayonnaise
1/2	cup freshly grated Parmesan cheese
1	large heart of romaine lettuce
1	tablespoon olive oil
3/4	teaspoon salt
1 1/4	pounds ground chicken or turkey
1/2	teaspoon ground black pepper
	nonstick cooking spray
4	(4-inch) squares focaccia bread, 1 inch thick, each split horizontally in half and toasted

1. Prepare outdoor grill for direct grilling over medium heat, or lightly spray a ridged grill pan with nonstick cooking spray, then heat on medium until hot.

2. From lemon, grate 1 teaspoon peel and squeeze 2 tablespoons juice. In small bowl, stir together lemon peel and juice, anchovies, garlic, mayonnaise, and 1/4 cup Parmesan. Set Caesar sauce aside. Makes about 1/2 cup.

3. Quarter romaine heart lengthwise. Place romaine and any loose leaves on plate; drizzle with oil and sprinkle with 1/4 teaspoon salt.

4. In medium bowl, combine chicken, pepper, and remaining 1/2 teaspoon salt and 1/4 cup Parmesan just until blended. Shape into four 3/4-inch-thick burgers. Spray both sides of burgers with cooking spray.

5. Place burgers on hot grill rack or pan. If grill has widely spaced grates, place burgers on perforated grill topper to keep them intact. Cook, turning once, until juices run clear when center of burger is pierced with tip of knife, 12 to 14 minutes. (An instant-read meat thermometer inserted horizontally into center should register 170°F.)

6. About 5 minutes before burgers are done, add romaine to grill rack and cook until lightly browned and softened, about 5 minutes, turning occasionally and transferring quarters and leaves to platter as they are done.

7. Serve burgers on focaccia with romaine and Caesar sauce.

EACH BURGER: About 680 calories, 42g protein, 54g carbohydrate, 33g total fat (4g saturated), 25mg cholesterol, 1,550mg sodium

Your Basic Turkey Burger

When you are trying to build a better burger, ground turkey is a great place to start because it plays so well with other flavors. Start with the basic version, then have fun with all the variations.

PREP: 10 minutes   **GRILL:** 12 to 14 minutes
MAKES: 4 burgers

1   pound ground turkey (85% lean)
½   teaspoon salt
¼   teaspoon ground black pepper
4   hamburger buns, toasted
4   lettuce leaves
4   tomato slices

1. Prepare outdoor grill for direct grilling over medium heat, or lightly spray a ridged grill pan with nonstick cooking spray, then heat on medium until hot.

2. In medium bowl, combine ground turkey, salt, and pepper until blended, but do not overmix. On waxed paper, shape mixture into four ¾-inch-thick patties, handling as gently as possible.

3. Place patties on hot grill rack or pan. If grill has widely spaced grates, place burgers on a perforated grill topper to keep them intact. Grill, turning once, until juices run clear when center of burger is pierced with tip of knife, 12 to 14 minutes. (An instant-read meat thermometer inserted horizontally into center should register 170°F.)

4. To serve, place burgers on bottom halves of buns; top with lettuce, tomato, and bun tops.

EACH BURGER: About 325 calories, 27g protein, 22g carbohydrate, 13g total fat (3g saturated), 87mg cholesterol, 625mg sodium

CHEESY CHILE TURKEY BURGERS: Prepare basic turkey burgers as above but in step 1, add *1 cup shredded Monterey Jack cheese (4 ounces), 1 can (4 ounces) drained, chopped mild green chiles, and 1 small seeded and chopped plum tomato* to meat mixture. In step 3, in place of lettuce and tomato, top burgers with *⅓ cup mild salsa.*

EACH CHEESY CHILE TURKEY BURGER: About 440 calories, 34g protein, 25g carbohydrate, 22g total fat (9g saturated), 112mg cholesterol, 1,045mg sodium

ASIAN BARBECUE TURKEY BURGERS: Prepare basic turkey burgers as above but in step 1, add *¼ cup chopped fresh cilantro, 2 finely chopped green onions, 2 tablespoons soy sauce*, and *1 tablespoon minced, peeled fresh ginger* to meat mixture. In step 3, in place of lettuce and tomato, top burgers with *½ cup hoisin sauce.*

EACH ASIAN BARBECUE TURKEY BURGER: About 370 calories, 28g protein, 31g carbohydrate, 14g total fat (4g saturated), 87mg cholesterol, 1,375mg sodium

Jerk Turkey Burgers

When ground turkey is spiced up with Jamaican jerk seasoning and fresh thyme, burger night takes on juicy and flavorful edge.

PREP: 10 minutes   **GRILL: 12 to 14 minutes**
MAKES: 4 burgers

⅓   cup light mayonnaise
2   teaspoons chopped fresh thyme
¼   teaspoon freshly grated orange peel
1¼ pounds ground turkey or chicken
2   green onions, chopped
1   small jalapeño chile with seeds, chopped
¾   teaspoon salt
4   teaspoons Jamaican jerk seasoning
nonstick cooking spray
4   hamburger buns, split and toasted
4   lettuce leaves

1. Prepare outdoor grill for direct grilling over medium heat, or lightly spray a ridged grill pan with nonstick cooking spray, then heat on medium until hot.

2. In small bowl, stir mayonnaise, thyme, and orange peel until well blended. Set sauce aside. Makes about ⅓ cup.

3. In medium bowl, combine turkey, green onions, jalapeño, and salt just until blended. Shape mixture into four ¾-inch-thick burgers. On a sheet of waxed paper, pat jerk seasoning onto both sides of burgers. Lightly spray both sides of burgers with cooking spray.

4. Place burgers on hot grill rack or pan; cook, turning once, until juices run clear when center of burger is pierced with tip of knife, 12 to 14 minutes. (An instant-read meat thermometer inserted horizontally into center should register 170°F.)

5. Serve burgers on buns with lettuce and seasoned mayonnaise.

EACH BURGER: About 445 calories, 33g protein, 24g carbohydrate, 23g total fat (6g saturated), 115mg cholesterol, 122mg sodium

Fresh Salmon Burgers with Capers and Dill

When you want a burger, but you're craving something out of the ordinary, think salmon.

PREP: 25 minutes   GRILL: 6 to 8 minutes
MAKES: 4 burgers

1   large lemon
¼   cup light mayonnaise
1   tablespoon capers, drained and coarsely chopped
1   salmon fillet (1 pound), skin removed
¼   cup loosely packed fresh dill fronds, chopped
2   green onions, thinly sliced
½   cup plain dried bread crumbs
¾   teaspoon salt
nonstick cooking spray
4   whole-wheat hamburger buns, split and toasted
4   green-leaf lettuce leaves

1. Prepare outdoor grill for direct grilling over medium heat, or lightly spray a ridged grill pan with nonstick cooking spray, then heat on medium until hot.

2. Meanwhile, from lemon, grate 1 teaspoon peel and squeeze 1 tablespoon juice.

3. In small bowl, stir lemon juice and ¹/₂ teaspoon lemon peel with mayonnaise and capers until blended. Set lemon-caper sauce aside. Makes about ¹/₃ cup.

4. Remove any pin bones from salmon. With large chef's knife, finely chop salmon; place in medium bowl. Add dill, green onions, ¹/₄ cup bread crumbs, salt, and remaining ¹/₂ teaspoon lemon peel to salmon; gently mix with fork until

combined. Shape salmon mixture into four 3-inch round burgers.

5. Sprinkle both sides of burgers with remaining ¹/₄ cup bread crumbs. Spray both sides of burgers with cooking spray.

6. Place burgers on hot grill rack or pan over medium heat. Cook burgers 6 to 8 minutes, until browned on the outside and still slightly pink in the center for medium, or to desired doneness, turning burgers over once.

7. Serve burgers on buns with lettuce and lemon-caper mayonnaise.

EACH BURGER: About 380 calories, 27g protein, 34g carbohydrate, 15g total fat (3g saturated), 65mg cholesterol, 990mg sodium

Asian Tuna Burgers

Finely chop the fish by hand for a light texture; using a food processor will make the patties dense and dry. Serve with or without a bun, with pickled ginger or Cucumber Relish (page 283).

PREP: 15 minutes   GRILL: 6 to 7 minutes
MAKES: 4 burgers

1	tuna steak (about 1 pound)
1	green onion, thinly sliced
2	tablespoons reduced-sodium soy sauce
1	teaspoon grated, peeled fresh ginger
¼	teaspoon coarsely ground black pepper
¼	cup plain dried bread crumbs
2	tablespoons sesame seeds
	nonstick cooking spray

1. Prepare outdoor grill for direct grilling over medium heat.

2. With large chef's knife, finely chop tuna and place in medium bowl. Add green onion, soy sauce, ginger, and pepper; mix until combined (mixture will be very soft and moist). Shape tuna mixture into four 3-inch round patties.

3. On waxed paper, combine bread crumbs and sesame seeds. Carefully press patties into mixture, turning to coat both sides. Spray both sides of tuna patties with cooking spray.

4. Place patties on hot grill rack and grill, turning once, until browned on the outside and still slightly pink in the center for medium-rare, 6 to 7 minutes, or to desired doneness.

EACH BURGER: About 210 calories, 26g protein, 7g carbohydrate, 8g total fat (2g saturated), 38mg cholesterol, 400mg sodium

Portobello Mushroom Burgers

Richly flavored, meaty-textured, portobellos are a satisfying substitute for real burgers— the swap saves you 16 grams fat, 76 milligrams cholesterol, and 200-plus calories.

PREP: 10 minutes   GRILL: 10 to 11 minutes
MAKES: 4 burgers

2	packages (6 ounces each) portobello mushroom caps (4 large)
3	tablespoons bottled balsamic vinaigrette
⅓	cup light mayonnaise
¼	cup drained, jarred roasted red peppers
4	whole-wheat hamburger buns, split
1	large ripe tomato (10 to 12 ounces), thinly sliced
4	Boston lettuce leaves
2	large carrots, sliced diagonally

1. Heat ridged grill pan on medium-high until hot. Place mushrooms, stem sides down, in pan. Brush with half of vinaigrette and grill 5 minutes. Turn mushrooms over; brush with remaining vinaigrette and grill 5 to 6 minutes longer or until very tender.

2. Place mayonnaise and red pepper in blender. Pulse until peppers are chopped but not pureed, turning off blender and scraping down sides several times. Toast buns.

3. To serve, spread red pepper mayonnaise on bottom buns. Layer on mushrooms, tomato, lettuce, then bun tops. Serve with carrot slices.

EACH SERVING: About 270 calories, 8g protein, 33g carbohydrate, 12g total fat (2g saturated), 7mg cholesterol, 590mg sodium

Bulgur Bean Burgers

Satisfy vegetarians and meat eaters alike with these healthful, Middle Eastern–style burgers.

PREP: **20 minutes**   GRILL: **15 minutes**
MAKES: **4 burgers**

1	cup water
¾	teaspoon salt
½	cup bulgur
1	can (15 to 19 ounces) reduced-sodium black beans, rinsed and drained
1	container (6 ounces) plain low-fat yogurt
¼	teaspoon ground allspice
¼	teaspoon ground cinnamon
¼	teaspoon ground cumin
¼	cup loosely packed fresh mint leaves, finely chopped
	nonstick cooking spray
1	small Kirby cucumber, shredded
⅛	teaspoon ground black pepper
4	lettuce leaves
1	ripe medium tomato (6 to 8 ounces), sliced
4	whole-wheat hamburger buns, split

1. In 1-quart saucepan, heat water and ½ teaspoon salt to boiling over high heat. Stir in bulgur. Reduce heat to low; cover and simmer until water is absorbed, 12 to 14 minutes.

2. Meanwhile, in large bowl, with potato masher or fork, mash beans with 2 tablespoons yogurt until almost smooth. Stir in bulgur, allspice, cinnamon, cumin, and half of mint until combined. With lightly floured hands, shape bean mixture into four 3-inch round patties. (Patties can be made ahead. Cover and refrigerate up to 1 day.) Spray both sides of each patty lightly with cooking spray.

3. Heat ridged grill pan over medium heat until hot. Add burgers and cook until lightly browned and heated through, about 15 minutes, turning them over once.

4. While burgers are cooking, prepare yogurt sauce: In small bowl, combine cucumber, pepper, remaining yogurt, remaining mint, and remaining ¼ teaspoon salt. Makes about 1¼ cups.

5. To serve, divide lettuce, tomato slices, and burgers among buns; top with some yogurt sauce. Serve with remaining yogurt sauce on the side.

EACH BURGER: About 295 calories, 16g protein, 58g carbohydrate, 3g total fat (1g saturated), 3mg cholesterol, 960mg sodium

Southwestern Black-Bean Burgers

For an even easier weeknight meal, make a double batch and freeze the uncooked burgers. Then all you need to do is defrost them for ten minutes and cook until heated through, about twelve minutes, turning once.

PREP: **10 minutes**   GRILL: **6 minutes**
MAKES: **4 burgers**

1   can (15 to 19 ounces) black beans, rinsed and drained
2   tablespoons light mayonnaise
¼   cup loosely packed fresh cilantro leaves, chopped
1   tablespoon plain dried bread crumbs
½   teaspoon ground cumin
½   teaspoon hot pepper sauce
nonstick cooking spray
1   cup loosely packed sliced lettuce
4   (4-inch) mini whole-wheat pitas, warmed
½   cup mild salsa

1. Prepare outdoor grill for direct grilling over medium heat, or lightly spray a ridged grill pan with nonstick cooking spray, then heat on medium until hot.

2. In large bowl, with potato masher or fork, mash beans with mayonnaise until almost smooth (some lumps of beans should remain). Stir in cilantro, bread crumbs, cumin, and pepper sauce until combined. With lightly floured hands, shape bean mixture into four 3-inch round patties. Spray both sides of each patty lightly with cooking spray.

3. Place burgers on hot grill rack or pan. Cook burgers until lightly browned, 6 minutes, turning over once.

4. Arrange lettuce on pitas; top with burgers then salsa.

EACH BURGER: About 210 calories, 13g protein, 42g carbohydrate, 3g total fat (0g saturated), 0mg cholesterol, 715mg sodium

Vegetarian Rice and Beans Burgers

Who needs meat when you have delicious vegetarian choices like this for the grill?

PREP: 20 minutes   **GRILL:** 10 to 12 minutes
MAKES: 4 burgers

1	lemon
1	container (6 ounces) plain low-fat yogurt
4	tablespoons well-stirred tahini (sesame paste)
3/4	teaspoon salt
1	package (8.8 ounces) precooked whole-grain brown rice
1	can (15 to 19 ounces) garbanzo beans (chickpeas)
1	garlic clove, crushed with garlic press
1/2	teaspoon fennel seeds
	nonstick cooking spray
4	burrito-size spinach or sun-dried tomato tortillas
2	medium carrots, shredded
2	plum tomatoes, thinly sliced
1	Kirby cucumber, thinly sliced

1. Prepare outdoor grill for covered direct grilling over medium heat, or lightly spray a ridged grill pan with nonstick cooking spray, then heat on medium until hot.

2. Meanwhile, from lemon, grate 1 1/2 teaspoons peel and squeeze 2 tablespoons juice. In small serving bowl, stir lemon juice, yogurt, 2 tablespoons tahini, and 1/2 teaspoon salt until blended. Set yogurt sauce aside. Makes about 3/4 cup.

3. Heat rice in microwave oven as package label directs; set aside.

4. Reserve 1/4 cup liquid from beans. Rinse beans and drain well. In medium bowl, combine beans, lemon peel, garlic, fennel seeds, remaining 1/4 teaspoon salt and 2 tablespoons tahini, and reserved bean liquid. With potato masher, coarsely mash bean mixture until well blended but still lumpy. Add rice and continue to mash just until blended.

5. Shape bean mixture into eight 1-inch-thick burgers. Spray both sides of burgers with cooking spray.

6. Place burgers on hot grill rack or pan. Cook until well browned on the outside, 10 to 12 minutes, turning over once.

7. To serve, place 2 burgers in center of each tortilla; top with yogurt sauce, carrots, tomatoes, and cucumbers. Fold opposite sides of each tortilla over filling, then fold ends over to form a package.

EACH BURGER: About 490 calories, 15g protein, 83g carbohydrate, 11g total fat (2g saturated), 3mg cholesterol, 1,260mg sodium

Poultry

Poultry can pose a challenge to some cooks. How to make sure it's cooked through all the way without incinerating it? Follow our easy directions and we guarantee your days of burned on the outside/raw on the inside will be over. We've also included a chart of approximate cook times for different chicken parts (legs, thighs, etc.), as well as the internal temperature they should be cooked to, and our strategies for cooking chicken safely.

Whether you want to grill your chicken or turkey whole or cut it up into kabobs, we've got a toothsome collection of recipes to pick from. We've also included recipes that are tailor made to serve at a party, like Ginger-Grilled Chicken for a Crowd, Grilled Chicken and Steak Fajitas for a Crowd, and Sweet and Tangy BBQ Chicken, where the chicken is oven-steamed in advance. And don't forget Cornish hens—cut in half, they cook up on the grill in just 30 minutes, and make an elegant change of pace from chicken.

Lemon-Mint Chicken Cutlets on Watercress, page 111

Ginger-Grilled Chicken for a Crowd

When you have a crowd to feed at a backyard bash, try this honey-and-ginger party pleaser.

PREP: 10 minutes plus overnight to marinate
GRILL: 30 to 35 minutes

MAKES: 12 main-dish servings

1¼	cups soy sauce
¾	cup honey
¼	cup fresh lemon juice (about 2 large lemons)
2	tablespoons vegetable oil
2	tablespoons minced, peeled fresh ginger
2	garlic cloves, crushed with garlic press
3	chickens (3 pounds each), each cut into quarters

1. In small bowl, combine soy sauce, honey, lemon juice, oil, ginger, and garlic until well blended. Divide chicken and marinade among three zip-tight plastic bags, turning chicken to coat; place in 15" by 9" baking dish. Seal bags, pressing out as much air as possible. Refrigerate overnight to marinate.

2. Prepare outdoor grill for covered direct grilling over medium heat.

3. Remove chicken from marinade; discard marinade. Place chicken on grill, cover, and cook until golden brown, about 5 minutes per side. Move chicken to perimeter of grill (where it is cooler); cover and cook until juices run clear when thickest part of chicken is pierced with tip of knife, 20 to 25 minutes longer.

EACH SERVING: About 410 calories, 42g protein, 10g carbohydrate, 22g total fat (6g saturated), 132mg cholesterol, 988mg sodium

---

GRILLING CHICKEN

Different chicken parts require different amounts of time to cook, but it is nice to be able to remove all the chicken from the grill at the same time so it is equally hot. Here's an easy way to accomplish this: When grilling a cut-up chicken, put the legs on first. After 5 minutes, place the breast on the grill. After another 10 minutes, put the thighs on the grill to cook.

CUT	COOK-TO INTERNAL TEMPERATURE	APPROXIMATE COOK TIME
Legs, bone-in	170°F	30–35 minutes
Thighs, bone-in	170°F	12–15 minutes
Thighs, boneless	170°F	10–12 minutes
Breasts, bone-in	165°F	25–30 minutes
Breasts, boneless	160°F	10–12 minutes
Whole chicken (about 3½ pounds)	170°F	1 hour to 1 hour 15 minutes

Beer-Can Chicken

Your favorite brew keeps this chicken moist and juicy. If using a charcoal grill, you will need to add ten fresh charcoal briquettes per side if more than an hour of cooking is required.

PREP: 15 minutes plus standing
GRILL: 1 hour to 1 hour 15 minutes
MAKES: 8 main-dish servings

3	tablespoons paprika
1	tablespoon sugar
1	tablespoon salt
2	teaspoons coarsely ground black pepper
1	teaspoon onion powder
1	teaspoon garlic powder
1	teaspoon ground red pepper (cayenne)
2	chickens (about 3½ pounds each)
2	cans beer (12 ounces each)

1. Prepare charcoal fire for covered indirect-heat grilling with drip pan as manufacturer directs or preheat gas grill for covered indirect grilling over medium heat.

2. In small bowl, combine paprika, sugar, salt, black pepper, onion powder, garlic powder, and ground red pepper.

3. Remove giblets and necks from chickens. Rinse chickens with cold running water; drain well and pat dry with paper towels. Sprinkle 1 tablespoon spice mixture inside cavity of each chicken. Rub remaining spice mixture all over chickens.

4. Wipe beer cans clean. Open beer cans; pour off ½ cup beer from each can and reserve for another use. With can opener (church key), make four more holes in top of each can. Place 1 partially filled beer can on flat surface; hold 1 chicken upright, with opening of body cavity down, and slide chicken over top of can so can fits inside cavity. Repeat with remaining chicken and can. Carefully set chickens over drip pan or away from the heat source on a gas grill. Spread out legs to balance chickens on rack. Cover grill and cook chickens until juices run clear when thickest part of thigh is pierced with tip of knife, 1 hour to 1 hour 15 minutes.

5. With tongs and barbecue mitts, carefully remove chickens and cans from grill, being careful not to spill beer. Let chicken stand 10 minutes before lifting from cans. Transfer chickens to large platter or carving board; discard beer. Cut each chicken into 8 serving pieces.

EACH SERVING: About 350 calories, 39g protein, 4g carbohydrate, 19g total fat (5g saturated), 152mg cholesterol, 985mg sodium

Grilled Chicken Quarters, Your Way

Choose either a simple mix of herbs, white wine, and lemon juice modeled after a classic French tarragon roast chicken, or a more exotic blend of yogurt, garlic, and warm spices based on a northern Indian tradition.

PREP: 15 minutes plus marinating
GRILL: 20 to 30 minutes
MAKES: 4 main-dish servings

Tandoori Marinade or Tarragon Marinade (right)
1   chicken (about 3½ pounds), cut into quarters, skin removed from all but wings

1. Prepare marinade of your choice as directed.

2. Pour marinade into large zip-tight plastic bag; add chicken, turning to coat. Seal bag, pressing out excess air. Place bag on plate; let stand 15 minutes at room temperature or refrigerate 1 hour (or up to 24 hours), turning bag over occasionally.

3. Prepare outdoor grill for covered direct grilling over medium heat.

4. Remove chicken from bag; discard marinade. Place chicken on hot grill rack. Cover grill and cook chicken, turning once and transferring pieces to platter as they are done, until juices run clear when thickest part of chicken is pierced with tip of knife, 20 to 30 minutes.

TANDOORI MARINADE: In blender at medium speed, puree until smooth *1 (8-ounce) container plain low-fat yogurt; 3 tablespoons coarsely chopped, peeled fresh ginger; 2 tablespoons fresh lemon juice; 1 tablespoon ground coriander; 2 teaspoons ground cumin; 1 teaspoon salt; ¼ teaspoon ground red pepper (cayenne)*; and *2 garlic cloves*, cut up.

EACH SERVING TANDOORI CHICKEN: About 285 calories, 41g protein, 3g carbohydrate, 11g total fat (3g saturated), 123mg cholesterol, 430mg sodium

TARRAGON MARINADE: In bowl, stir *2 small shallots*, minced (¼ cup); *1 cup dry white wine; 2 tablespoons chopped fresh tarragon; 1 teaspoon freshly grated lemon peel; ½ teaspoon salt*; and *¼ teaspoon coarsely ground black pepper.*

EACH SERVING TARRAGON CHICKEN: About 150 calories, 27g protein, 1g carbohydrate, 3g total fat (1g saturated), 72mg cholesterol, 210mg sodium

All-American BBQ Chicken

Try this sweet and spicy sauce on pork spareribs, too. If you'd prefer, substitute chicken thighs or bone-in breasts for the whole chickens. Wait until the chicken has cooked for twenty minutes before brushing it with sauce, and it will become beautifully glazed without burning.

PREP: 1 hour   **GRILL:** 35 to 40 minutes
MAKES: 8 main-dish servings

2   tablespoons olive oil
1   large onion (12 ounces), chopped
2   cans (15 ounces each) tomato sauce
1   cup red wine vinegar
½   cup light (mild) molasses
¼   cup Worcestershire sauce
⅓   cup packed brown sugar
¾   teaspoon ground red pepper (cayenne)
2   chickens (3½ pounds each), each cut
     into quarters

1. In 10-inch skillet, heat oil over medium heat. Add onion and cook until tender, about 10 minutes, stirring a few times. Stir in tomato sauce, vinegar, molasses, Worcestershire, brown sugar, and ground red pepper; heat to boiling over high heat. Reduce heat to medium-low and cook, uncovered, until sauce thickens slightly, about 45 minutes. (If not using sauce right away, cover and refrigerate to use within 2 weeks.) Reserve 1½ cups sauce to serve with chicken.

2. Meanwhile, prepare outdoor grill for direct grilling over medium heat.

3. Place chicken quarters on hot grill rack over medium heat and grill, turning over once, for 20 minutes. Generously brush chicken with some of the remaining barbecue sauce; grill, turning pieces often and brushing frequently with sauce, until juices run clear when thickest part of chicken is pierced with tip of knife, 15 to 20 minutes longer.

4. Serve chicken with reserved sauce.

EACH SERVING: About 590 calories, 50g protein, 36g carbohydrate, 27g total fat (7g saturated), 154mg cholesterol, 880mg sodium

> **TIP:** For a lighter version, remove skin from the chicken before grilling. Before heating the grill, brush the rack with a little oil to prevent sticking and proceed with the recipe as directed. Removing the skin also lessens flare-ups.

Sweet and Tangy BBQ Chicken

It wouldn't be an American summer get-together without grilled chicken brushed with our delicious homemade barbecue sauce. To help you enjoy more time with your guests and not worry about undercooking, completely precook the chicken in the oven and keep it refrigerated up to a day. Then, when you're ready to dine, just warm up the chicken on the grill and brush on the sauce.

PREP: 15 minutes plus oven-steaming
GRILL: 15 to 20 minutes

MAKES: 12 main-dish servings

OVEN-STEAMED CHICKEN

3   chickens (about 4 pounds each), each cut into quarters, skin removed if you like

1½ teaspoons salt

2   lemons, cut into wedges

1   large onion (12 ounces), cut into wedges

SWEET AND TANGY BARBECUE SAUCE

1   tablespoon olive oil

1   large onion (12 ounces), chopped

3   garlic cloves, crushed with garlic press

¼   cup chili powder

1   can (28 ounces) tomato puree

1   jar (12 ounces) apricot preserves

½   cup cider vinegar

3   tablespoons spicy brown mustard

2   tablespoons Worcestershire sauce

1   teaspoon salt

1. Prepare oven-steamed chicken: Preheat oven to 425°F. Arrange chicken quarters in large roasting pan (17" by 11½"), overlapping pieces if necessary. Sprinkle chicken with salt; top with lemon wedges and onion. Cover roasting pan tightly with heavy-duty foil. Oven-steam chicken until juices run clear when thickest part of chicken is pierced with tip of knife, about 1¼ hours, turning chicken halfway through baking time to ensure even cooking. Discard lemons and onion. Refrigerate broth for use another day. Transfer chicken to large platter; cover and refrigerate until ready to grill.

2. Prepare barbecue sauce: In 5- to 6-quart saucepot, heat oil over medium heat until hot. (Do not use a smaller pan; sauce bubbles up and splatters during cooking—the deeper the pan, the better.) Add chopped onion and cook until tender and golden, about 10 minutes, stirring occasionally. Add garlic and chili powder; cook 1 minute. Remove saucepot from heat; carefully stir in remaining sauce ingredients. Heat sauce to boiling over medium-low heat and cook, partially covered, 10 minutes to thicken slightly, stirring occasionally.

3. Transfer sauce to bowl; if not using right away, cover and store up to 1 week in refrigerator or 2 months in freezer. Makes about 6 cups.

4. Prepare outdoor grill for covered direct grilling over medium heat. Reserve 3 cups barbecue sauce for serving. Place chicken on hot grill rack; cover grill and cook 10 minutes, turning chicken once. Cook chicken 5 to 10 minutes longer, turning occasionally and frequently brushing with remaining sauce until chicken is heated through and sauce is browned. Heat reserved sauce to serve with chicken.

EACH SERVING: About 315 calories, 44g protein, 6g carbohydrate, 12g total fat (3g saturated), 135mg cholesterol, 540mg sodium

Grilled Whole Chicken with Lemon and Garlic

Use a covered grill to cook this deliciously seasoned chicken. If using a charcoal grill, you will need to add ten fresh charcoal briquettes per side if more than an hour of cooking is required.

PREP: 15 minutes   **GRILL:** about 1 hour 15 minutes
MAKES: 4 main-dish servings

1	chicken (about 3½ pounds)
1	lemon
1	small bunch fresh thyme
6	garlic cloves, peeled
½	teaspoon salt
¼	teaspoon coarsely ground black pepper

1. Preheat gas grill for covered indirect grilling over medium heat. If using a charcoal grill, prepare it for covered indirect-heat grilling with drip pan as manufacturer directs.

2. Remove giblets and neck from chicken; reserve for another use. Rinse chicken with cold running water; drain well and pat dry with paper towels.

3. From lemon, grate 2 teaspoons peel. Cut lemon into quarters and set aside. Chop enough thyme to equal 1 teaspoon; reserve remaining sprigs. Into cup, crush 2 garlic cloves with garlic press; reserve remaining 4 cloves. To garlic in cup, add lemon peel, chopped thyme, salt, and pepper; set aside. Place lemon quarters, whole garlic cloves, and 3 thyme sprigs inside cavity of chicken. Reserve remaining thyme sprigs for garnish, if you like.

4. With chicken breast side up, lift wings up toward neck, then fold wing tips under back of chicken so they stay in place. With string, loosely tie legs together. Rub lemon mixture on outside of chicken.

5. Place chicken on hot grill rack over drip pan or away from the heat source on a gas grill. Cover grill and cook chicken until juices run clear when thickest part of chicken is pierced with tip of knife, about 1 hour 15 minutes.

6. Place chicken on platter; let stand 10 minutes to allow juices to set for easier carving. Cut into 8 serving pieces and garnish with thyme sprigs, if using. Remove skin from chicken before eating, if you like.

EACH SERVING WITHOUT SKIN: About 235 calories, 36g protein, 1g carbohydrate, 9g total fat (3g saturated), 109mg cholesterol, 395mg sodium

Portuguese Mixed Grill

We've used chorizo instead of the less readily available Portuguese sausage linguiça. Chorizo, a spicy Spanish cured sausage, is often available in packages of two in the meat or deli section of your supermarket. Be sure to purchase fully cooked chorizo.

PREP: 30 minutes plus marinating
GRILL: 20 to 25 minutes
MAKES: 6 main-dish servings

¼ cup red wine vinegar

1 teaspoon salt

½ teaspoon coarsely ground black pepper

3 tablespoons olive oil

2 tablespoons chopped fresh oregano

8 large bone-in chicken thighs (about 3 pounds total), skin removed

3 medium red onions

3 (12-inch) metal skewers

¾ pound fully cooked chorizo sausage links, each cut crosswise in half

⅔ cup assorted olives such as Kalamata, cracked green, and picholine (optional)

1. In large bowl, combine vinegar, salt, pepper, 2 tablespoons oil, and 1 tablespoon oregano. Add chicken; toss until evenly coated. Cover and let stand 30 minutes in the refrigerator.

2. Prepare outdoor grill for direct grilling over medium heat.

3. Meanwhile, peel and cut each onion into 6 wedges; thread onto 3 skewers.

4. Place onion skewers on hot grill rack. Brush with remaining 1 tablespoon oil; grill 5 minutes. Place chicken on grill with onions; grill, turning onions and chicken once, until onions are browned and tender and juices run clear when chicken thighs are pierced with tip of knife, 15 to 20 minutes longer.

5. About 10 minutes before onions and chicken are done, add chorizo pieces to grill and cook, turning chorizo occasionally, until lightly browned and heated through.

6. To serve, place onion skewers on platter with chicken and chorizo. Sprinkle with remaining 1 tablespoon oregano and serve with olives, if you like.

EACH SERVING: About 550 calories, 48g protein, 10g carbohydrate, 35g total fat (11g saturated), 187mg cholesterol, 1,240mg sodium

Grilled Bone-In Chicken Breasts, Three Ways

This simple recipe for grilled chicken breasts on the bone with crisp skin and juicy meat takes on a new dimension when one of our flavorful mixtures is rubbed under the skin: Sun-Dried Tomato and Basil, Garlic-Herb, or Sage-Butter.

PREP: 15 minutes   GRILL: about 25 minutes
MAKES: 4 main-dish servings

choice of seasoning mixture (right)
2   whole bone-in chicken breasts, split
     (about 2½ pounds total)
½   teaspoon salt
¼   teaspoon coarsely ground black pepper

1. Prepare outdoor grill for direct grilling over medium heat.

2. Prepare one seasoning mixture as directed.

3. With fingertips, separate skin from meat on each breast half. Rub equal amounts of seasoning mixture under skin of each breast. Sprinkle chicken with salt and pepper.

4. Place chicken on hot grill rack and grill, turning over once, until juices run clear when thickest part of breast is pierced with tip of knife, about 25 minutes.

SUN-DRIED TOMATO AND BASIL SEASONING: In small bowl, mix *2 sun-dried tomatoes packed in seasoned olive oil*, minced, and *¼ cup loosely packed fresh basil leaves*, finely chopped.

EACH SERVING SUN-DRIED TOMATO AND BASIL CHICKEN: About 305 calories, 46g protein, 0g carbohydrate, 12g total fat (3g saturated), 129mg cholesterol, 405mg sodium

GARLIC-HERB SEASONING: In small bowl, mix *2 garlic cloves*, crushed with garlic press; *1 tablespoon chopped fresh rosemary leaves; 1 tablespoon olive oil*; and *1 teaspoon freshly grated lemon peel*.

EACH SERVING GARLIC-HERB CHICKEN: About 335 calories, 46g protein, 1g carbohydrate, 15g total fat (4g saturated), 129mg cholesterol, 400mg sodium

SAGE-BUTTER SEASONING: In small bowl, mix *1 tablespoon softened butter or margarine* and *1 tablespoon chopped fresh sage*.

EACH SERVING SAGE-BUTTER CHICKEN: About 330 calories, 46g protein, 0g carbohydrate, 15g total fat (5g saturated), 137mg cholesterol, 417mg sodium

Lemon Chicken with Grilled Summer Squash

For this easy summer supper, simply toss the sliced squash on the grill along with the marinated chicken. You can use zucchini, yellow squash, or a combination.

PREP: 15 minutes plus marinating
GRILL: 10 to 12 minutes
MAKES: 4 main-dish servings

1	large lemon
1	tablespoon olive oil
½	teaspoon salt
¼	teaspoon coarsely ground black pepper
4	medium skinless, boneless chicken thighs (about 1¼ pounds)
4	medium yellow summer squash and/or zucchini (about 6 ounces each), each cut lengthwise into 4 wedges
¼	cup snipped fresh chives

1. From lemon, grate 1 tablespoon peel and squeeze 3 tablespoons juice. In medium bowl, whisk together lemon peel and juice, oil, salt, and pepper; transfer 2 tablespoons marinade to cup and reserve.

2. Add chicken to bowl with marinade; toss until evenly coated. Cover and let stand 15 minutes at room temperature or 30 minutes in the refrigerator.

3. Meanwhile, prepare outdoor grill for covered direct grilling over medium heat.

4. Discard chicken marinade. Place chicken and squash on hot grill rack. Cover grill and cook, turning chicken and squash over once and removing pieces as they are done, until juices run clear when thickest part of thigh is pierced with tip of knife and squash is tender and browned, 10 to 12 minutes.

5. Transfer chicken and squash to cutting board. Cut chicken into 1-inch-wide strips; cut each squash wedge crosswise in half.

6. To serve, on large platter, toss squash with reserved lemon-juice marinade, then toss with chicken and sprinkle with chives.

EACH SERVING: About 255 calories, 29g protein, 8g carbohydrate, 8g total fat (3g saturated), 101mg cholesterol, 240mg sodium

Grilled Chicken Quarters with Grape Tomato Salad

To mellow the strong flavor and take the bite out of a raw onion, we like to soak it, sliced or chopped, in ice water for 10 minutes—or a little longer for an even sweeter flavor.

PREP: 25 minutes   **GRILL:** 30 to 40 minutes
MAKES: 4 main-dish servings

4 to 5 lemons

3   garlic cloves, crushed with garlic press

1   teaspoon olive oil

1¼   teaspoons kosher salt

¾   teaspoon coarsely ground black pepper

1   chicken (about 4 pounds), cut into quarters (see Tip, right)

¼   cup finely chopped red onion

¼   cup loosely packed fresh basil leaves, chopped

2   pints (about 4 cups) grape or cherry tomatoes, each cut in half

1. Prepare outdoor grill for covered direct grilling over medium heat.

2. From 3 to 4 lemons, grate 3 tablespoons plus 1 teaspoon peel and squeeze 1 tablespoon juice. Cut remaining lemon into 4 wedges and reserve for serving with chicken.

3. In small bowl, combine 3 tablespoons lemon peel with garlic, oil, 1 teaspoon salt, and ½ teaspoon pepper. With fingertips, gently separate chicken skin from meat on chicken breasts and thighs. Rub half of lemon-peel mixture on meat under skin; rub remaining mixture all over skin.

4. Place chicken on hot grill rack. Cover grill and cook chicken until juices run clear when thickest part of thigh is pierced with tip of knife, 30 to 40 minutes, turning over once. Transfer chicken pieces to platter as they are done.

5. Meanwhile, place chopped onion in *cup of ice water* and soak 10 minutes; drain well. In medium bowl, combine onion, basil, tomato halves, lemon juice, and remaining ¼ teaspoon salt, ¼ teaspoon pepper, and 1 teaspoon lemon peel. Makes about 4 cups.

6. Arrange each chicken quarter on a dinner plate and top with grape tomato salad. Garnish each plate with a reserved lemon wedge.

EACH SERVING: About 455 calories, 47g protein, 11g carbohydrate, 24g total fat (7g saturated), 182mg cholesterol, 755mg sodium

> **TIP:** To deliver this irresistible dish to the dinner table even faster, replace the chicken quarters with 1½ pounds turkey cutlets or thin-sliced chicken cutlets. Proceed as above, but reduce grilling time to 5 to 7 minutes, turning cutlets over once.

A Guide to Grilling Chicken

GREASE YOUR GRILL: Chances are you won't have a sticking problem if your chicken has skin, or if it's marinated or rubbed with some oil. But play it safe. Before you light the grill, spray the rack with nonstick cooking spray or brush it with oil.

KEEP IT HOT: Sear the chicken on a hot grill—this makes it easier to turn the chicken over.

WATCH SEASONINGS CAREFULLY: Marinades and basting sauces, many of which have a high sugar content, will burn if the grill temperature is too hot or if exposed to heat for too long. A hot grill is normally not a problem with quick-cooking chicken cuts (such as skinless, boneless breasts), but longer-cooking cuts (such as bone-in chicken parts) should be cooked over a lower heat. And don't start basting until the chicken is almost fully cooked.

CLOSE THE TOP: If your grill has a cover, cook bone-in chicken with the cover down. It will make your grill more ovenlike, and your food will cook more evenly. Also, because the cover cuts off some of the oxygen, you'll have fewer flare-ups.

BE PATIENT: Resist the urge to continuously move the poultry around while it cooks. The chicken will cook more evenly (and more quickly!) if you follow the recipe cooking instructions or turn it over only once midway through grilling.

USE THE RIGHT UTENSIL: Use long-handled tongs or a wide metal spatula to move the chicken. Poking it with a fork will allow precious juices to escape.

TEST FOR DONENESS: Don't risk serving undercooked chicken. When in doubt, make a small cut into the thickest part so you can be positive that it's no longer pink inside. You can also use an instant-read meat thermometer to see if your meat has reached a safe internal temperature, 170°F for whole chicken and 160°F for breasts.

BE SURE TO CLEAN UP: Scrape your grill rack after each use; otherwise, the chicken will pick up charred bits from your last barbecue. Chicken has a tendency to stick to a dirty grill.

Hoisin-Glazed Chicken with Plums and Green Onions

What a wonderful combination of flavors—the richly satisfying taste of hoisin-basted chicken with the sweetness of plums and bite of grilled green onions.

PREP: 20 minutes plus marinating
GRILL: 34 to 48 minutes

MAKES: 4 main-dish servings

- ¼   cup rice vinegar
- 1   tablespoon Asian sesame oil
- 1   tablespoon grated, peeled fresh ginger
- 1   teaspoon Chinese five-spice powder
- ¼   teaspoon ground red pepper (cayenne)
- 1   chicken (4 pounds), cut into 8 serving pieces, skin removed if you like
- 4   plums
- 2   bunches green onions
- 1   tablespoon olive oil
- ¼   teaspoon salt
- ⅛   teaspoon coarsely ground pepper
- ⅓   cup hoisin sauce
- 1   tablespoon low-sodium soy sauce
- 1   teaspoon sesame seeds

1. In large bowl, stir together vinegar, sesame oil, ginger, five-spice powder, and red pepper. Add chicken to spice mixture and toss until evenly coated. Let marinate 15 minutes at room temperature, turning occasionally.

2. Meanwhile, prepare outdoor grill for covered direct grilling over medium heat.

3. Cut each plum in half; discard pits. Brush green onions with olive oil and sprinkle with salt and black pepper. In small bowl, mix hoisin sauce and soy sauce.

4. Remove chicken from marinade and place on hot grill rack. Discard marinade. Cover grill and cook chicken until juices run clear when thickest part of chicken is pierced with knife, 25 to 35 minutes, turning pieces over once. Reserve ¼ cup hoisin mixture for serving; brush chicken with remaining mixture for last minute of cooking. Transfer chicken to platter. Cover; keep warm.

5. Place plums and green onions on hot grill rack. Cook onions until lightly charred and tender, 3 to 5 minutes, turning over once; cook plums until lightly charred and softened, 6 to 8 minutes, turning over once. Transfer onions and plums to platter with chicken.

6. To serve, sprinkle chicken with sesame seeds. Pass a bowl with reserved hoisin mixture.

EACH SERVING WITHOUT SKIN: About 465 calories, 48g protein, 25g carbohydrate, 19g total fat (4g saturated), 138mg cholesterol, 770mg sodium

Chicken with Gremolata Salsa

Gremolata, a sprightly combination of parsley, lemon peel, and garlic, is tossed with sun-ripened tomatoes for a full-flavored summer treat. For a change, try grated orange peel instead of the lemon, and basil instead of the parsley. If you like, remove the skin from the chicken and brush the quarters with a tablespoon of oil before cooking to lighten the dish.

PREP: 15 minutes   GRILL: 40 to 45 minutes
MAKES: 4 main-dish servings

4   ripe medium tomatoes (6 to 8 ounces each),
     cut into ¼-inch pieces
2   tablespoons finely chopped fresh parsley
1   teaspoon freshly grated lemon peel
1   small garlic clove, minced
1   teaspoon olive oil
1   teaspoon salt
½   teaspoon coarsely ground black pepper
1   chicken (about 3½ pounds), cut into
     quarters

1. Prepare outdoor grill for direct grilling over medium heat.

2. In small bowl, stir tomatoes, parsley, lemon peel, garlic, oil, ¹/₂ teaspoon salt, and ¹/₄ teaspoon pepper; set salsa aside. Makes about 3 cups.

3. Sprinkle chicken with remaining ¹/₂ teaspoon salt and ¹/₄ teaspoon pepper.

4. Place chicken on hot grill rack and grill 20 minutes. Turn over and grill until juices run clear when thickest part of chicken is pierced with tip of knife, 20 to 25 minutes longer.

5. Serve chicken with salsa.

EACH SERVING: About 460 calories, 49g protein, 6g carbohydrate, 25g total fat (7g saturated), 154mg cholesterol, 740mg sodium

> **TIP:** Mix up a batch of this lemon-scented tomato salsa to spoon over grilled zucchini, eggplant, or a mixture of vegetables.

Lemon-Mint Chicken Cutlets on Watercress

The tang of lemon and the peppery punch of watercress make this a refreshing choice on a hot summer night. Another plus is that these thin cutlets will cook up in just a few minutes. For photo, see page 94.

PREP: 15 minutes   **GRILL:** 4 to 5 minutes
MAKES: 4 main-dish servings

1¼	pounds thinly sliced skinless, boneless chicken breasts
2	lemons
2	tablespoons olive oil
2	tablespoons chopped fresh mint, plus more for garnish
½	teaspoon salt
½	teaspoon coarsely ground black pepper
1	bag (4 ounces) baby watercress

1. Heat ridged grill pan over medium-high heat (or prepare outdoor grill for direct grilling over medium-high heat).

2. Pound chicken to uniform ¼-inch thickness if necessary (see below).

3. From lemons, grate 1 tablespoon plus 1½ teaspoons peel and squeeze 3 tablespoons juice. In large bowl, mix lemon peel and juice, oil, 2 tablespoons mint, salt, and pepper until dressing is blended.

4. Reserve ¼ cup dressing. In large bowl, toss chicken cutlets with remaining dressing. Place chicken in grill pan and cook until juices run clear when breast is pierced with tip of knife, 4 to 5 minutes, turning over once.

5. To serve, toss watercress with reserved dressing and top with chicken. Sprinkle with additional chopped mint for garnish.

EACH SERVING: About 225 calories, 34g protein, 2g carbohydrate, 9g total fat (1g saturated), 82mg cholesterol, 375mg sodium

THE GENTLE ART OF POUNDING

Here's how to pound a chicken breast to a uniform thickness.

1. Place a skinless, boneless chicken breast half between 2 sheets of plastic wrap and place on a cutting board or work surface. The plastic wrap will protect the surface of the chicken and prevent the meat from sticking to the mallet and the cutting board—and it won't rip as easily as waxed paper. The same 2 sheets of plastic wrap can be reused for remaining chicken breasts.

2. Use the smooth side of a metal or wood meat mallet. (The textured side is good for tough cuts of meat that need to be tenderized.) If you don't have a meat mallet, you can use a sturdy rolling pin or the flat side of a heavy skillet. Gently strike the chicken breast until it has an even thickness, ⅛ to ¼ inch thick, depending on the recipe. It's not necessary to strike the breast with a great deal of force; let the mallet do the work!

Curried Chicken with Mango-Cantaloupe Slaw

Here, curry, crystallized ginger, and crushed red pepper bring out the flavor of the fresh fruit.

PREP: 25 minutes plus marinating
GRILL: 10 to 12 minutes
MAKES: 4 main-dish servings

1 to 3 limes
1   small container (6 ounces) plain low-fat yogurt
¾   teaspoon curry powder
4   tablespoons chopped crystallized ginger
1   teaspoon salt
¼   teaspoon crushed red pepper
4   medium skinless, boneless chicken breast halves (about 1¼ pounds total)
½   small cantaloupe, rind removed, seeded and cut into julienne strips (2 cups)
1   large mango, peeled and cut into julienne strips (2 cups)
½   cup loosely packed fresh cilantro leaves, chopped
1   head Boston lettuce

1. Grease grill rack. Prepare outdoor grill for direct grilling over medium heat, or lightly spray a ridged grill pan with nonstick cooking spray, then heat on medium until hot.

2. From 1 or 2 limes, grate ½ teaspoon peel and squeeze 2 tablespoons juice. In large bowl, combine 1 tablespoon lime juice and ¼ teaspoon lime peel with yogurt, curry powder, 2 tablespoons ginger, ¾ teaspoon salt, and ⅛ teaspoon crushed red pepper; whisk until blended. Add chicken, turning to coat. Cover and let stand 15 minutes at room temperature or 30 minutes in refrigerator, turning occasionally.

3. Meanwhile, in medium bowl, with rubber spatula, gently stir cantaloupe and mango with cilantro, remaining 2 tablespoons ginger, 1 tablespoon lime juice, ¼ teaspoon lime peel, ¼ teaspoon salt, and ⅛ teaspoon crushed red pepper; set slaw aside. Makes about 4 cups.

4. Remove chicken from marinade; discard marinade. Place chicken on hot grill rack or pan. Cover and cook until juices run clear when thickest part of breast is pierced with tip of knife, 10 to 12 minutes, turning over once. Transfer chicken to cutting board; cool slightly to allow juices to set for easier slicing, then cut into long, thin slices.

5. To serve, divide lettuce leaves among 4 dinner plates; top with chicken and slaw. If you like, cut remaining lime into wedges and use for garnish.

EACH SERVING WITH LETTUCE: About 205 calories, 34g protein, 5g carbohydrate, 4g total fat (1g saturated), 92mg cholesterol, 330mg sodium

EACH ½ CUP SLAW: About 50 calories, 1g protein, 13g carbohydrate, 0g total fat, 0mg cholesterol, 150mg sodium

Indian-Style Chicken with Grilled Mango Chutney

If you've ever tried to cut a mango and mangled the flesh, ending up with a mushy mess, check out the GHRI-tested OXO Good Grips mango splitter. It easily cuts through a firm-ripe mango, separating the seed from the flesh.

PREP: **20 minutes plus marinating**
GRILL: **28 to 33 minutes**
MAKES: **4 main-dish servings**

3	tablespoons plain low-fat yogurt
1	tablespoon paprika
1½	teaspoons ground cumin
1½	teaspoons ground coriander
½	teaspoon ground red pepper (cayenne)
1	garlic clove, crushed with garlic press
4½	teaspoons grated, peeled fresh ginger
¾	teaspoon salt
4	medium bone-in chicken breast halves (about 2 pounds total), skin removed
2	firm, ripe mangoes
1	tablespoon light brown sugar
1	tablespoon cider vinegar
1	small green onion, thinly sliced

cooked basmati rice (optional)

1. In small bowl, mix yogurt, paprika, cumin, coriander, red pepper, garlic, 4 teaspoons ginger, and ½ teaspoon salt until blended. Pour yogurt marinade into large zip-tight plastic bag; add chicken, turning to coat. Seal bag, pressing out excess air. Place on plate and refrigerate at least 1 hour or up to 4 hours.

2. Prepare outdoor grill for covered direct grilling over medium heat.

3. Peel mangoes and cut lengthwise; slice from each side of long, flat seed, as close to seed as possible. Cut away remaining flesh from around seed in as few pieces as possible. Place mango on hot grill rack and cook until lightly charred and tender, about 8 minutes, turning over halfway through grilling. Transfer mangoes to cutting board and set aside until cool enough to handle.

4. Coarsely chop grilled mangoes and place in medium bowl. Add brown sugar, vinegar, green onion, remaining ¼ teaspoon salt, and remaining ½ teaspoon ginger; stir to combine. Makes about 2 cups.

5. Remove chicken from marinade; discard marinade. Place chicken on hot grill rack. Cover grill and cook until juices run clear when thickest part of breast is pierced with tip of knife, 20 to 25 minutes, turning over once. Place on platter and serve with mango chutney and, if you like, basmati rice.

EACH SERVING CHICKEN: About 170 calories, 35g protein, 2g carbohydrate, 2g total fat (1g saturated), 85mg cholesterol, 375mg sodium

EACH ¼ CUP CHUTNEY: About 40 calories, 0g protein, 11g carbohydrate, 1g total fat (0g saturated), 0mg cholesterol, 75mg sodium

Grilled Basil Chicken with Garden Tomatoes and Baby Greens

Fragrant basil leaves turn everyday chicken breasts into something special.

PREP: **20 minutes**   GRILL: **about 25 minutes**
MAKES: **4 main-dish servings**

1	large bunch fresh basil
4	medium chicken breast halves (1¼ pounds total)
¾	teaspoon salt
¼	teaspoon coarsely ground black pepper
3	ripe medium tomatoes (6 to 8 ounces each), chopped
¼	cup olive oil
2	tablespoons white wine vinegar
2	teaspoons freshly grated lemon peel
½	teaspoon Dijon mustard
4	ounces (8 cups) mixed baby greens or sliced romaine lettuce leaves

1. From bunch of basil, reserve 8 large leaves and measure 1 cup loosely packed small leaves. Finely slice enough of remaining leaves to equal ½ cup loosely packed (see Tip). Cover and refrigerate small and sliced leaves.

2. Prepare outdoor grill for direct grilling over medium heat.

3. Place 2 reserved large basil leaves under skin of each chicken breast half. Sprinkle with ¼ teaspoon salt and ⅛ teaspoon pepper. Place chicken, skin side up, on hot grill rack. Grill until juices run clear when thickest part of breast is pierced with tip of knife and skin is brown and crisp, about 25 minutes, turning over once.

4. Meanwhile, in small bowl, stir tomatoes, oil, vinegar, lemon peel, mustard, remaining ½ teaspoon salt, and remaining ⅛ teaspoon pepper.

5. To serve, in large bowl, toss baby greens with small basil leaves. Stir sliced basil leaves into tomato mixture. Toss greens with ½ cup tomato mixture. Divide greens among 4 dinner plates; top with chicken breasts. Spoon remaining tomato mixture over chicken.

EACH SERVING: About 340 calories, 31g protein, 6g carbohydrate, 22g total fat (5g saturated), 83mg cholesterol, 490mg sodium

> **TIP:** Slicing basil can be a breeze: Stack the leaves one on top of the other, then roll them up into a compact cylinder. Use a sharp knife to thinly slice the whole stack of leaves at once.

Grilled Boneless Chicken Breasts with a Trio of Sauces

It's easy to grill chicken breasts a day or two ahead, so they are perfect party fare. Serve cold or at room temperature with sauce of choice.

PREP: **10 minutes**   GRILL: **10 to 12 minutes**
MAKES: **16 main-dish servings**

16   medium skinless, boneless chicken-breast halves (about 5 pounds total)
2   tablespoons olive oil
2   teaspoons freshly grated lemon peel
1   teaspoon salt
½   teaspoon coarsely ground black pepper
lemon leaves for garnish
Peach Salsa, Walnut Sauce, and/or Parsley-Caper Sauce (right)

1. Prepare outdoor grill for direct grilling over medium heat, or lightly spray a ridged grill pan with nonstick cooking spray, then heat on medium until hot.

2. In large bowl, toss chicken breasts with oil, lemon peel, salt, and pepper until evenly coated.

3. Place chicken on hot grill rack or pan (in batches if necessary) and cook until juices run clear when thickest part of breast is pierced with tip of knife, 10 to 12 minutes, turning over once. Transfer chicken to platter; cover and refrigerate up to 2 days if not serving right away.

4. To serve, garnish platter with lemon leaves. Provide sauces on the side.

EACH SERVING CHICKEN: About 190 calories, 33g protein, 0g carbohydrate, 6g total fat (1g saturated), 90mg cholesterol, 225mg sodium

PEACH SALSA: Stir *3 pounds ripe peaches*, peeled, pitted, and cut into ½-inch cubes; *1 green onion*, finely chopped; *2 tablespoons fresh lime juice; 1 small hot red pepper*, seeded and minced, and *½ teaspoon salt* until mixed. Refrigerate up to 4 hours. Makes 4 cups.

EACH ¼ CUP PEACH SALSA: About 30 calories, 1g protein, 7g carbohydrate, 0g total fat, 0mg cholesterol, 75mg sodium

WALNUT SAUCE: In food processor, blend *2 cups walnuts*, toasted; *1 garlic clove*; and *3 slices firm white bread*, torn into large pieces until finely ground. Add *1 cup reduced-sodium chicken broth, ⅓ cup reduced-fat sour cream, ¾ teaspoon salt, ½ teaspoon sweet paprika,* and *⅛ teaspoon ground red pepper (cayenne)* and blend until combined. Refrigerate up to 3 days. Sprinkle with *paprika* for garnish. Makes 2 ½ cups.

EACH TABLESPOON WALNUT SAUCE: About 45 calories, 1g protein, 2g carbohydrate, 4g total fat (1g saturated), 1g cholesterol, 70mg sodium

PARSLEY-CAPER SAUCE: In food processor, blend together *3 cups loosely packed fresh parsley leaves, ⅓ cup olive oil, ¼ cup drained capers, ⅛ teaspoon ground red pepper (cayenne), 1 garlic clove,* and *4 teaspoons water* until very finely chopped. Refrigerate up to 2 days. Makes 1 cup.

EACH 2 TABLESPOONS PARSLEY-CAPER SAUCE: About 45 calories, 0g protein, 1g carbohydrate, 5g total fat (1g saturated), 0mg cholesterol, 70mg sodium

Grilled Chicken Breasts with Tomato-Olive Relish

Our tasty no-cook relish was inspired by Italian puttanesca sauce. Serve with a crisp green vegetable or a Mediterranean side dish like Grilled Eggplant with Feta and Fresh Mint (page 260).

PREP: 15 minutes GRILL: 10 to 12 minutes
MAKES: 4 main-dish servings

2 ripe medium tomatoes (6 to 8 ounces each), cut into ¼-inch pieces

¼ cup Kalamata olives, pitted and coarsely chopped, plus whole olives for garnish

2 tablespoons minced red onion

2 tablespoons capers, drained

1 teaspoon red wine vinegar

3 teaspoons olive oil

4 small skinless, boneless chicken breast halves (about 1 pound total)

¼ teaspoon salt

¼ teaspoon coarsely ground black pepper

1. In small bowl, mix tomatoes, olives, onion, capers, vinegar, and 1 teaspoon oil; set aside.

2. Prepare outdoor grill for direct grilling over medium heat, or lightly spray a ridged grill pan with nonstick cooking spray, then heat on medium until hot.

3. In medium bowl, toss chicken with salt, pepper, and remaining 2 teaspoons oil until evenly coated.

4. Place chicken on hot grill rack or pan and grill until juices run clear when thickest part of breast is pierced with tip of knife, 10 to 12 minutes, turning over once.

5. To serve, top chicken with tomato-olive relish and garnish with olives.

EACH SERVING: About 200 calories, 27g protein, 5g carbohydrate, 7g total fat (1g saturated), 66mg cholesterol, 565mg sodium

> **TIP:** If you'd like, double the tomato-olive mixture and toss half with 8 ounces cooked corkscrew pasta. Serve the pasta at room temperature alongside the chicken.

Lemon-Oregano Chicken with Mint Zucchini

For even cooking, it's a good idea to pound chicken breasts to a uniform thickness. See the box on page 111 for directions on how to do it.

PREP: **15 minutes**   GRILL: **8 to 12 minutes**
MAKES: **4 main-dish servings**

3   medium zucchini (8 ounces each)
2   tablespoons olive oil
½   teaspoon salt
½   cup loosely packed fresh mint leaves, chopped
4   medium skinless, boneless chicken-breast halves (about 1½ pounds total)
3   lemons
1   tablespoon chopped fresh oregano
½   teaspoon coarsely ground black pepper

1. Prepare outdoor grill for direct grilling over medium heat, or lightly spray a ridged grill pan with nonstick cooking spray, then heat on medium until hot.

2. With mandoline or sharp knife, slice zucchini very thinly lengthwise. In large bowl, toss zucchini with 1 tablespoon oil, ¼ teaspoon salt, and half of mint.

3. Pound chicken breasts to uniform ¼-inch thickness. From 2 lemons, grate 1 tablespoon peel and squeeze 2 tablespoons juice. Cut remaining lemon into 4 wedges; set aside. In medium bowl, combine lemon peel and juice with oregano, pepper, and remaining 1 tablespoon oil and ¼ teaspoon salt. Add chicken to bowl and toss until evenly coated.

4. Place zucchini slices, in batches, on hot grill rack and cook until grill marks appear and zucchini is tender, 2 to 4 minutes, turning over once. Remove zucchini from grill; place on large platter and sprinkle with remaining mint.

5. Place chicken on hot grill rack or pan. Cover and cook until juices run clear when chicken is pierced with tip of knife, 6 to 8 minutes, turning over once. Transfer chicken to platter with zucchini; serve with lemon wedges.

EACH SERVING: About 280 calories, 42g protein, 8g carbohydrate, 9g total fat (2g saturated), 99mg cholesterol, 390mg sodium

Poultry Safety Strategies

Chicken and turkey are deliciously simple choices for dinner, but because of the possibility of salmonella, they need to be treated with respect. Here are some sensible tips for keeping it safe in the kitchen and on the grill:

PROMOTE GOOD HYGIENE: Proper hand washing—20 seconds with hot, soapy water—is absolutely essential before and after handling raw poultry. Try this tactic: Wash as long as it takes to sing two rousing choruses of "Happy Birthday." You may even encourage good hygiene in your child with this tactic!

TACKLE CROSS-CONTAMINATION: Place the package of raw poultry in a plastic bag to separate it from other groceries. Take it straight home from the store and refrigerate it immediately (35° to 40°F). Set wrapped raw poultry on a plate on the bottom shelf of the refrigerator so juices don't drip onto other foods. Always thoroughly wash cutting boards, knives, utensils, and countertops after they come in contact with raw poultry. Never place cooked food on a plate that previously held raw poultry.

MAKE SEASONING SAFE: Always marinate in the refrigerator. If using a marinade as a basting or dipping sauce, set aside a portion before adding the raw food. Wash basting brushes with hot, soapy water after using them on poultry. Discard leftover marinade that comes in contact with raw poultry, or bring it to a boil for 1 minute before serving.

REFRIGERATE OR COOK: Thaw poultry in the refrigerator or in the microwave; never leave it at room temperature. When you thaw in the microwave, cook the poultry immediately and completely to destroy harmful bacteria. Never partially grill and finish cooking it later.

Stuffed Chicken Breasts with Lemon and Basil Couscous

Garlic-and-herb cheese and roasted peppers are the surprise filling for these boneless breasts. Accompanied by a lemony herb couscous, this dish is elegant enough for guests but easy enough for a weeknight family dinner.

PREP: 20 minutes   GRILL: 12 to 15 minutes
MAKES: 4 main-dish servings

STUFFED CHICKEN BREASTS

4	medium skinless, boneless chicken breast halves (about 1¼ pounds total)
¼	cup light garlic-and-herb spreadable cheese (about half 4.4-ounce package)
¼	cup drained and chopped jarred roasted red peppers
8	fresh basil leaves, chopped
1	teaspoon extra-virgin olive oil
½	teaspoon salt
¼	teaspoon coarsely ground black pepper

LEMON AND BASIL COUSCOUS

1	tablespoon extra-virgin olive oil
½	teaspoon salt
¼	teaspoon coarsely ground black pepper
1⅓	cups water
1	cup couscous
1	cup loosely packed fresh basil leaves, coarsely chopped
2	tablespoons fresh lemon juice

1. Prepare chicken breasts: With tip of knife, cut each chicken breast along one long side, keeping knife parallel to surface of breast, to form a deep pocket with as small an opening as possible.

2. Prepare outdoor grill for direct grilling over medium heat.

3. In small bowl, combine cheese, peppers, and basil. Stuff one-fourth cheese mixture into each chicken pocket. Rub oil on outside of chicken and sprinkle with salt and pepper.

4. Prepare couscous: In 2-quart saucepan, heat oil, salt, pepper, and water to boiling over high heat; stir in couscous. Cover pan; remove from heat and let stand at least 5 minutes.

5. Meanwhile, place chicken on hot grill rack and grill until juices run clear when thickest part of breast is pierced with tip of knife, 12 to 15 minutes, turning over once.

6. To serve, add basil and lemon juice to couscous; fluff with fork until well mixed. Spoon onto 4 dinner plates; top with chicken breasts.

EACH SERVING CHICKEN: About 255 calories, 35g protein, 4g carbohydrate, 10g total fat (5g saturated), 113mg cholesterol, 560mg sodium

EACH SERVING COUSCOUS: About 205 calories, 6g protein, 37g carbohydrate, 4g total fat (1g saturated), 0mg cholesterol, 295mg sodium

Chicken Grilled in a Foil Packet

We took three of our favorite chicken recipes usually prepared in a skillet and adapted them to the grill.

PREP: 15 minutes   **GRILL: 15 minutes**
MAKES: 4 main-dish servings

4	medium skinless, boneless chicken breast halves (about 1¼ pounds total)
3	tablespoons drained capers, chopped
2	tablespoons butter or margarine, cut into pieces
¼	teaspoon coarsely ground black pepper
¼	cup loosely packed fresh parsley leaves, chopped
	heavy-duty foil
2	teaspoons cornstarch
1	tablespoon water

1. Prepare outdoor grill for direct grilling over medium heat.

2. Make foil pouch: Cut two 24" by 18" sheets heavy-duty foil; layer to make a double thickness. Place chicken, capers, butter, peppers, and 2 tablespoons parsley in center of foil. In cup, stir cornstarch with water, then pour over chicken. To seal foil packet, bring short ends of foil up and over ingredients and fold two or three times to seal well. Fold remaining sides of foil the same way to seal in juices.

3. Place packet on hot grill rack and cook 15 minutes, turning once halfway through. Remove packet from grill; let stand 5 minutes.

4. Before serving, with kitchen shears, cut an X in top of packet to let steam escape. Open packet and check to make sure juices run clear when thickest part of chicken is pierced with tip of knife. Sprinkle chicken with remaining parsley.

EACH SERVING: About 215 calories, 33g protein, 2g carbohydrate, 8g total fat (5g saturated), 98mg cholesterol, 342mg sodium

MUSHROOM AND MARSALA CHICKEN: Prepare recipe as directed, but omit capers and add *8 ounces sliced mushrooms, 2 tablespoons dry or sweet marsala wine, ½ teaspoon salt*, and *1 garlic clove*, crushed with garlic press, to packet before grilling. In step 4, sprinkle with an additional *1 tablespoon marsala wine* before serving.

EACH SERVING MUSHROOM AND MARSALA CHICKEN: About 230 calories, 34g protein, 4g carbohydrate, 8g total fat (5g saturated), 98mg cholesterol, 632mg sodium

BUFFALO-STYLE CHICKEN: Prepare recipe as directed, but omit capers and add *3 tablespoons cayenne pepper sauce* to packet before grilling. Serve chicken with *3 medium carrots*, peeled and cut into 3-inch-long sticks; *3 stalks celery*, cut into 3-inch-long sticks; and *¼ cup crumbled blue cheese* (1 ounce).

EACH SERVING BUFFALO-STYLE CHICKEN: About 265 calories, 35g protein, 8g carbohydrate, 10g total fat (6g saturated), 104mg cholesterol, 882mg sodium

Coffee-Spice Chicken and Fruit-Basil Salsa

A jerk-style seasoning of allspice and java gives this Caribbean chicken its caffeinated kick. Balancing the heat: a cooling summer salsa of just-picked nectarines and juicy watermelon.

PREP: 30 minutes   GRILL: 8 to 10 minutes
MAKES: 8 main-dish servings

3	cups seedless watermelon cubes, cut into ½-inch chunks (from 4-pound piece of watermelon)
1	large ripe nectarine, pitted and cut into ½-inch chunks
3	tablespoons finely chopped red onion
1	tablespoon fresh lemon juice
2	tablespoons instant coffee
1	tablespoon grated peeled fresh ginger
1	tablespoon olive oil
1¼	teaspoons ground allspice
¾	teaspoon salt
8	skinless, boneless chicken-breast halves (about 3 pounds total)
½	cup packed fresh basil leaves, coarsely chopped

1. In medium bowl, combine watermelon, nectarine, red onion, and lemon juice. Cover and refrigerate salsa while preparing chicken. Makes 4 cups.

2. Prepare outdoor grill for direct grilling over medium heat, or lightly spray a ridged grill pan with nonstick cooking spray, then heat on medium until hot.

3. In large bowl, with spoon or fingers, press coffee to pulverize. Add ginger, oil, allspice, and ½ teaspoon salt; stir to combine. Add chicken and toss to evenly coat with spice mixture (you may need to pat spice mixture onto chicken with fingers).

4. Place chicken breasts on hot grill grate or pan. Cover and cook 8 to 10 minutes or until juices run clear when thickest part of chicken is pierced with tip of knife, turning once. Transfer chicken to cutting board and let rest 5 minutes. Meanwhile, stir basil and remaining ¼ teaspoon salt into salsa. Slice chicken crosswise and serve with salsa alongside.

EACH SERVING: About 235 calories, 40g protein, 8g carbohydrate, 4g total fat (1g saturated), 99mg cholesterol, 310mg sodium

Grilled Chicken and Steak Fajitas for a Crowd

Fajitas are fun party food. Set up a buffet area with all the fajita components and let your guests make their own!

PREP: 15 minutes plus marinating
GRILL: 16 to 21 minutes
MAKES: 24 servings

¼ cup tequila

½ cup fresh lime juice

2 teaspoons ground cumin

6 garlic cloves, minced

2¼ teaspoons salt

2 pounds beef skirt steaks

4 medium skinless, boneless chicken-breast halves (about 1¼ pounds total)

12 (12-inch) bamboo skewers

3 medium red onions, cut into ½-inch-thick slices

2 tablespoons olive oil

4 large red and/or green peppers, stems and seeds removed, each cut lengthwise in half

24 (6-inch) flour tortillas, warmed

salsa, sour cream, and cilantro leaves

1. In cup, combine tequila, lime juice, cumin, garlic and 1 teaspoon salt. Divide marinade between 2 large zip-tight plastic bags. Add steaks to 1 bag and chicken to remaining bag, turning meat to coat with marinade. Seal bags, pressing out excess air; refrigerate at least 2 hours or overnight, turning over several times.

2. Soak skewers in water to cover at least 20 minutes. Meanwhile, prepare outdoor grill for covered direct grilling over medium heat.

3. Thread skewers horizontally through onion slices. Brush onions with some oil; sprinkle with ¼ teaspoon salt. In medium bowl, toss ½ teaspoon salt and remaining oil with peppers.

4. Place onions and peppers on hot grill rack. Cover grill and cook vegetables until tender, 10 to 12 minutes, turning over once. Remove vegetables to large platter as they are done. Remove skewers from onions. Transfer peppers to cutting board; cut into ½-inch-wide slices. Return to platter with onions. Set aside.

5. Remove steaks and chicken from bags; discard marinade. Place steaks and chicken on grill; sprinkle with remaining ½ teaspoon salt. Cover grill and cook steak 6 to 8 minutes for medium-rare or until desired doneness, turning over once. Cook chicken until juices run clear when thickest part of chicken breast is pierced, 7 to 9 minutes, turning over once.

6. Transfer steaks and chicken to cutting board; let steak stand 10 minutes for easier slicing. Thinly slice chicken; transfer to platter with vegetables. Thinly slice steak against the grain; place on platter.

7. To serve, set the platter out, along with the warm tortillas in a towel-lined basket and accompaniments in separate bowls so guests can custom assemble fajitas.

EACH SERVING: About 485 calories, 33g protein, 42g carbohydrate, 20g total fat (6g saturated), 84mg cholesterol, 660mg sodium

Jamaican Jerk Chicken Kabobs

Originally, jerk seasoning was only used to season pork shoulder, which was "jerked" apart into shreds before serving. Nowadays, this very popular power-packed seasoning rub is enjoyed on fish and chicken as well.

PREP: **15 minutes plus marinating**
GRILL: **about 10 minutes**

MAKES: **4 main-dish servings**

2 green onions, chopped
1 jalapeño chile, seeded and minced
1 tablespoon minced, peeled fresh ginger
2 tablespoons white wine vinegar
2 tablespoons Worcestershire sauce
3 teaspoons vegetable oil
1 teaspoon ground allspice
1 teaspoon dried thyme
½ teaspoon plus ⅛ teaspoon salt
1 pound skinless, boneless chicken breast halves, cut into 12 pieces
1 red pepper, stem and seeds removed, cut into 1-inch pieces
1 green pepper, stem and seeds removed, cut into 1-inch pieces
4 (10-inch) metal skewers

1. In blender or in food processor with knife blade attached, process green onions, jalapeño, ginger, vinegar, Worcestershire, 2 teaspoons oil, allspice, thyme, and ½ teaspoon salt until paste forms.

2. Place chicken in small bowl or zip-tight plastic bag and add green-onion mixture, turning to coat. Cover bowl or seal bag and refrigerate 1 hour to marinate.

3. Meanwhile, in small bowl, toss red and green peppers with remaining 1 teaspoon oil and remaining ⅛ teaspoon salt.

4. Prepare outdoor grill for direct grilling over medium heat, or lightly spray a ridged grill pan with nonstick cooking spray, then heat on medium until hot. Alternately thread chicken and pepper pieces on each skewer.

5. Place kabobs on hot grill rack or pan. Brush with any remaining marinade. Cook 5 minutes; turn and cook until chicken loses its pink color throughout, about 5 minutes longer.

EACH SERVING: About 181 calories, 27g protein, 6g carbohydrate, 5g total fat (1g saturated), 66mg cholesterol, 525mg sodium

Flame-Cooked Chicken Saltimbocca

So simple, yet so flavorful, this dish will quickly become a part of your outdoor repertoire. Remember, cutlets are thin, so make sure you don't overcook them. These would be delicious served between two layers of grilled focaccia.

PREP: 15 minutes   **GRILL: about 8 minutes**
MAKES: 8 main-dish servings

2   tablespoons fresh lemon juice
1   tablespoon olive oil
8   chicken cutlets or skinless, boneless chicken breast halves with tenderloins removed (2 pounds total)
24   large fresh sage leaves
8   thin slices prosciutto (4 ounces; see Tip)

1. Prepare outdoor grill for direct grilling over medium heat, or lightly spray a ridged grill pan with nonstick cooking spray, then heat on medium until hot.

2. In large bowl, with fork, mix lemon juice and oil. Add chicken and toss to coat.

3. Place 3 sage leaves on each cutlet or breast half, then wrap each with 1 slice prosciutto. Place chicken on hot grill rack or pan and grill until juices run clear when thickest part of breast is pierced with tip of knife, about 8 minutes, turning over once.

EACH SERVING: About 195 calories, 31g protein, 1g carbohydrate, 7g total fat (2g saturated), 83mg cholesterol, 410mg sodium

> **TIP:** If you can't find prosciutto, substitute slices of lean bacon or Canadian bacon.

Honey and Spice Cornish Hens

These honey-grilled Cornish hens boast intense flavor and tender, succulent meat.

PREP: 15 minutes   **GRILL: 32 to 33 minutes**
MAKES: 4 main-dish servings

2   Cornish hens (1½ pounds each), fresh or frozen (thawed)
1¾   teaspoons Chinese five-spice powder
1¼   teaspoons salt
2   tablespoons honey

1. Prepare outdoor grill for direct grilling over medium heat.

2. Remove giblets and necks from hens; reserve to use in soup another day. With kitchen shears, cut each hen in half. Rinse with running cold water; drain well.

3. In cup, mix five-spice powder and salt. Rub mixture on hen halves.

4. Place hen halves on hot grill rack; cook, turning hens occasionally, until juices run clear when thickest part is pierced with a knife, about 30 minutes. Brush hens with honey; grill 2 to 3 minutes longer, until hens are golden.

EACH SERVING: About 360 calories, 38g protein, 9g carbohydrate, 19g total fat (1g saturated), 71mg cholesterol, 755mg sodium

Cornish Hens with Ginger-Plum Glaze

The hens are cut in half for fast, even cooking, then brushed with a gingery plum jam. Glazed plum halves are grilled right alongside.

PREP: 25 minutes   **GRILL:** about 30 minutes
MAKES: 4 servings

2/3	cup plum jam or preserves
3	teaspoons grated, peeled fresh ginger
4	large plums, each cut in half and pitted
2	Cornish hens (about 1¾ pounds each), fresh or frozen (thawed)
2	tablespoons reduced-sodium soy sauce
1	teaspoon Chinese five-spice powder
¾	teaspoon salt
¼	teaspoon coarsely ground black pepper
2	small garlic cloves, crushed with garlic press

1. Prepare outdoor grill for direct grilling over medium heat.

2. In 1-quart saucepan, heat jam and 1 teaspoon ginger over low heat, stirring, until jam melts, 1 to 2 minutes. Spoon 2 tablespoons glaze into medium bowl; add plums and toss to coat.

3. Remove giblets and necks from hens; reserve for another use. With kitchen shears, cut each hen in half. Rinse with cold running water and drain well; pat dry with paper towels.

4. In small bowl, mix remaining 2 teaspoons ginger with soy sauce, five-spice powder, salt, pepper, and garlic. Brush mixture on hen halves.

5. Place hen halves, skin side down, on hot grill rack and grill, turning once, 15 minutes. Brush skin side of hens with plum glaze from saucepan; turn hens over and grill 5 minutes. Brush hens with remaining glaze; turn and grill until juices run clear when thickest part of thigh is pierced with tip of knife and hens are golden, about 10 minutes longer.

6. Just before hens are done, place plums on grill rack and cook, turning once, until plums are hot and lightly browned, about 6 minutes. Serve each hen half with 2 plum halves.

EACH SERVING: About 620 calories, 39g protein, 47g carbohydrate, 31g total fat (8g saturated), 219mg cholesterol, 920mg sodium

THE POWER OF FIVE-SPICE POWDER

Five-spice powder is a fragrant blend of seasonings that work together in harmony—just as, according to Chinese lore, the five elements of the universe (wood, metal, water, fire, and earth) do. A staple in Chinese cuisine, the blend sometimes contains more or less of each component, or even varied ingredients, depending on the brand. The usual mix is star anise, cinnamon, Szechuan peppercorns, fennel (or anise seeds), and cloves. But some versions have licorice root or ginger. In any form, the powder is slightly sweet and very pungent; shake it on sparingly. We love it stirred into soy sauce and honey to make a quick glaze for everything from pork to poultry.

Charcoal-Grilled Turkey

Cooking a turkey on a covered charcoal grill gives it a delightful smoky flavor. Using an outdoor grill also frees up the kitchen for other holiday dinner preparations, and it cuts down considerably on cleanup.

PREP: 15 minutes
GRILL: 2 hours 30 minutes to 3 hours
MAKES: 16 main-dish servings

2   cups mesquite chips
1   turkey (12 pounds), fresh or frozen (thawed)
1 to 2 (8-inch) metal skewers and kitchen string or stuffing clamp
2   tablespoons vegetable oil
2   teaspoons dried rosemary, crumbled
2   teaspoons dried thyme
2   teaspoons salt
½   teaspoon ground black pepper
rosemary sprigs for garnish

1. Soak mesquite chips in enough *water* to cover for about 1 hour.

2. To prepare coals: In bottom of covered charcoal grill, with vents open and grill uncovered, ignite 60 charcoal briquettes (not self-starting). Allow briquettes to burn until all coals are covered with a thin coating of gray ash, about 30 minutes. Push hot briquettes to two sides of grill; place sturdy disposable foil pan (about 13″ by 9″ by 2″) in between coals. Drain chips well and scatter over hot coals.

3. Meanwhile, remove giblets and neck from turkey; reserve for use in soup another day. Rinse turkey with cold running water and drain well. Fasten neck skin to back with 1 or 2 skewers. With turkey breast side up, fold wings under back of turkey so they stay in place. Depending on brand of turkey, with string, tie legs and tail together, or push drumsticks under band of skin, or use stuffing clamp. In cup, mix oil, dried rosemary, thyme, salt, and pepper; rub mixture all over turkey.

4. Place turkey, breast side up, on hot grill rack directly over foil pan (to catch drips). Cover grill and roast turkey 2 hours 15 minutes to 3 hours (11 to 13 minutes per pound for unstuffed bird), adding 8 to 9 briquettes to each side of pan every hour to maintain a grill temperature of 325°F on oven or grill thermometer. Turkey is done when thigh temperature on meat thermometer reaches 175 to 180°F and juices run clear when thickest part of thigh is pierced with tip of knife; breast temperature should reach 165 to 170°F. (Upon standing, temperature will rise 5 to 10°F.)

5. When turkey is done, place on cutting board; let stand 15 minutes to allow juices to set for easier carving. Carefully remove drip pan from grill; skim fat from drippings. Carve turkey and arrange on warm large platter; garnish with rosemary sprigs. Serve drippings along with turkey.

EACH SERVING: About 250 calories, 43g protein, 0g carbohydrate, 8g total fat (2g saturated), 112mg cholesterol, 190mg sodium

Spiced Grilled Turkey Breast

Soaking a whole turkey breast overnight in a spiced salt solution, or brine, produces exceptionally tender and flavorful meat. You can also brine a whole chicken before roasting.

PREP: 35 minutes plus brining and standing
GRILL: 25 to 30 minutes
MAKES: 12 main-dish servings

SPICED TURKEY BREAST

¼ cup sugar

¼ cup kosher salt

2 tablespoons cracked black pepper

2 tablespoons ground ginger

1 tablespoon ground cinnamon

4 cups water

1 whole boneless turkey breast (about 4 pounds), skin removed, breast cut in half

4 garlic cloves, crushed with side of chef's knife

CHIPOTLE HONEY MUSTARD GLAZE

2 tablespoons honey

2 tablespoons Dijon mustard

1 chipotle chile in adobo, minced

1 teaspoon balsamic vinegar

1 recipe Peach Salsa (page 116)

1. Prepare turkey: In 2-quart saucepan, heat sugar, salt, pepper, ginger, cinnamon, and 1 cup water to boiling over high heat. Reduce heat to low; simmer 2 minutes. Meanwhile, stir remaining water with ice cubes to chill. Remove pan from heat; stir in 3 cups ice water.

2. Place turkey breast in large zip-tight plastic bag; add brine and garlic. Seal bag, pressing out excess air. Place bag in bowl and refrigerate, turning occasionally, 24 hours.

3. Prepare outdoor grill for covered direct grilling over medium heat. With long-handled basting brush, oil grill rack.

4. Meanwhile, prepare glaze: In small bowl, stir honey, mustard, chipotle, and vinegar until blended. Set aside.

5. Remove turkey from bag and discard brine and garlic. With paper towels, pat turkey dry and brush off most of pepper. Place turkey on hot grill rack. Cover grill and cook turkey 20 minutes, turning over once. Brush turkey with glaze and cook 5 to 10 minutes longer (depending on thickness of breast), brushing and turning frequently, until temperature on instant-read meat thermometer inserted into thickest part of breast reaches 165°F. (Internal temperature will rise 5°F upon standing.) Place turkey on cutting board and let stand 10 minutes to allow juices to set for easier slicing.

6. While turkey rests, prepare Peach Salsa.

7. Serve turkey hot, or cover and refrigerate to serve cold, with the salsa on the side.

EACH SERVING TURKEY: About 170 calories, 34g protein, 4g carbohydrate, 1g total fat (0g saturated), 94mg cholesterol, 555mg sodium

Southwestern Turkey Fajitas with Tomatillo Salsa

Broiling the tomatillos adds a subtle smokiness to this luscious salsa. Fajita seasoning mixes vary among manufacturers, especially with regard to salt content. Add salt to taste if necessary.

PREP: 20 minutes   **GRILL:** 15 to 20 minutes
MAKES: 6 servings

TOMATILLO SALSA

1	pound tomatillos, husked and rinsed
1	small poblano chile, cut in half, stems and seeds discarded
1	small shallot, finely chopped
3	tablespoons fresh lime juice
¾	teaspoon salt
¾	teaspoon sugar
⅓	cup loosely packed fresh cilantro leaves, chopped

TURKEY AND ONION FAJITAS

2	turkey breast tenderloins (about 1¾ pounds total) or 6 medium skinless, boneless chicken breast halves (about 1¾ pounds total)
2	tablespoons fajita seasoning
4	teaspoons olive oil
3	large onions (12 ounces each), cut into ½-inch-thick slices
12	(6-inch) corn tortillas

1. Prepare salsa: Preheat broiler. Place tomatillos in broiling pan without rack. Broil tomatillos 5 to 6 inches from heat source, turning once, until blackened in spots and blistering, about 10 minutes. When tomatillos are turned, add poblano, skin side up, to pan and broil until charred, about 6 minutes.

2. In blender or food processor, pulse tomatillos, poblano, shallot, lime juice, salt, and sugar until chopped. Stir in cilantro. Refrigerate salsa up to 3 days if not serving right away. Makes about 2 cups.

3. Prepare outdoor grill for direct grilling over medium heat.

4. Prepare fajitas: In medium bowl, toss turkey or chicken with fajita seasoning and 2 teaspoons oil until evenly coated. Brush onion slices with remaining 2 teaspoons oil. Place turkey or chicken and onions on hot grill rack. Grill, turning once, until instant-read meat thermometer registers 170°F and juices run clear when thickest part of meat is pierced with tip of knife, 15 to 20 minutes for turkey (10 to 12 minutes for chicken), turning over once. Grill onions until tender and golden, 12 to 15 minutes, turning over once.

6. While turkey or chicken is grilling, place tortillas in batches on grill rack and heat until lightly browned. Wrap in foil and keep warm.

7. Transfer turkey or chicken to cutting board and thinly slice. Top tortillas with equal amounts of turkey or chicken and onion. Spoon some salsa on each and fold to eat out of hand. Serve with any remaining onions and salsa.

EACH SERVING TURKEY: About 350 calories, 36g protein, 35g carbohydrate, 7g total fat (1g saturated), 88mg cholesterol, 440mg sodium

EACH ¼ CUP SALSA: About 30 calories, 1g protein, cholesterol, 220mg sodium

Prosciutto-Wrapped Turkey Cutlets with Basil-Melon Salsa

When buying turkey cutlets for this recipe, make sure not to get the ones that are very thinly sliced for scaloppine.

PREP: 20 minutes   GRILL: 5 to 7 minutes
MAKES: 4 main-dish servings

2	limes
1½	cups chopped, peeled cantaloupe
1½	cups chopped, peeled honeydew melon
1	small Kirby cucumber, shredded (½ cup)
1	jalapeño chile, seeded and finely chopped
¼	cup loosely packed fresh basil leaves, chopped
¼	teaspoon salt
4	turkey breast cutlets (1 pound total)
¼	teaspoon coarsely ground black pepper
4	ounces thinly sliced prosciutto

1. Grease grill rack. Prepare outdoor grill for direct grilling over medium heat, or lightly spray a ridged grill pan with nonstick cooking spray, then heat on medium until hot.

2. From 1 lime, grate 1 teaspoon peel and squeeze 2 tablespoons juice. Cut remaining lime into 4 wedges and set aside. In medium bowl, combine lime juice, cantaloupe, honeydew, cucumber, jalapeño, basil, and salt. Makes about 3 cups salsa.

3. Sprinkle turkey cutlets with lime peel and pepper. Wrap cutlets with prosciutto, pressing prosciutto firmly to turkey.

4. Place cutlets on hot grill rack or pan and cook until turkey loses its pink color throughout, 5 to 7 minutes, turning over once. Transfer turkey to plate; serve with salsa and lime wedges.

EACH SERVING TURKEY: About 185 calories, 35g protein, 0g carbohydrate, 4g total fat (1g saturated), 86mg cholesterol, 815mg sodium

EACH ¼ CUP SALSA: About 10 calories, 0g protein, 3g carbohydrate, 0g total fat, 0mg cholesterol, 50mg sodium

Orange-Rosemary Turkey Cutlets with Couscous and Arugula

Turkey cutlets keep this dish lean, while flavor-packed citrus and rosemary keep guests coming back for more.

PREP: 15 minutes **GRILL:** 4 to 5 minutes
MAKES: 4 main-dish servings

3	navel oranges
1½	cups water
3	tablespoons olive oil
½	teaspoon salt
1½	cups whole-wheat couscous
1	tablespoon fresh rosemary leaves, chopped
¼	teaspoon ground black pepper
4	turkey cutlets (1 pound total)
2	tablespoons seasoned rice vinegar
1	bag (5 ounces) baby arugula

1. From oranges, grate 2 tablespoons peel and squeeze ³/₄ cup juice. In 4-quart saucepan, heat water, ¹/₂ cup orange juice, 1 tablespoon orange peel, 2 teaspoons oil, and ¹/₄ teaspoon salt to boiling over high heat. Stir in couscous; cover saucepan and remove from heat. Let stand until ready to serve.

2. Heat ridged grill pan over medium-high heat, or prepare outdoor grill for direct grilling over medium-high heat. In cup, combine remaining 1 tablespoon orange peel with rosemary, 1 teaspoon oil, remaining ¹/₄ teaspoon salt, and pepper. Pat turkey cutlets dry with paper towels, then rub both sides of each cutlet with rosemary mixture.

3. Add cutlets to hot grill pan or rack and cook until cutlets just lose their pink color throughout, 4 to 5 minutes, turning over once.

4. In small bowl, prepare orange vinaigrette: Whisk together vinegar and remaining ¹/₄ cup orange juice; slowly whisk in remaining 2 tablespoons oil until blended.

5. To serve, fluff couscous with fork. Toss arugula with ¹/₄ cup vinaigrette. Arrange arugula on 4 dinner plates; top with couscous and turkey. Drizzle with remaining vinaigrette.

EACH SERVING: About 410 calories, 33g protein, 44g carbohydrate, 12g total fat (2g saturated), 71mg cholesterol, 610mg sodium

Turkey Cutlets, Indian Style

These are delicious with a squeeze of fresh lime or Pineapple Salsa (page 278) served alongside. For a festive presentation, set out bowls of yogurt, store-bought mango chutney, fluffy basmati rice, and chopped fresh cilantro.

PREP: 15 minutes   GRILL: 5 to 7 minutes
MAKES: 6 main-dish servings

2	large limes
⅓	cup plain low-fat yogurt
1	tablespoon vegetable oil
2	teaspoons minced, peeled fresh ginger (see Tip)
1	teaspoon ground cumin
1	teaspoon ground coriander
1	teaspoon salt
1	garlic clove, crushed with garlic press
6	turkey cutlets (1½ pounds total)

1. Prepare outdoor grill for direct grilling over medium heat, or lightly spray a ridged grill pan with nonstick cooking spray, then heat on medium until hot.

2. From 1 lime, grate 1 teaspoon peel and squeeze 1 tablespoon juice. Cut remaining lime into wedges; reserve.

3. In large bowl, mix lime peel and juice, yogurt, oil, ginger, cumin, coriander, salt, and garlic until blended.

4. Just before grilling, add turkey cutlets to bowl with yogurt mixture; stir to coat. (Do not let cutlets marinate in yogurt mixture; their texture will become mealy.)

5. Place cutlets on hot grill rack or pan and grill until they just lose their pink color throughout, 5 to 7 minutes, turning over once. Serve with lime wedges.

EACH SERVING: About 160 calories, 29g protein, 3g carbohydrate, 3g total fat (1g saturated), 71mg cholesterol, 450mg sodium

> **TIP:** Freeze any extra unpeeled fresh ginger, wrapped well in plastic wrap. It will keep for up to six months.

Turkey Kabobs with Garden Tomato Jam

Cut lean turkey breast into cubes, then marinate in a savory spice mixture. After grilling, serve with a quickly cooked combination of tomato and onion, sweetened with raisins and orange juice.

PREP: **30 minutes plus marinating**
GRILL: **about 10 minutes**

MAKES: **6 main-dish servings**

TURKEY KABOBS

1	garlic clove, crushed with garlic press
1	tablespoon olive oil
1½	teaspoons chili powder
¾	teaspoon paprika
¾	teaspoon salt
¼	teaspoon ground red pepper (cayenne)
¼	teaspoon ground black pepper
2	pounds skinless, boneless turkey breast, cut into 1½-inch cubes

GARDEN TOMATO JAM

1	navel orange
1	tablespoon olive oil
1	onion, chopped
7	large plum tomatoes (about 1 pound total), seeded and cut into ¼-inch dice
⅓	cup golden raisins
¼	teaspoon salt
¼	cup loosely packed fresh cilantro leaves, chopped
4	(12-inch) metal skewers

cilantro sprigs for garnish

1. Prepare kabobs: In large zip-tight plastic bag, combine garlic, oil, chili powder, paprika, salt, ground red pepper, and black pepper. Add turkey to bag, tossing to coat with spice mixture. Seal bag, pressing out excess air. Place bag on plate; refrigerate at least 15 minutes or up to 1 hour.

2. Prepare outdoor grill for direct grilling over medium heat, or lightly spray a ridged grill pan with nonstick cooking spray, then heat on medium until hot.

3. Meanwhile, prepare tomato jam: From orange, grate 1 teaspoon peel and squeeze ¼ cup juice. In 10-inch skillet, heat oil over medium-low heat. Add onion and cook until golden, about 5 minutes, stirring occasionally. Add tomatoes, raisins, salt, and orange peel and juice. Increase heat to medium-high; cook until tomatoes soften and liquid evaporates, about 6 minutes. Remove skillet from heat. Stir chopped cilantro into tomato jam just before serving. Makes about 1½ cups.

4. Thread turkey on skewers. Place skewers on hot grill rack or pan. Cook until juices run clear when turkey is pierced with tip of knife, about 10 minutes, turning over once.

5. To serve, place skewers on platter; garnish with cilantro sprigs. Serve with tomato jam.

EACH SERVING TURKEY: About 175 calories, 34g protein, 1g carbohydrate, 3g total fat (1g saturated), 94mg cholesterol, 355mg sodium

EACH ¼ CUP JAM: About 75 calories, 1g protein, 13g carbohydrate, 3g total fat (0g saturated), 0mg cholesterol, 105mg sodium

Beef, Veal, and Lamb

Steak was made for the grill. With a flame-charred outside and tender pink inside it's irresistible. If cooking the perfect steak has eluded you, you'll find plenty of help in this chapter—tips for grilling, a chart with grill times, and advice for determining doneness, plus a mouthwatering collection of recipes for every kind of beef steak—filet mignon, sirloin, Porterhouse, flank, and skirt. Entertaining a crowd? Try our cheater smoked brisket (Brisket with Chunky BBQ Sauce), which is cooked low and slow on the stovetop in advance, then gets a smoky turn on the grill, sopped with sauce. Or give beef short ribs a try, either Korean style or deviled.

Veal isn't something you see often on the grill, but don't miss our Stuffed Veal Chops, filled with a mix of Fontina, roasted red peppers, and fresh basil and served on a bed of arugula. And if you haven't tried lamb on the grill, make sure you do—whether you choose a recipe for butterflied leg of lamb or kabobs, the flavor is superb.

Filet Mignon with Horseradish Salsa, page 140

Spice-Rubbed Beef Tenderloin

Make a double batch of this rub and use it the next time you're grilling pork chops, pork tenderloin, or a leg of lamb.

PREP: 10 minutes plus standing
GRILL: 30 to 40 minutes
MAKES: 10 main-dish servings

1	tablespoon fennel seeds
2	teaspoons salt
½	teaspoon ground ginger
½	teaspoon crushed red pepper
1	beef tenderloin roast (about 2½ pounds; see Tip)

1. Prepare outdoor grill for covered direct grilling over medium heat.

2. In mortar with pestle or in zip-tight plastic bag with rolling pin, crush fennel seeds. In small bowl, combine fennel seeds, salt, ginger, and crushed red pepper.

3. Rub beef tenderloin with spice mixture. Place spice-rubbed beef in zip-tight plastic bag and refrigerate several hours or overnight before grilling.

4. Place beef on hot grill rack. Cover grill and cook beef, turning occasionally, until meat thermometer inserted in center reaches 135°F, 30 to 40 minutes. Internal temperature of meat will rise to 140°F (medium-rare) upon standing. Or cook until meat reaches desired doneness. Transfer to cutting board and let stand 10 minutes to set juices for easier slicing.

EACH SERVING: About 225 calories, 19g protein, 0g carbohydrate, 16g total fat (6g saturated), 66mg cholesterol, 510mg sodium

> **TIP:** Ask your butcher to cut this roast from a whole tenderloin for you. The center-cut roast should be 2½ pounds after trimming; the ends make deliciously tender kabobs.

GRILLING BEEF

To test for doneness, insert an instant-read meat thermometer into the center or thickest part of the meat. If it is ½ inch thick or less, insert the thermometer horizontally into the meat, halfway in. Always let steak rest approximately 10 minutes before serving or slicing, so the juices have time to redistribute throughout the meat. During the resting time, the internal temperature of the meat will rise about 5 degrees.

CUT	COOK-TO INTERNAL TEMPERATURE	APPROXIMATE COOK TIME
Steaks (porterhouse, T-bone, sirloin, rib-eye, top round):		
3/4" thick	145°F	6–8 minutes
1" thick	145°F	11–14 minutes
Steaks (flank or skirt)	145°F	15–20 minutes
Tenderloin, whole	135°F	30–40 minutes

Pepper-Crusted Filet Mignon

These very tender steaks are great company fare, plus they're a snap to make ahead. Simply coat them with crushed spices as directed, then cover and refrigerate for up to one day until ready to cook.

PREP: 15 minutes plus standing
GRILL: 16 to 20 minutes

MAKES: 4 main-dish servings

1	tablespoon whole black peppercorns
1	teaspoon fennel seeds
4	beef tenderloin steaks (filet mignon), 1 inch thick (about 4 ounces each)
3	medium peppers (red, yellow, and/or orange), each stemmed, seeded, and cut in half lengthwise
1	tablespoon minced fresh parsley
1	teaspoon olive oil
¾	teaspoon salt

1. Prepare outdoor grill for covered direct grilling over medium-high heat, or lightly spray a ridged grill pan with nonstick cooking spray, then heat on medium until hot.

2. Meanwhile, in mortar with pestle or in zip-tight plastic bag with rolling pin, crush peppercorns and fennel seeds. With hands, pat spice mixture around edges of steaks. Cover and refrigerate steaks until ready to cook. If you like, steaks can be prepared up to 1 day ahead.

3. With hand, flatten each pepper half and place, skin side down, on hot grill rack or pan. Cover and cook until skins are charred and blistered, 8 to 10 minutes. Transfer peppers to bowl; cover with plate and let steam at room temperature until cool enough to handle, about 15 minutes. If using gas grill, reset temperature to medium.

4. Remove peppers from bowl. Peel skins and discard. Cut peppers lengthwise into ¼-inch-wide strips. Return peppers to same bowl and toss with parsley, oil, and ¼ teaspoon salt.

5. Sprinkle steaks with remaining ½ teaspoon salt. Place steaks on hot grill rack. Cover grill and cook, turning once, 8 to 10 minutes for medium-rare or until desired doneness. Serve steaks topped with peppers.

EACH SERVING: About 230 calories, 26g protein, 9g carbohydrate, 10g total fat (3g saturated), 71mg cholesterol, 495mg sodium

Filet Mignon with Roquefort

Tangy Roquefort cheese is such a luxuriously flavorful topping that just a tablespoon per serving is enough.

PREP: 5 minutes   GRILL: 10 minutes
MAKES: 4 main-dish servings

4   beef tenderloin steaks (filet mignon),
    1 inch thick (4 ounces each)
2   teaspoons olive oil
½   teaspoon salt
¼   teaspoon coarsely ground pepper
1   ounce Roquefort cheese, crumbled (¼ cup)

1. Heat ridged grill pan on medium-high heat until hot, or prepare outdoor grill for direct grilling over medium-high heat. Pat steaks dry with paper towels. Rub oil all over steaks and sprinkle with salt and pepper.

2. Place steaks in hot grill pan or on hot rack and cook 8 to 10 minutes for medium-rare, or to desired doneness, turning over once. Transfer steaks to 4 dinner plates; top with Roquefort.

EACH SERVING: About 205 calories, 25g protein, 0g carbohydrate, 11g total fat (4g saturated), 63mg cholesterol, 470mg sodium

Filet Mignon with Horseradish Salsa

Juicy steaks taste even better with our flavor-packed salsa. (For photo, see page 136.) For an extra-special company dinner, grill portobello mushrooms as you would in Portobello and Prosciutto Salad (page 57) and serve thickly sliced alongside.

PREP: 15 minutes   GRILL: 10 to 12 minutes
MAKES: 4 main-dish servings

1   recipe Horseradish Salsa (page 276)
1   teaspoon cracked black pepper
1   teaspoon olive oil
½   teaspoon salt
¼   teaspoon dried thyme
1   garlic clove, crushed with garlic press
4   beef tenderloin steaks (filet mignon),
    1 inch thick (about 6 ounces each)

1. Prepare Horseradish Salsa.

2. Prepare outdoor grill for direct grilling over medium heat, or lightly spray a ridged grill pan with nonstick cooking spray, then heat on medium until hot.

3. In cup, mix pepper, oil, salt, thyme, and garlic. Rub pepper mixture all over steaks.

4. Place steaks on hot grill rack or pan and grill, turning over once, 10 to 12 minutes for medium-rare or until desired doneness. Serve steaks with Horseradish Salsa.

EACH SERVING: About 330 calories, 39g protein, 9g carbohydrate, 15g total fat (4g saturated), 89mg cholesterol, 710mg sodium

The Perfect Steak

A high price alone won't guarantee great results from beef. Our tips for shopping, prepping, and cooking it right help you get the most from your splurge.

BETTER RED? Bright crimson meat has always been the standard by which a good steak is judged. But if the meat is vacuum packed, it will be purplish brown. Not to worry: Once it's exposed to oxygen, the meat will turn a satisfying red.

PAT IT DRY: To get a good sear on your steak, dry it well with paper towels. If there's any surface moisture, the meat will steam, not brown.

SLASH THE FAT? Today most meat is trimmed, leaving only ¼ inch of fat, so there's no need to make slashes in the fat to keep the steak from curling as it cooks. If your butcher does leave on a thicker layer, you can make shallow vertical slits in the fat, taking care not to cut through to the meat.

A TIME TO SEASON: Don't salt in advance—you'll draw out the juices. Preheat your grill or pan, then just before adding the steak, sprinkle it with salt and pepper.

CHECK FOR DONENESS: Here's a general formula for cooking a 1-inch-thick steak over medium-high heat. Rare: about 6 minutes per side (135°F). Medium: about 8 minutes per side (145°F). Well done: about 10 minutes per side (160°F). These times are only guidelines, however, so check your steak earlier to avoid overcooking it.

LEFTOVERS: Don't even try to reheat steak—the fat will oxidize, giving the meat an off flavor (think steam table). Our recommendation: Let the meat sit out of the fridge for 10 to 15 minutes, then serve it with horseradish, grainy mustard, or, if you have leftover sauce, heat it to boiling and pour it over.

Chili-Glazed Porterhouse Steak with Grilled Salad

This is steak-house fare—a big porterhouse with grilled greens on the side.

PREP: 15 minutes   **GRILL:** 20 to 30 minutes
MAKES: 5 main-dish servings

CHILI-GLAZED PORTERHOUSE STEAK

- ¼ cup chili sauce
- ¼ cup balsamic vinegar
- ¾ teaspoon salt
- 1 garlic clove, crushed with garlic press
- 1 beef loin porterhouse or T-bone steak, 2 inches thick (about 2¼ pounds)

GRILLED SALAD

- 1 large head radicchio, cut into 6 wedges
- 3 medium heads Belgian endive, each cut lengthwise in half
- 3 tablespoons olive oil
- 1 tablespoon chopped fresh rosemary leaves, or 1 teaspoon dried rosemary, crushed
- ½ teaspoon salt

1. Prepare outdoor grill for direct grilling over medium heat.

2. Prepare the steak: In a pie plate or deep dish, mix chili sauce, vinegar, salt, and garlic. Trim all fat from steak; add steak to chili-sauce mixture and turn to coat on both sides.

3. Place steak on hot grill rack and brush with half the chili-sauce mixture remaining in plate. Cook steak 20 to 30 minutes for medium-rare or until of desired doneness, turning steak occasionally and brushing with chili-sauce mixture remaining in plate halfway through grilling.

4. Meanwhile, prepare the salad: In small bowl, mix oil, rosemary, and salt. Place radicchio and endive on grill over medium heat with the steak; brush with olive-oil mixture. Cook, turning them occasionally, until vegetables are tender-crisp, 5 to 10 minutes.

5. Transfer steak to cutting board; let stand 10 minutes to allow juices to set for easier slicing. Slice steak and serve with the grilled salad.

EACH SERVING: About 205 calories, 22g protein, 5g carbohydrate, 10g total fat (4 saturated fat), 57mg cholesterol, 590mg sodium

Red-Wine and Rosemary Porterhouse

This robust marinade can season a thick, juicy steak in fifteen minutes. Give it up to one hour for more intense flavor. It's also good on lamb, pork, or poultry. The steak is terrific served with Lemon-Garlic Potato Packet (page 253) and Crumb-Topped Tomatoes (page 261).

PREP: 10 minutes plus marinating
GRILL: 15 to 20 minutes

MAKES: 4 main-dish servings

½ cup dry red wine (see Tip)
1 tablespoon Worcestershire sauce
1 tablespoon tomato paste
1 tablespoon Dijon mustard
1 tablespoon balsamic vinegar
1 tablespoon chopped fresh rosemary
1 large garlic clove, crushed with garlic press
1 beef loin porterhouse or T-bone steak, 1½ inches thick (about 1½ pounds)
1 lemon, cut into wedges

1. In small bowl, stir together wine, Worcestershire, tomato paste, mustard, vinegar, rosemary, and garlic.

2. Place steak in large zip-tight plastic bag. Pour wine marinade over steak, turning to coat. Seal bag, pressing out excess air. Let stand 15 minutes at room temperature or refrigerate up to 1 hour, turning once.

3. Prepare outdoor grill for direct grilling over medium heat.

4. Remove steak from bag; discard marinade. Place steak on hot grill rack and grill, turning once, 15 to 20 minutes for medium-rare, or to desired doneness.

5. Transfer steak to cutting board; let stand 10 minutes to allow juices to set for easier slicing. Thinly slice steak and serve with lemon wedges.

EACH SERVING: About 395 calories, 32g protein, 1g carbohydrate, 28g total fat (11g saturated), 104mg cholesterol, 125mg sodium

> **TIP:** For a dry red wine that would work well in this recipe, try a Shiraz, Merlot, Chianti, or Cabernet.

PORTERHOUSE VERSUS T-BONE

Both steaks are cut from the beef short loin and have a T-shaped bone. But the defining characteristic is the size of the tenderloin (the smaller portion of meat on one side of the T). The T-bone's tenderloin starts at ½ inch in diameter. The more expensive porterhouse—so named because in the early 1800s, travelers dined on steak and ale at coach stops, or porter houses—contains a tenderloin that's at least 1¼ inches in diameter. Either steak works very well for our Red-Wine and Rosemary Porterhouse (above) and Chili-Glazed Porterhouse Steak with Grilled Salad (opposite).

Lemon-Soy-Marinated Sirloin Steak

Want to use a less tender cut? Marinate meat four hours or overnight to tenderize it.

PREP: 15 minutes plus marinating
GRILL: 12 to 15 minutes
MAKES: 6 main-dish servings

2   lemons
2   tablespoons soy sauce
1   tablespoon olive oil
1   clove garlic, crushed with garlic press
¼   teaspoon ground black pepper
¼   teaspoon ground red pepper (cayenne)
1   boneless beef top sirloin steak,
    1¼ inches thick (about 1½ pounds)
2   tablespoons water

1. Remove 3 strips lemon peel (3" by 1" each) and squeeze ⅓ cup juice. In bowl, mix lemon peel and juice, soy sauce, oil, garlic, black pepper, and red pepper.

2. Pour marinade into large zip-tight plastic bag; add steak, turning to coat. Seal bag, pressing out excess air; refrigerate 30 minutes.

3. Prepare outdoor grill for direct grilling over medium heat. Remove steak from bag. Pour marinade into 1-quart saucepan, add water, and reserve.

4. Place steak on hot grill rack and cook 12 to 15 minutes for medium-rare or until desired doneness, turning once. Transfer steak to cutting board; let stand 10 minutes to allow juices to set for easier slicing.

5. Meanwhile, heat reserved marinade to boiling over high heat; boil 1 minute. To serve, thinly slice steak and serve with cooked marinade.

EACH SERVING: About 265 calories, 24g protein, 2g carbohydrate, 18g total fat (7g saturated), 77mg cholesterol, 395mg sodium

---

IS THAT STEAK DONE YET?

You've got three options when it comes to determining the doneness of a steak.

1. Using an instant-read meat thermometer, check the steak's internal temperature (see The Perfect Steak, page 141).

2. Cut a small slit in the meat near the bone or center of a boneless steak. Rare steak will be bright red in the center and pinkish toward the surface; medium-rare, very pink in the center and slightly brown toward the surface; medium, light pink in the center with a brown outer portion; and well done, brown throughout. (Unlike hamburgers, steak can safely be eaten rare or medium-rare.)

3. To test doneness without cutting, try the chef's method: Compare the feel of the meat in the top center to the skin between the thumb and index finger when your hand is relaxed (hanging loosely), lightly fisted, and tightly clenched. A rare steak feels soft and spongy when pressed, similar to a relaxed hand. A medium-rare steak is springy to the touch, as on a loosely clenched hand. Medium steak feels firm, with minimal give, like a tight fist.

Coriander Steak with Warm Corn Salad

A simple Mexican-inspired corn salad tops luscious peppery steak.

PREP: 15 minutes   **GRILL:** about 8 minutes
MAKES: 4 main-dish servings

2	teaspoons olive oil
1	tablespoon coriander seeds, crushed
1	teaspoon cracked black peppercorns
3/4	teaspoon salt
2	boneless beef top sirloin steaks, 3/4 inch thick (about 10 ounces each)
1	small red pepper, stems and seeds removed, cut into 1/4-inch dice
1/2	small red onion, finely chopped
2	cups fresh corn kernels (from 4 ears)
1	tablespoon chopped fresh cilantro
1	tablespoon fresh lime juice
1/2	teaspoon ground cumin

1. Heat 10-inch ridged grill pan over medium-high heat until very hot. Brush pan with 1 teaspoon oil. On waxed paper, mix coriander, black pepper, and 1/2 teaspoon salt; use to coat both sides of steaks.

2. Place steaks in grill pan; cook about 8 minutes for medium-rare or until desired doneness, turning over once.

3. Meanwhile, in 2-quart saucepan, heat remaining 1 teaspoon oil over medium-high heat. Add red pepper and onion; cook until soft, about 5 minutes, stirring a few times. Add corn; heat through. Stir in cilantro, lime juice, cumin, and remaining 1/4 teaspoon salt. Makes about 2 1/2 cups salad.

4. Transfer steak to cutting board; let stand 10 minutes to allow juices to set for easier slicing. Thinly slice steak and serve with corn salad.

EACH SERVING: About 430 calories, 31g protein, 25g carbohydrate, 25g total fat (9g saturated), 84mg cholesterol, 705mg sodium

TIP: If you don't have a mortar and pestle to crush spices, place them in a zip-tight plastic bag. Seal the bag, then pound several times with a meat mallet, rolling pin, or heavy skillet.

Orange-Glazed Top Round Steak

We marinate the beef in a soy and garlic mixture, then brush it with orange marmalade on the grill. Serve with Orange-Chipotle Salsa (page 277) on the side.

PREP: 5 minutes plus marinating
GRILL: 20 to 25 minutes
MAKES: 6 main-dish servings

¼	cup soy sauce
2	cloves garlic, crushed with garlic press
1	teaspoon coarsely ground black pepper
1	beef top round steak, 1¼ inches thick (about 2 pounds), well trimmed
⅓	cup orange marmalade

1. In a 13" by 9" glass baking dish, mix soy sauce, garlic, and pepper. Add steak to soy sauce mixture, turning to coat. Cover and refrigerate 30 minutes, turning once.

2. Prepare outdoor grill for direct grilling over medium heat.

3. Place steak on hot grill rack; spoon remaining marinade over steak. Cook steak 20 to 25 minutes for medium-rare or until of desired doneness, brushing with orange marmalade during last 10 minutes of cooking, turning occasionally.

EACH SERVING: About 400 calories, 36g protein, 13g carbohydrate, 7g total fat (3g saturated), 95mg cholesterol, 415mg sodium

Garlic and Rosemary Flank Steak with Grilled Vegetable "Lasagna"

Add a loaf of crusty bread to round out this flavorful menu.

PREP: 30 minutes   **GRILL:** about 35 minutes
MAKES: 4 main-dish servings

1	medium red pepper
2	tablespoons soy sauce
1	tablespoon finely chopped fresh rosemary leaves
1	garlic clove, minced
5	tablespoons balsamic vinegar
4	tablespoons extra-virgin olive oil
1	beef flank steak (about 1¼ pounds), well trimmed
2	small zucchini (about 6 ounces each)
1	small yellow summer squash (about 6 ounces)
1	large portobello mushroom (about 6 ounces), stem discarded
¾	teaspoon salt
¼	teaspoon plus ⅛ teaspoon ground black pepper
2	tablespoons finely chopped fresh basil
1	tablespoon finely chopped fresh oregano
2	ounces feta cheese, crumbled (about ½ cup)

fresh rosemary sprigs for garnish

1. Heat large ridged grill pan over medium-high heat until very hot. Cut pepper lengthwise in half; discard membrane and seeds. With hand, flatten each pepper half. Place pepper halves, skin side down, in grill pan and cook until skin is charred and blistered, 3 to 4 minutes. Wrap pepper with foil; allow to steam at room temperature until cool enough to handle, about 10 minutes.

2. Meanwhile, in large zip-tight plastic bag, mix soy sauce, rosemary, garlic, 3 tablespoons vinegar, and 1 tablespoon oil. Add steak to marinade, turning to coat both sides. Seal bag, pressing out excess air. Place bag on plate and refrigerate until ready to cook.

3. Cut each zucchini and yellow squash lengthwise into 4 slices. Cut mushroom into 1/2-inch-thick slices. In large bowl, toss vegetables with 1 tablespoon oil, 1/2 teaspoon salt, and 1/4 teaspoon black pepper; set aside.

4. Remove red pepper from foil. Peel off skin and discard. Cut pepper into 1/4-inch dice. In small bowl, mix red pepper with basil, oregano, remaining 2 tablespoons vinegar, 2 tablespoons oil, 1/4 teaspoon salt, and 1/8 teaspoon black pepper. Set relish aside. Makes about 1 cup.

5. Heat same grill pan over medium-high heat until hot. Add zucchini, yellow squash, and mushroom, in batches, and cook until lightly browned on both sides and tender, about 6 minutes, turning over once. Remove vegetables to plate as they are done.

6. Remove steak from marinade; discard marinade. Pat steak dry with paper towels. In same hot grill pan over medium-high heat, cook steak 12 to 15 minutes for medium-rare or until desired doneness, turning steak over once. Transfer steak to cutting board; let rest 10 minutes to allow juices to set for easier slicing.

7. While steak is resting, assemble "lasagna": On each of 4 dinner plates, stack yellow squash, zucchini, and mushroom alternately with red-pepper relish and feta, ending with feta.

8. To serve, thinly slice steak diagonally against the grain. Arrange steak slices on plates with "lasagna." Garnish with rosemary sprigs.

EACH SERVING: About 430 calories, 33g protein, 11g carbohydrate, 28g total fat (9g saturated), 85mg cholesterol, 810mg sodium

TIP: In warm weather, this recipe works well on an outdoor grill. Prepare it for direct grilling over medium-high heat. Grill as described in recipe.

Five-Spice Flank Steak with Glazed Eggplant

You're going to love this eggplant, first grilled directly over the fire for great smoky flavor, then coated with an intense marinade and wrapped in foil to continue its cooking on the grill. It partners perfectly with flank steak perfumed with Chinese five-spice powder.

PREP: 10 minutes   GRILL: 17 to 23 minutes
MAKES: 4 main-dish servings

2	teaspoons Chinese five-spice powder
½	teaspoon salt
1	beef flank steak (1¼ pounds), well trimmed
3	tablespoons teriyaki sauce
2	teaspoons brown sugar
1½	teaspoons minced, peeled fresh ginger
¼	teaspoons Asian sesame oil
1	garlic clove, crushed with garlic press
4	medium Japanese eggplants (about 5 ounces each)
	heavy-duty aluminum foil
1	bunch green onions, trimmed (optional)

1. Prepare outdoor grill for covered direct grilling over medium heat.

2. In cup, combine five-spice powder and salt; use to rub all over flank steak. Set steak aside. In small bowl, with fork, mix teriyaki sauce, brown sugar, ginger, sesame oil, and garlic; set aside.

3. With knife, trim eggplant stems, then cut each eggplant lengthwise in half. Score cut side of each half with ¼-inch-deep slits to form a diamond pattern. With tongs, place eggplants, cut sides down, on hot grill rack. Grill until cut sides are lightly browned, about 5 minutes.

4. Fold 30" by 18" sheet of heavy-duty foil crosswise in half. Place grilled eggplants on double thickness of foil. Pour teriyaki mixture over. Bring long sides of foil up and over eggplants; fold several times, then fold in ends to seal tightly. Set aside.

5. Place steak on hot grill rack. Cover grill and cook steak 12 to 15 minutes for medium-rare or until desired doneness, turning over once. After steak has grilled 5 minutes, add foil packet with eggplants to same grill rack. Cook eggplants until very tender, about 7 minutes.

6. When eggplants are done, transfer packet to plate. When steak is done, transfer to cutting board and let stand 10 minutes to allow juices to set for easier slicing. If you like, add whole green onions to grill and cook until tender, 2 to 3 minutes, turning occasionally.

7. To serve, with kitchen shears, cut an X in top of packet to let steam escape, then carefully pull back foil to open. Thinly slice steak diagonally across the grain. Serve with eggplants with their sauce and green onions, if using.

EACH SERVING STEAK: About 245 calories, 28g protein, 1g carbohydrate, 13g total fat (6g), 72mg cholesterol, 385mg sodium

EACH SERVING EGGPLANT: About 55 calories, 2g protein, 12g carbohydrate, 1g total fat (0g saturated), 0mg cholesterol, 520mg sodium

Flank Steak with Flame-Roasted Veggies

To boost the flavor, this steak is sprinkled with balsamic vinegar just before serving.

PREP: 30 minutes GRILL: 24 to 35 minutes
MAKES: 6 main-dish servings

4   (10-inch) wooden skewers
2   tablespoons fresh rosemary leaves, chopped
2   teaspoons salt
¾   teaspoon coarsely ground black pepper
1   beef flank steak (1½ pounds), well trimmed
5   tablespoons olive oil
2   large onions (about 12 ounces each),
    cut into ¾-inch-thick slices
3   ripe medium tomatoes (6 to 8 ounces each),
    each cut in half
1   small eggplant (1 to 1¼ pounds),
    cut crosswise into ½-inch-thick slices
1   tablespoon balsamic vinegar
rosemary sprigs for garnish (optional)

1. Soak wooden skewers in water at least 20 minutes. Meanwhile, in cup, mix chopped rosemary, salt, and pepper. Rub flank steak with 4 teaspoons herb mixture; set aside. Stir remaining herb mixture together in cup with oil. Reserve for brushing on vegetables.

2. Prepare outdoor grill for direct grilling over medium heat.

3. Thread onion slices onto skewers. Place skewered onions on hot grill rack; brush with some rosemary oil. Cook until tender and lightly browned, 25 to 30 minutes, turning skewers occasionally. At same time, place tomato halves and eggplant slices on grill, brushing with remaining rosemary oil. Cook until lightly browned, 12 to 15 minutes, turning occasionally.

4. As tomatoes and eggplant finish cooking, transfer to large platter; keep warm. Place steak on grill with onions and cook 12 to 15 minutes for medium-rare or until desired doneness.

5. Transfer steak to cutting board; let stand 10 minutes to allow juices to set for easier slicing. Transfer onions to platter, removing them from skewers. Thinly slice steak; sprinkle with vinegar. Serve with grilled vegetables; garnish with rosemary sprigs if you like.

EACH SERVING: About 390 calories, 30g protein, 21g carbohydrate, 21g total fat (5g saturated), 47mg cholesterol, 780mg sodium

Flank Steak with Chimichurri Sauce

Chimichurri is a thick green herb sauce that is served with grilled meats in Argentina. Prepare ahead and refrigerate for up to two days. Bring it to room temperature before serving.

PREP: 15 minutes   GRILL: 12 to 15 minutes
MAKES: 4 main-dish servings

1½	cups loosely packed fresh parsley leaves, chopped
1½	cups loosely packed fresh cilantro leaves, chopped
¼	cup olive oil
3	tablespoons red wine vinegar
1	garlic clove, crushed with garlic press
¾	teaspoon salt
¼	teaspoon ground black pepper
1	pinch crushed red pepper
½	teaspoon chili powder
½	teaspoon sugar
¼	teaspoon ground coriander
¼	teaspoon ground cumin
1	beef flank steak (1½ pounds), well trimmed

1. Prepare outdoor grill for direct grilling over medium heat, or lightly spray a ridged grill pan with nonstick cooking spray, then heat on medium until hot.

2. Meanwhile prepare chimichurri sauce: In small bowl, combine parsley, cilantro, oil, vinegar, garlic, ¼ teaspoon salt, black pepper, and crushed red pepper; set aside.

3. In cup, combine chili powder, sugar, coriander, cumin, and remaining ½ teaspoon salt. Use to rub on flank steak.

4. Place steak on hot grill rack or pan and cook, turning once, 12 to 15 minutes for medium-rare or until desired doneness.

5. Transfer steak to cutting board; let stand 10 minutes to allow juices to set for easier slicing. Holding knife in slanting position, almost parallel to cutting board, slice steak thinly across the grain. Serve with sauce.

EACH SERVING WITH 1 TABLESPOON SAUCE: About 239 calories, 25g protein, 2g carbohydrate, 14g total fat (5g saturated), 62mg cholesterol, 497mg sodium

Coffee-and-Spice Steak with Watermelon Salsa

A dry rub of instant coffee, cinnamon, and allspice adds a rich, caramelized flavor to the steak. Our crisp watermelon and cucumber salsa is a refreshing go-along with any meat.

PREP: 30 minutes   **GRILL:** 12 to 15 minutes
MAKES: 6 main-dish servings

COOL WATERMELON SALSA

1	lime
2	cups ¼-inch cubes watermelon
½	English (seedless) cucumber, unpeeled, cut into ¼-inch cubes
1	green onion, minced
¼	teaspoon salt
⅛	teaspoon coarsely ground black pepper

COFFEE-AND-SPICE STEAK

2	teaspoons instant-coffee granules
1	teaspoon sugar
1	teaspoon salt
1	teaspoon coarsely ground black pepper
½	teaspoon ground cinnamon
¼	teaspoon ground allspice
1	beef flank steak (about 1½ pounds), well trimmed
2	teaspoons olive oil

1. Prepare salsa: From lime, grate 1 teaspoon peel and squeeze 2 tablespoons juice. In medium bowl, toss lime peel and juice with watermelon, cucumber, green onion, salt, and pepper. Cover and refrigerate salsa up to 2 hours if not serving right away. Makes about 3½ cups.

2. Prepare outdoor grill for direct grilling over medium heat, or lightly spray a ridged grill pan with nonstick cooking spray, then heat on medium until hot.

3. Prepare steak: In cup, mix coffee granules, sugar, salt, pepper, cinnamon, and allspice. Coat both sides of steak with oil, then rub with coffee mixture.

4. Place steak on hot grill rack or pan and grill, turning once, 12 to 15 minutes for medium-rare or until desired doneness.

5. Transfer steak to cutting board and let stand 10 minutes to allow juices to set for easier slicing. Thinly slice steak and serve with salsa.

EACH SERVING: About 215 calories, 27g protein, 1g carbohydrate, 11g total fat (4g saturated), 47mg cholesterol, 445mg sodium

EACH ¼ CUP SALSA: About 20 calories, 0g protein, 4g carbohydrate, 0g total fat, 0mg cholesterol, 80mg sodium

Pastrami-Spiced Flank Steak

Pastrami, a popular New York City deli item, probably came to us via the Romanians, who prepared many of their meats by smoking. Although our tribute to pastrami isn't smoked, it is similarly coated with coarse pepper and other aromatic spices. Serve it on sliced rye with a side of coleslaw, deli style!

PREP: 15 minutes plus marinating
GRILL: 12 to 15 minutes

MAKES: 6 main-dish servings

1	tablespoon coriander seeds
1	tablespoon paprika
1	tablespoon cracked black pepper
2	teaspoons ground ginger
1½	teaspoons salt
1	teaspoon sugar
½	teaspoon crushed red pepper
3	garlic cloves, crushed with garlic press
1	beef flank steak (about 1½ pounds), well trimmed
12	slices rye bread
	deli-style mustard

1. In mortar with pestle or in zip-tight plastic bag with rolling pin, crush coriander seeds (see Tip). In cup, mix coriander, paprika, black pepper, ginger, salt, sugar, and crushed red pepper.

2. Rub garlic on both sides of steak, then pat with spice mixture. Place steak in large zip-tight plastic bag; seal bag, pressing out excess air. Place bag on plate; refrigerate at least 2 hours, or up to 24 hours.

3. Prepare outdoor grill for direct grilling over medium heat.

4. Remove steak from bag. Place steak on hot grill rack and grill, turning once, 12 to 15 minutes for medium-rare, or to desired doneness.

5. Place bread slices on grill rack and toast, without turning, just until grill marks appear on underside of bread.

6. Transfer steak to cutting board and let stand 10 minutes to allow juices to set for easier slicing. Thinly slice steak across the grain and serve with grilled rye bread and mustard.

EACH SERVING: About 380 calories, 33g protein, 35g carbohydrate, 12g total fat (4g saturated), 47mg cholesterol, 1,015mg sodium

> **TIP:** Grinding whole spices in a mortar with a pestle releases their flavorful oils, which makes the steak even tastier.

Flank Steak with Corn and Red-Pepper Quesadillas

If you have the time, let the spice-rubbed flank steak sit in the fridge up to 1 hour before grilling for more intense flavor.

PREP: 15 minutes   **GRILL:** 14 to 16 minutes
MAKES: 4 main-dish servings

1   lime
4   teaspoons chili powder
1½   teaspoons ground cumin
1   teaspoon brown sugar
¼   teaspoon salt
1   beef flank steak (about 1¼ pounds), well trimmed
3   ears corn, husks and silk removed
1   large red pepper, stem and seeds removed, cut into quarters
4   (8-inch) flour tortillas
3   ounces reduced-fat (2%) Mexican-style cheese, shredded (¾ cup)
2   green onions, thinly sliced
     plain fat-free Greek yogurt or low-fat sour cream (optional)

1. Prepare outdoor grill for covered direct grilling over medium heat.

2. From lime, grate 1 teaspoon peel and squeeze 1 teaspoon juice. In small bowl, combine lime peel and juice, chili powder, cumin, brown sugar, and salt. Rub steak with chili powder mixture to season both sides.

3. Place steak, corn, and pepper on hot grill rack. Cover grill and cook steak and vegetables until corn is browned in spots, pepper is lightly charred and tender (turning vegetables occasionally), and steak reaches desired doneness (turning steak over once), 12 to 15 minutes, for medium-rare.

4. As vegetables are done, transfer to cutting board. Transfer steak to another cutting board; let stand 10 minutes to allow juices to set for easier slicing.

5. When vegetables are cool enough to handle, cut corn kernels from cobs and coarsely chop pepper. Place tortillas on work surface. Evenly distribute cheese, green onions, corn, and peppers, mounding fillings on one side of each tortilla. Fold each tortilla over filling to make 4 quesadillas. Grill quesadillas until browned on both sides, about 2 minutes, carefully turning over once. Return quesadillas to same cutting board; cut each in half.

6. Thinly slice steak and serve with quesadillas and yogurt, if using.

EACH SERVING: About 515 calories, 41g protein, 46g carbohydrate, 20g total fat (8g saturated), 81mg cholesterol, 745mg sodium

Mexican Skirt Steak

Here is a flavor-packed change of pace for dinner: Garlic- and chili-rubbed beef is wrapped in warm flour tortillas with crisp lettuce and a spoonful of creamy cilantro-spiked yogurt. If skirt steak (also called top round steak) is difficult to find, flank steak is a good alternative.

PREP: 15 minutes plus standing
GRILL: 10 to 15 minutes
MAKES: 5 main-dish servings

1	lime
½	cup plain low-fat yogurt
⅓	cup chopped fresh cilantro leaves
¼	cup light mayonnaise
⅛	teaspoon plus ¾ teaspoon salt
3	tablespoons chili powder
1	teaspoon ground coriander
1	teaspoon ground cumin
1	beef skirt steak (about 1¼ pounds), well-trimmed
1	large garlic clove, cut lengthwise in half
10	(6- to 7-inch) flour tortillas
3	cups shredded romaine lettuce

1. Prepare outdoor grill for direct grilling over medium heat, or lightly spray a ridged grill pan with nonstick cooking spray, then heat on medium until hot.

2. Grate ¼ teaspoon peel and squeeze 1 teaspoon juice from lime. In small bowl, mix lime peel and juice, yogurt, cilantro, mayonnaise, and ⅛ teaspoon salt until blended. Cover and refrigerate until serving time.

3. In cup, mix chili powder, coriander, cumin, and remaining ¾ teaspoon salt. Rub steak on both sides with cut sides of garlic clove. Then rub with chili powder mixture.

4. Place steak on hot grill rack or pan and grill 5 minutes. Turn steak over and grill 5 to 10 minutes longer, for medium or until desired doneness. Transfer steak to cutting board; let stand 5 minutes to allow juices to set for easier slicing.

5. Meanwhile, wrap tortillas in foil and heat at edge of grill over low heat until heated through.

6. To serve, thinly slice steak crosswise on the diagonal. Placed sliced steak in warm tortillas; top with cilantro-yogurt sauce and lettuce.

EACH SERVING: About 450 calories, 36g protein, 40g carbohydrate, 16g total fat (5g saturated), 52 mg cholesterol, 885 mg sodium

Red Wine–Marinated London Broil

This herbed marinade not only adds flavor—it tenderizes the meat. Fresh rosemary will taste sensational, but if you can't find it, use 2 teaspoons dried rosemary, crumbled.

PREP: 10 minutes plus marinating
GRILL: 12 to 15 minutes
MAKES: 8 main-dish servings

¼   cup dry red wine
2   tablespoons soy sauce
2   tablespoons balsamic vinegar
2   tablespoons chopped fresh rosemary leaves
1   tablespoon tomato paste
1   tablespoon Dijon mustard
¼   teaspoon crushed red pepper
4   large garlic cloves, crushed with garlic press
1   beef top round steak, 1 inch thick (about 2 pounds), well trimmed

1. In small bowl, with wire whisk, mix together wine, soy sauce, vinegar, rosemary, tomato paste, mustard, crushed red pepper, and garlic. Pour marinade into large zip-tight plastic bag. Add steak to marinade, turning to coat. Seal bag, pressing out excess air. Place bag on plate; refrigerate 4 to 6 hours, turning several times.

2. Prepare outdoor grill for covered direct grilling over medium heat, or lightly spray a ridged grill pan with nonstick cooking spray, then heat on medium until hot.

3. Remove steak from bag; discard marinade. Place steak on hot grill rack or pan. Cover and cook steak, turning once, 12 to 15 minutes for medium-rare or until desired doneness. Transfer steak to cutting board; let stand 10 minutes to allow juices to set for easier slicing.

4. To serve, thinly slice steak on the diagonal across the grain. Arrange on platter.

EACH SERVING: About 185 calories, 26g protein, 1g carbohydrate, 8g total fat (3g saturated), 72mg cholesterol, 115mg sodium

WHAT IS LONDON BROIL?

London broil was originally a recipe for a beef flank steak, which was marinated, broiled or grilled, and carved across the grain into thin slices. Despite its name, the recipe is said to be American in origin. Today the term applies not only to flank steak but also to other boneless cuts of beef such as top sirloin, top round, and chuck shoulder steaks. These are also meant to be prepared in the same manner and served thinly sliced across the grain.

Korean Steak

Set out bowls of crisp romaine lettuce, rice, green onions, and sesame seeds and let each person assemble his or her own package.

PREP: 40 minutes plus marinating
GRILL: 14 to 15 minutes

MAKES: 6 main-dish servings

½	cup reduced-sodium soy sauce
2	tablespoons sugar
2	tablespoons minced, peeled fresh ginger
2	tablespoons seasoned rice vinegar
1	tablespoon Asian sesame oil
¼	teaspoon ground red pepper (cayenne)
3	garlic cloves, crushed with garlic press
1	beef top round or sirloin steak, 1 inch thick (1½ pounds)
1	cup regular long-grain rice
¼	cup water
3	green onions, thinly sliced
1	tablespoon sesame seeds, toasted (see Tip)
1	head romaine lettuce, separated into leaves

1. In large zip-tight plastic bag, combine soy sauce, sugar, ginger, vinegar, sesame oil, ground red pepper, and garlic; add steak, turning to coat. Seal bag, pressing out excess air. Place bag on plate; refrigerate 1 to 4 hours to marinate, turning once.

2. Prepare outdoor grill for direct grilling over medium heat, or lightly spray a ridged grill pan with nonstick cooking spray, then heat on medium until hot. Prepare rice as label directs; keep warm.

3. Remove steak from bag; reserve marinade. Place steak on hot grill rack or pan and grill, turning once, 14 to 15 minutes for medium-rare or until desired doneness. Transfer steak to cutting board; let stand 10 minutes to allow juices to set for easier slicing.

4. In saucepan, heat reserved marinade and water to boiling over high heat; boil 2 minutes.

5. To serve, thinly slice steak. Let each person place some steak slices, rice, green onions, and sesame seeds on a lettuce leaf, then drizzle with cooked marinade. Fold sides of lettuce leaf over filling to form a packet to eat like a sandwich.

EACH SERVING: About 370 calories, 30g protein, 35g carbohydrate, 11g total fat (3g saturated), 69mg cholesterol, 960mg sodium

> **TIP:** Toasting brings out the nutty flavor of sesame seeds. To toast, heat seeds in a small, dry skillet over moderate heat, stirring constantly, until fragrant and a shade darker.

Anise Beef Kabobs

We like to buy a sirloin steak and cut it into chunks to ensure equal-size pieces for even grilling. But, if you prefer, use precut beef cubes from your supermarket for the kabobs. The rub and meat can easily be doubled to feed a larger crowd. Serve with bowls of rice.

PREP: 10 minutes plus marinating
GRILL: 8 to 10 minutes
MAKES: 4 main-dish servings

1	teaspoon anise seeds or fennel seeds
2	teaspoons olive oil
½	teaspoon salt
¼	teaspoon coarsely ground black pepper
	pinch crushed red pepper (optional)
1	boneless beef top sirloin steak, 1 inch thick (about 1 pound), cut into 1¼-inch chunks
4	(8-inch) metal skewers

1. Prepare outdoor grill for direct grilling over medium heat, or lightly spray a ridged grill pan with nonstick cooking spray, then heat on medium until hot.

2. In mortar with pestle or in zip-tight plastic bag with rolling pin, crush anise seeds. In medium bowl, combine anise seeds, oil, salt, black pepper, and crushed red pepper, if using. Add beef chunks, tossing until well coated. Cover and let beef stand 10 minutes at room temperature to marinate.

3. Loosely thread meat onto skewers. Place skewers on hot grill rack or pan; grill, turning occasionally, 8 to 10 minutes for medium-rare or until desired doneness.

EACH SERVING: About 220 calories, 21g protein, 0g carbohydrate, 14g total fat (5g saturated), 68mg cholesterol, 340mg sodium

> **TIP:** If you like, toss chunks of onion and peppers in a tablespoon of olive oil and thread them onto the skewers along with the meat.

Jerk Steak Kabobs with Pineapple Salsa

The hot Caribbean coating on the meat is the perfect foil for our cool tropical salsa. If you like, flame-cook pineapple wedges next to the kabobs instead of making the salsa.

PREP: 30 minutes plus marinating
GRILL: 8 to 10 minutes

MAKES: 4 main-dish servings

1	recipe Pineapple Salsa (page 278)
2	green onions, minced
2	tablespoons fresh lime juice
2	tablespoons brown sugar
1	tablespoon Worcestershire sauce
1	tablespoon grated, peeled fresh ginger
1	teaspoon vegetable oil
1	teaspoon salt
1	teaspoon dried thyme
1	teaspoon ground allspice
½	teaspoon ground red pepper (cayenne)
1	boneless beef top sirloin steak, 1¼ inches thick (1½ pounds), cut into 1¼-inch cubes
4	(12-inch) metal skewers

1. Prepare Pineapple Salsa.

2. In large bowl, mix green onions, lime juice, brown sugar, Worcestershire, ginger, oil, salt, thyme, allspice, and red pepper. Add steak cubes and toss to coat well; let stand 15 minutes to marinate.

3. Prepare outdoor grill for direct grilling over medium heat, or lightly spray a ridged grill pan with nonstick cooking spray, then heat on medium until hot.

4. Thread steak cubes on skewers. Place skewers on hot grill rack or pan; cook 8 to 10 minutes for medium-rare or until desired doneness, turning occasionally. Serve kabobs with salsa.

EACH SERVING KABOBS ONLY: About 295 calories, 34g protein, 10g carbohydrate, 13g total fat (5g saturated), 102mg cholesterol, 650mg sodium

EACH ¼ CUP SALSA: About 20 calories, 0g protein, 5g carbohydrate, 0g total fat, 0mg cholesterol, 35mg sodium

Deviled Beef Short Ribs

When buying short ribs, choose the beefiest ones you can find and trim away any excess fat.

PREP: 10 minutes   **GRILL:** about 30 minutes
MAKES: 6 main-dish servings

- 1/3 cup spicy brown mustard
- 1/4 cup prepared white horseradish
- 3 tablespoons Worcestershire sauce
- 4 pounds beef chuck short ribs, cut into serving-size pieces
- unseasoned meat tenderizer
- 3 ripe medium tomatoes (6 to 8 ounces each), sliced (optional)

1. Prepare outdoor grill for direct grilling over medium heat, or lightly spray a ridged grill pan with nonstick cooking spray, then heat on medium until hot.

2. In small bowl, mix mustard, horseradish, and Worcestershire.

3. Sprinkle beef short ribs with meat tenderizer as label directs.

4. Place short ribs on hot grill rack. Cook about 30 minutes for medium-rare or until of desired doneness, turning ribs often and brushing with mustard mixture frequently during last 10 minutes of cooking. Serve with sliced tomatoes if you like.

EACH SERVING: About 315 calories, 31g protein, 6g carbohydrate, 18g total fat (8g saturated), 88mg cholesterol, 700mg sodium

Korean-Style Short Ribs

Marinating overnight makes these meaty ribs irresistible. Serve with a spicy cabbage slaw or a cool rice salad. If you like, sprinkle them with sesame seeds and thinly sliced green onion just before serving.

PREP: 15 minutes plus marinating overnight
GRILL: 20 to 25 minutes
MAKES: 6 main-dish servings

- 4 pounds beef chuck short ribs, cut into 2-inch pieces
- 1/2 cup reduced-sodium soy sauce
- 4 teaspoons minced, peeled fresh ginger
- 2 teaspoons Asian sesame oil
- 3 large garlic cloves, minced

1. With sharp knife, cut 1/4-inch-deep slashes in meaty side of short ribs at 1/2-inch intervals.

2. In large zip-tight plastic bag, combine soy sauce, ginger, sesame oil, and garlic. Add short ribs, turning to coat. Seal bag, pressing out as much air as possible. Place bag on plate and refrigerate overnight, turning once.

3. Prepare outdoor grill for direct grilling over medium heat.

4. Lift ribs from bag and place on hot grill rack; brush with remaining marinade in bag. Grill, turning occasionally, 20 to 25 minutes for medium-rare or until desired doneness.

EACH SERVING: About 745 calories, 34g protein, 3g carbohydrate, 65g total fat (27g saturated), 142 mg cholesterol, 880mg sodium

Brisket with Chunky BBQ Sauce

This is a great do-ahead main dish for a summer picnic. You can slow-cook the brisket on the stovetop up to several days ahead. Then, 20 minutes before serving, brush it with the sauce and grill until heated through.

PREP: 15 minutes
COOK: 3 hours   GRILL: 20 minutes
MAKES: 12 main-dish servings

1   beef brisket (4½ pounds), well trimmed
1   medium onion, cut into quarters
1   large carrot, peeled and cut
     into 1½-inch pieces
1   bay leaf
1   teaspoon whole black peppercorns
¼   teaspoon whole allspice
Chunky BBQ Sauce (page 273)

1. In 8-quart Dutch oven, place brisket, onion, carrot, bay leaf, peppercorns, and allspice. Add enough water to cover and heat to boiling over high heat. Reduce heat; cover and simmer until meat is tender, about 3 hours.

2. Meanwhile, prepare Chunky BBQ Sauce.

3. When brisket is done, transfer to large platter. If desired, cover and refrigerate until ready to serve.

4. Prepare outdoor grill for covered direct grilling over medium heat. Place brisket on hot grill rack over medium heat, cover, and cook 10 minutes. Turn brisket and cook 5 minutes longer. Spoon 1 cup barbecue sauce on top of brisket and cook until brisket is heated through, about 5 minutes longer. (Do not turn brisket after topping with sauce.) Transfer to cutting board.

6. To serve, reheat remaining sauce in small saucepan on grill. Slice brisket thinly across the grain and serve with sauce.

EACH SERVING: About 241 calories, 26g protein, 6g carbohydrate, 11g total fat (4g saturated), 81mg cholesterol, 174mg sodium

EACH ¼ CUP SAUCE: About 61 calories, 1g protein, 13g carbohydrate, 1g total fat (0g saturated), 0mg cholesterol, 328mg sodium

---

THE SKINNY ON BEEF RIBS

You know, it's not all about pork when you're talking ribs. Here are some tasty beef alternatives when you're looking for something a little different:

■ Beef back ribs are the large bones left when a standing rib roast is cut to make a boneless rib-eye roast. The ribs are trimmed and divided into single-rib portions.

■ Short ribs, cut from the shoulder, are rectangular. They contain a cross section of rib bones with alternating layers of lean meat and fat.

■ Flanken-style ribs are similar to short ribs (they're from the same area of the cow) but are cut across rather than between the ribs.

Stuffed Veal Chops

Thick, juicy veal chops, stuffed with a mixture of creamy cheese, roasted peppers, and basil, sit atop a bed of spicy greens. The combination of warm chop and cool greens is a real winner. Use a small paring knife to cut the pocket so that it is deep but not wide.

PREP: 15 minutes   GRILL: 10 to 12 minutes
MAKES: 4 main-dish servings

¼	cup store-bought roasted red peppers, drained and chopped
3	tablespoons chopped fresh basil
4	veal rib chops, 1 inch thick (about 10 ounces each)
2	ounces Fontina cheese, sliced
½	plus ⅛ teaspoon salt
½	plus ⅛ teaspoon coarsely ground black pepper
1	tablespoon olive oil
1	tablespoon balsamic vinegar
½	teaspoon Dijon mustard
4	ounces arugula, watercress, or baby spinach, trimmed

1. Prepare outdoor grill for direct grilling over medium-high heat, or lightly spray a ridged grill pan with nonstick cooking spray, then heat on medium until hot.

2. In small bowl, mix roasted red peppers and 2 tablespoons basil. Set aside.

3. Holding knife parallel to surface, cut a horizontal pocket in each chop. Tuck cheese slices into veal pockets; spread red-pepper mixture over cheese. Sprinkle veal chops with ½ teaspoon salt and ½ teaspoon pepper.

4. Place chops on hot grill rack or pan and grill, turning chops once, until they are lightly browned on both sides and just lose their pink color throughout, 10 to 12 minutes.

5. Meanwhile, in medium bowl, with wire whisk, mix oil, vinegar, mustard, and remaining 1 tablespoon basil, ⅛ teaspoon salt, and ⅛ teaspoon pepper; add arugula, tossing to coat.

6. To serve, spoon salad onto platter; arrange chops on top.

EACH SERVING: About 440 calories, 40g protein, 2g carbohydrate, 29g total fat (11g saturated), 181mg cholesterol, 655mg sodium

Butterflied Lamb with Moroccan Flavors

Enjoy fabulous, exotic flavors with very little work! Serve with a refreshing cucumber salad.

PREP: **15 minutes plus marinating**
GRILL: **15 to 25 minutes**

MAKES: **12 main-dish servings**

⅓	cup loosely packed fresh cilantro leaves, chopped
¼	cup olive oil
2	tablespoons dried mint, crumbled
2	teaspoons ground coriander
1	teaspoon ground ginger
1	teaspoon salt
½	teaspoon coarsely ground black pepper
½	teaspoon chili powder
1	butterflied boneless leg of lamb (3½ pounds), trimmed (see Tip)

1. In small bowl, stir cilantro, oil, mint, coriander, ginger, salt, pepper, and chili powder.

2. Place lamb in 13" by 9" glass baking dish. Rub cilantro mixture on lamb to coat completely. Cover and refrigerate at least 1 hour or up to 4 hours.

3. Prepare outdoor grill for covered direct grilling over medium heat.

4. Place lamb on hot grill rack. Cover grill and cook lamb, turning occasionally, 15 to 25 minutes for medium-rare or until desired doneness. Thickness of butterflied lamb will vary throughout; cut off sections of lamb as they are cooked and place on cutting board. Let stand 10 minutes to allow juices to set for easier slicing. Thinly slice lamb to serve.

EACH SERVING: About 225 calories, 28g protein, 1g carbohydrate, 12g total fat (3g saturated), 88mg cholesterol, 270mg sodium

> **TIP:** Ask your butcher to bone a 4½-pound lamb leg shank half and slit the meat lengthwise to spread open like a thick steak.

Indian-Spiced Butterflied Lamb

For a cool and tangy sauce, a jar of mango chutney can be chopped, added to yogurt, and served with the lamb. A crisp green or cucumber salad tossed with chopped fresh cilantro and a side of basmati rice would also be welcome additions to this Indian-style entrée.

PREP: 10 minutes plus marinating
GRILL: 20 to 30 minutes
MAKES: 10 main-dish servings

1   cup (8 ounces) plain low-fat yogurt
8   garlic cloves, peeled
1   piece fresh ginger (about 2 inches), peeled and coarsely chopped
1   tablespoon ground coriander
1   tablespoon ground cumin
2   tablespoons fresh lemon juice (see Tip)
2   teaspoons salt
¼ to ½ teaspoon ground red pepper (cayenne)
1   butterflied boneless leg of lamb (3 pounds), trimmed (see Tip, opposite)

1. In blender, puree yogurt, garlic, ginger, coriander, cumin, lemon juice, salt, and ground red pepper until smooth. Pour yogurt mixture into large zip-tight plastic bag; add lamb, turning to coat. Seal bag, pressing out excess air. Place bag on plate; refrigerate 1 hour, turning occasionally. (Do not marinate more than 2 hours, or texture of meat will change.)

2. Prepare outdoor grill for direct grilling over medium heat.

3. Remove lamb from bag. Pour marinade into small bowl and reserve.

4. Place lamb on hot grill rack. Cover grill and cook lamb, turning once, 15 minutes. Brush both sides of lamb with reserved marinade and cook, turning lamb occasionally, 5 to 15 minutes longer for medium-rare or until desired doneness. Thickness of butterflied lamb will vary throughout; cut off sections of lamb as they are cooked and place on cutting board. Let stand 10 minutes to allow juices to set for easier slicing. Thinly slice lamb to serve.

EACH SERVING: About 280 calories, 27g protein, 3g carbohydrate, 17g total fat (7g saturated), 95mg cholesterol, 550mg sodium

> **TIP:** For seedless lemon juice, place a lemon half, cut side down, on a square of cheesecloth. Bring cheesecloth up over the top and fasten with a twist-tie, then squeeze out the juice, seed free.

Spicy Garlic Lamb with Minted Cucumber Raita

Leg of lamb isn't only for the oven; it's divine cooked on the grill. The raita—cucumbers in minted yogurt—balances the spicy meat.

PREP: 30 minutes plus chilling
GRILL: 15 to 25 minutes
MAKES: 8 main-dish servings

MINTED CUCUMBER RAITA

6   Kirby cucumbers (about 1½ pounds)
1   teaspoon salt
2   cups (16 ounces) plain low-fat yogurt
½   cup loosely packed fresh mint leaves, chopped
1½   teaspoons sugar

SPICY GARLIC LAMB

1   tablespoon fennel seeds
1   tablespoon mustard seeds
1   tablespoon cumin seeds
2   teaspoons salt
1   teaspoon whole black peppercorns
1   teaspoon dried thyme
3   whole cloves
3   garlic cloves, crushed with garlic press
2   tablespoons fresh lemon juice
1   butterflied boneless leg of lamb (3½ pounds), trimmed (see Tip, page 166)

mint sprigs for garnish

1. Prepare raita: With vegetable peeler, remove several strips of peel from each cucumber. Cut each cucumber lengthwise in half; scoop out seeds; cut each piece lengthwise in half again, then crosswise into ½-inch-thick pieces. In medium bowl, toss cucumbers with ¼ teaspoon salt; let stand 10 minutes. Press cucumbers to remove as much liquid as possible. Stir in yogurt, mint, sugar, and remaining ¾ teaspoon salt. Cover and refrigerate until ready to serve or up to 6 hours. Makes about 4 cups.

2. Prepare outdoor grill for direct grilling over medium-low heat.

3. Prepare lamb: In spice grinder or coffee grinder, blend fennel, mustard, cumin, salt, peppercorns, thyme, and cloves until finely ground.

4. In small bowl, mix garlic and lemon juice with ground spices until blended. Rub spice mixture over both sides of lamb.

5. Place lamb on hot grill rack; cover and cook 15 to 25 minutes for medium-rare or until desired doneness, turning lamb once. Thickness of butterflied lamb will vary throughout; cut off sections of lamb as they are cooked and place on cutting board. Let stand 10 minutes to allow juices to set for easier slicing.

6. To serve, thinly slice lamb and arrange on platter; garnish with mint sprigs. Serve with Minted Cucumber Raita.

EACH SERVING LAMB: About 275 calories, 39g protein, 2g carbohydrate, 11g total fat (4g saturated), 121mg cholesterol, 675mg sodium

EACH ½ CUP RAITA: About 60 calories, 4g protein, 10g carbohydrate, 2g total fat (0g saturated), 4mg cholesterol, 260mg sodium

Butterflied Leg of Lamb with Almond-Mint Pesto

We top this juicy, chargrilled leg of lamb with our fresh mint-and-almond pesto—a flavor match made in heaven. The thickness of a butterflied leg of lamb will vary; check thinner pieces early for doneness, cut off those sections as they are cooked, and place them on a cutting board. Cover with foil to keep warm.

PREP: 10 minutes plus marinating
GRILL: 15 to 25 minutes

MAKES: 12 main-dish servings

4½ cups loosely packed fresh mint leaves

2 garlic cloves, crushed with garlic press

½ cup water

⅓ cup olive oil

1 teaspoon salt

1 teaspoon coarsely ground black pepper

1 butterflied boneless leg of lamb (4 pounds), trimmed (see Tip, page 166)

¾ cup whole blanched almonds

1. In food processor with knife blade attached, pulse mint, garlic, water, oil, salt, and pepper until well blended.

2. Place lamb in 13″ by 9″ glass baking dish. Remove ¼ cup mint mixture from food processor; spread on lamb to coat both sides. Cover and refrigerate at least 1 hour or up to 6 hours.

3. Meanwhile, add almonds to mint mixture remaining in food processor and pulse until almonds are finely chopped. Spoon pesto into serving bowl; cover and refrigerate until ready to serve.

4. Remove lamb from refrigerator about 15 minutes before cooking. Prepare outdoor grill for covered direct grilling over medium heat.

5. Place lamb on hot grill rack; cover and cook 15 to 25 minutes (depending on thickness) for medium-rare, turning over once halfway through cooking and removing pieces to cutting board as they are done. When remaining lamb is done, transfer to same cutting board and let stand 10 minutes to allow juices to set for easier slicing. Serve lamb with almond-mint pesto.

EACH SERVING: About 380 calories, 32g protein, 5g carbohydrate, 26g total fat (8g saturated), 99mg cholesterol, 270mg sodium

Aromatic Leg of Lamb

Once your butcher has boned a leg of lamb for you, ask for the lamb bone. Use it to cook up some flavorful lamb broth for an especially tasty stew or hearty soup.

PREP: 20 minutes   **GRILL: 15 to 25 minutes**
MAKES: 8 main-dish servings

1   butterflied boneless leg of lamb (3 pounds), trimmed (see Tip, page 166)
3   garlic cloves, each cut in half and crushed with side of chef's knife
1   tablespoon olive oil
2   teaspoons fennel seeds, crushed
2   teaspoons cumin seeds, crushed
2   teaspoons coriander seeds, crushed
1½ teaspoons salt
1   lemon, cut into wedges

1. Prepare outdoor grill for covered direct grilling over medium heat. Rub both sides of lamb with cut sides of garlic cloves; discard garlic.

2. In small bowl, combine oil, fennel seeds, cumin seeds, coriander seeds, and salt. Use to rub on lamb.

3. Place lamb on hot grill rack, cover and cook, turning lamb occasionally, 15 to 25 minutes for medium-rare or until desired doneness. Thickness of butterflied lamb will vary throughout; cut off sections of lamb as they are done and place on cutting board. Let stand 10 minutes to allow juices to set for easier slicing. Thinly slice the lamb and serve with lemon wedges.

EACH SERVING: About 265 calories, 36g protein, 1g carbohydrate, 12g total fat (4g saturated), 114mg cholesterol, 525mg sodium

Grilled Lamb Chops with Spice Rub

Grilling chops that have been seasoned with a rub is the easiest way to guarantee lots of flavor.

PREP: 5 minutes   **GRILL: about 10 minutes**
MAKES: 4 main-dish servings

1   recipe choice of dry spice rub (pages 266-268)
4   lamb shoulder chops, ¾ inch thick (each 8 ounces)

1. Prepare outdoor grill for direct grilling over medium heat.

2. In small bowl, combine rub ingredients; use to rub on lamb chops.

3. Place chops on hot grill rack and cook about 5 minutes per side for medium-rare or until desired doneness.

EACH SERVING: About 454 calories, 57g protein, 2g carbohydrate, 22g total fat (8g saturated), 196mg cholesterol, 470mg sodium

Lamb Kabobs and Salad Slaw with Peppery Orange Dressing

This is a delicious meal in one.

PREP: 25 minutes   GRILL: 10 to 12 minutes
MAKES: 4 main-dish servings

1   pound boneless leg of lamb, from shank
⅓   cup chili sauce
2   tablespoons teriyaki sauce
¼   cup orange juice
2   tablespoons low-fat mayonnaise dressing
1   tablespoon cider vinegar
1   teaspoon prepared mustard
¼   teaspoon cracked black pepper
⅛   teaspoon salt
¼   head red cabbage, thinly sliced
1   head romaine lettuce, cut crosswise into ¼-inch ribbons
1   bunch green onions, cut into 2-inch pieces
1   large navel orange, cut into 6 wedges, each wedge halved crosswise to make 12 pieces
4   (12-inch) metal skewers (see box, below)

1. Trim all fat then cut lamb into 12 chunks. In medium bowl, mix lamb, chili sauce, and teriyaki sauce until lamb is coated; set aside.

2. In large bowl, stir orange juice, mayonnaise dressing, vinegar, mustard, pepper, and salt until blended. Add cabbage and lettuce; toss well.

3. Prepare outdoor grill for direct grilling over medium heat, or lightly spray a ridged grill pan with nonstick cooking spray, then heat on medium until hot.

4. On skewers, alternately thread lamb, green onion, and orange pieces. Place on hot grill rack or pan. Cook 10 to 12 minutes for medium-rare, or to desired doneness, turning once.

5. Transfer skewers to platter. Serve kabobs with salad slaw and orange wedges.

EACH SERVING: About 265 calories, 28g protein, 20g carbohydrate, 9g total fat (3g saturated), 74mg cholesterol, 810mg sodium

SKEWER KNOW-HOW

■ If you use metal skewers, look for the kind that are twisted or square—not round. Food twirls around when you try to turn it on a round skewer. (Wooden and skinny bamboo skewers aren't slippery, so their round shape is no problem.)

■ Before using wooden or bamboo skewers, soak them in water for at least 20 minutes so they won't burn when exposed to the grill's heat and flames.

■ For even cooking, don't jam foods up against each other on the skewer—leave a space between items when you thread them.

■ Use two parallel skewers for unwieldy items like thick, large slices of onion.

■ Combine foods with similar cooking times on the same skewer.

Rosemary-Orange Lamb and Vegetable Kabobs

The fresh, clean flavors of orange and rosemary are wonderful with lamb. Serve alongside skewers of grilled cherry tomatoes and a bowl of yellow rice.

PREP: 30 minutes plus marinating
GRILL: 10 to 12 minutes
MAKES: 4 main-dish servings

3	oranges
1	tablespoon olive oil
1	tablespoon chopped fresh rosemary or 1½ teaspoons dried rosemary, crumbled
2	garlic cloves, each cut in half
¼	teaspoon salt
¼	teaspoon ground red pepper (cayenne)
1	pound boneless lamb leg, trimmed of all fat and cut into 1½-inch chunks
8	(12-inch) metal skewers
1	red pepper, stem and seeds removed, cut into 1½-inch squares
1	yellow pepper, stem and seeds removed, cut into 1½-inch squares
1	orange pepper, stem and seeds removed, cut into 1½-inch squares
1	pint cherry tomatoes
6	green onions, cut into 2-inch pieces
10	ounces small mushrooms, trimmed

1. Prepare outdoor grill for direct grilling over medium heat, or lightly spray a ridged grill pan with nonstick cooking spray, then heat on medium until hot.

2. Meanwhile, from oranges, grate 1 teaspoon peel and squeeze 1 cup juice. In large bowl, combine orange peel and juice, oil, rosemary, garlic, salt, and ground red pepper. Add lamb, turning to coat, and let stand, stirring occasionally, 10 minutes at room temperature.

3. Thread lamb onto 4 metal skewers and thread vegetables onto remaining 4 skewers, alternating vegetables. Place skewers on hot grill rack or pan. Cook lamb and vegetables, turning once, 10 to 12 minutes for medium-rare lamb, or to desired doneness. Transfer to platter.

EACH SERVING: About 245 calories, 28g protein, 12g carbohydrate, 10g total fat (3g saturated), 81mg cholesterol, 118mg sodium

Pork

Pork in all its forms is extremely versatile when it comes to the grill and the grill pan, whether it be a roast, tenderloin, chops, ribs, or kabobs. A single pork tenderloin will feed a family of four nicely, cooks up in just 20 minutes, and takes to a wide range of flavors. Consider Lime Pork Tenderloin with Grilled Plums, Bacon-Wrapped Pork Tenderloins, and Hoisin-Honey-Glazed Pork Tenderloin with Grilled Pineapple. Pork chops grill up in half the time—serve with one of our grilled accompaniments such as corn salad, brown sugar–glazed peaches, or tomato salad.

The big daddy of the pork grill, though, are ribs, and we've got some delicious recipes for you: Kansas City Ribs, Baby Back Ribs with Sweet and Hot Rub, and Barbecued Pork Spareribs with your choice of three sauces—Balsamic-Rosemary, Orange-Dijon, or Asian Barbecue Sauce. The big, meaty flavors of sausage and ham are enhanced by the fire-roasting of the grill. Try Spiced Kielbasa and Summer Fruit Kabobs, the classic Sausage and Pepper Grill, or enjoy the interplay of hot and sweet in Chile-Rubbed Ham with Peach-Cilantro Salsa.

Hoisin-Honey-Glazed Pork Tenderloin with Grilled Pineapple, page 176

Hoisin-Honey-Glazed Pork Tenderloin with Grilled Pineapple

When choosing a pineapple, pick one that is slightly soft with a deep, sweet fragrance. Pineapples are harvested ripe and will not get any sweeter with time. For photo of finished dish, see page 174.

PREP: 10 minutes   **GRILL:** 18 to 20 minutes
MAKES: 4 main-dish servings

¼ cup hoisin sauce
1 tablespoon honey
1 tablespoon grated, peeled fresh ginger
1 teaspoon Asian sesame oil
1 pork tenderloin (1¼ pounds), trimmed
½ medium pineapple
2 tablespoons brown sugar

1. Prepare outdoor grill for covered direct grilling over medium heat. In small bowl, combine hoisin sauce, honey, ginger, and sesame oil.

2. Place pork on hot grill rack. Cover grill and cook pork 18 to 20 minutes, turning occasionally, until browned outside and still slightly pink in center; an instant-read meat thermometer inserted in thickest part of tenderloin should read 150°F.

3. Meanwhile, with serrated knife, cut pineapple half into 4 wedges. Rub cut sides of pineapple with brown sugar.

4. Grill pineapple on rack with pork until browned on both sides, about 5 minutes, turning over once. While pineapple is grilling, brush pork with hoisin-honey glaze and turn frequently.

5. Transfer pork to cutting board; let stand 5 minutes to allow juices to set for easier slicing. Transfer pineapple to platter. Thinly slice pork and serve with pineapple wedges.

EACH SERVING: About 275 calories, 31g protein, 23g carbohydrate, 6g total fat (2g saturated), 92mg cholesterol, 245mg sodium

GRILLING PORK

Our top tip for succulent pork is not to overcook it. Use an instant-read meat thermometer to check the internal temperature.

CUT	COOK-TO INTERNAL TEMPERATURE	APPROXIMATE COOK TIME
Chops (rib or loin, 1" thick)	150°F	10–12 minutes
Tenderloin, whole (1 to 1¼ pounds)	150°F	13–23 minutes
Tenderloin steaks, ¼" thick	150°F	5–6 minutes

Pork Tenderloins with Oregano

A lemon-herb marinade gives this lean cut of pork a zippy flavor. Twenty minutes is all it needs; the lemon juice will start to break down the meat fibers if it marinates much longer. To complete the dinner, serve with Grilled Vegetables Vinaigrette (page 247).

PREP: 10 minutes plus marinating
GRILL: 15 to 20 minutes

MAKES: 6 main-dish servings

¼   cup fresh lemon juice

2   tablespoons chopped fresh oregano or 1 teaspoon dried oregano

2   tablespoons chopped fresh parsley

2   pork tenderloins (about 12 ounces each), trimmed

1   tablespoon olive oil

½   teaspoon salt

¼   teaspoon coarsely ground black pepper

1. In large zip-tight plastic bag, combine lemon juice and 1 tablespoon each oregano and parsley. Add tenderloins, turning to coat. Seal bag, pressing out excess air. Place bag on plate; refrigerate 20 minutes to marinate, turning once.

2. Prepare outdoor grill for direct grilling over medium heat, or lightly spray a ridged grill pan with nonstick cooking spray, then heat on medium until hot.

3. Remove tenderloins from bag; discard marinade. In cup, mix oil, salt, pepper, and remaining 1 tablespoon each oregano and parsley; rub mixture on tenderloins.

4. Place tenderloins on hot grill rack or pan and grill 20 minutes, turning occasionally, until browned outside and still slightly pink in center; an instant-read meat thermometer inserted in thickest part of tenderloin should register 150°F.

5. When tenderloins are done, transfer to warm large platter and let stand 5 minutes to allow juices to set for easier slicing. Thinly slice tenderloins to serve.

EACH SERVING: About 175 calories, 23g protein, 1g carbohydrate, 8g total fat (3g saturated), 71mg cholesterol, 240mg sodium

TIP: To prevent bacterial contamination from raw meat, always follow the "two-platter" rule: Use one platter for transporting meat, poultry, or fish to the grill, then use a second, clean one for the cooked food.

Pork Loin with Lemon, Thyme, and Garlic

A few minutes of prep yield deliciously spectacular results.

PREP: 15 minutes plus standing
GRILL: 50 minutes
MAKES: 8 main-dish servings

4	lemons
4	garlic cloves, crushed with garlic press
2	tablespoons fresh thyme leaves, chopped
1	tablespoon olive oil
½	teaspoon salt
½	teaspoon coarsely ground black pepper
1	boneless pork loin roast (3 pounds), trimmed

1. Prepare gas grill for covered indirect grilling over medium heat. If using a charcoal grill, prepare it for covered indirect-heat grilling with drip pan as manufacturer directs.

2. From 2 lemons, grate 1 tablespoon peel and squeeze 1 tablespoon juice. Cut each remaining lemon into 4 wedges.

3. In small bowl, combine lemon peel and juice, garlic, thyme, oil, salt, and pepper.

4. Make 10 to 12 (1-inch-long and ½-inch-deep) slits in pork. Rub pork all over with lemon mixture, pushing some into slits.

5. Place pork on hot grill rack and cook over direct heat 10 minutes, turning several times to sear all sides. Move pork to hot grill rack over drip pan or away from the heat source on a gas grill; cover grill and cook pork until instant-read meat thermometer inserted into center of pork registers 150°F, about 40 minutes.

6. Transfer pork to cutting board; let stand 5 minutes to allow juices to set for easier slicing. (Internal temperature of pork will rise 5°F to 10°F upon standing.)

7. Serve sliced pork with lemon wedges and any juices from cutting board.

EACH SERVING: About 350 calories, 35g protein, 3g carbohydrate, 21g total fat (7g saturated), 112mg cholesterol, 240mg sodium

Tarragon Pork Tenderloin with Grilled Grapes

Grapes on the grill are a wonderful treat, a warm and smoky burst of flavor. They're terrific in combination with these pork tenderloins slathered with a tasty mix of fresh tarragon and Dijon mustard.

PREP: 12 minutes   GRILL: 18 to 20 minutes
MAKES: 8 main-dish servings

½   small shallot, cut in half

3   tablespoons chopped fresh tarragon

2   tablespoons Dijon mustard

½   teaspoon ground black pepper

½   teaspoon salt

2   pork tenderloins (about 1 pound each), trimmed

1   bunch seedless red grapes (about 1½ pounds)

lemon, cut into slices

mint sprigs

1. Prepare outdoor grill for covered direct grilling over medium heat, or lightly spray a ridged grill pan with nonstick cooking spray, then heat on medium until hot.

2. Press shallot through garlic press into cup; stir in tarragon, Dijon, pepper, and salt. Spread tarragon mixture all over tenderloins.

3. Place tenderloins on hot grill rack or pan. Cover grill and cook 18 to 20 minutes, turning occasionally, until browned outside and still slightly pink in center; an instant-read meat thermometer inserted in thickest part of tenderloin should register 150°F.

4. After tenderloins have cooked 15 minutes, add grapes to grill rack and cook until grapes soften slightly and brown in spots, 4 to 5 minutes, turning occasionally.

5. Transfer tenderloins to cutting board; let stand 5 minutes to allow juices to set for easier slicing. Place grapes on large platter; with kitchen shears, cut into 8 clusters. To serve, thinly slice tenderloins and transfer to platter with grapes. Garnish with lemon and mint.

EACH SERVING: About 230 calories, 27g protein, 15g carbohydrate, 7g total fat (2g saturated), 78mg cholesterol, 215mg sodium

Lime Pork Tenderloin with Grilled Plums

For an easy all-on-the grill supper, serve this succulent pork with our Short-Cut Grilled Sweet Potatoes (see Tip).

PREP: 30 minutes   **GRILL:** 12 to 15 minutes
MAKES: 4 main-dish servings

1   pork tenderloin (about 1¼ pounds), trimmed
1   large lime
1   teaspoon coarsely ground black pepper
½   teaspoon salt
nonstick cooking spray
4   large plums (about 1¼ pounds total), each cut in half and pitted
1   tablespoon honey
pinch ground cloves

1. Prepare outdoor grill for covered direct grilling over medium heat, or lightly spray a ridged grill pan with nonstick cooking spray, then heat on medium until hot.

2. Cut pork lengthwise in half. From lime, grate 1 teaspoon peel and squeeze 2 tablespoons juice. In cup, mix lime peel, pepper, and salt; rub mixture on pork. Spray pork with cooking spray.

3. Place pork on hot grill rack or pan. Cover grill and cook 10 to 15 minutes, turning over once, until browned outside and still slightly pink in center; an instant-read meat thermometer inserted in thickest part of tenderloin should read 150°F. After grilling pork 2 to 3 minutes, add plums; grill until browned, about 10 minutes, turning over once.

4. Transfer pork and plums to cutting board. Let pork stand 5 minutes to allow juices to set for easier slicing. Cut plums into wedges and place in bowl. Add honey, cloves, and lime juice; toss until coated. Slice pork; serve with plums.

EACH SERVING: About 289 calories, 30g protein, 23g carbohydrate, 9g total fat (3g saturated), 90mg cholesterol, 351mg sodium

> **TIP:** As an accompaniment to the pork, try Short-Cut Grilled Sweet Potatoes: Cut *2 medium sweet potatoes* into ½-inch-thick slices. Spray both sides with *cooking spray*, then sprinkle with ½ *teaspoon salt*. Place potatoes on microwave-safe plate. Cook in microwave oven on High 5 minutes. Transfer potatoes to hot grill rack and cook, covered, until brown on both sides, about 10 minutes.

Bacon-Wrapped Maple-Glazed Pork Tenderloins

Use leftovers for a sandwich treat of thinly sliced pork topped with sharp Cheddar cheese and apple slices.

PREP: **10 minutes, plus refrigerating**
GRILL: **20 to 25 minutes**

MAKES: **6 main-dish servings**

2   pork tenderloins (12 ounces each), trimmed
8   wooden toothpicks
½   teaspoon salt
¼   teaspoon ground black pepper
6   slices bacon
½   cup maple or maple-flavored syrup

1. Prepare outdoor grill for direct grilling over medium heat. Soak toothpicks in water for 30 minutes.

2. Sprinkle tenderloins with salt and pepper. Place pork in bowl; cover and refrigerate 30 minutes.

3. Wrap 3 bacon slices around each tenderloin and secure with toothpicks. Place tenderloins on hot grill rack over medium heat and cook, brushing frequently with syrup and turning occasionally, until browned on the outside and still slightly pink in the center, 20 to 25 minutes; an instant-read meat thermometer inserted in thickest part of tenderloin should register 150°F. Transfer to cutting board and let stand 5 minutes to allow juices to set for easier slicing.

EACH SERVING: About 265 calories, 28g protein, 18g carbohydrate, 9g total fat (3g saturated), 86mg cholesterol, 352mg sodium

Spiced Pork Tenderloin Cutlets with Mango-Kiwi Salsa

A simple blend of warm spices lends exotic flavor to lean and tender pork "cutlets."

PREP: **20 minutes**   GRILL: **6 to 7 minutes**

MAKES: **8 main-dish servings**

Mango-Kiwi Salsa (page 281)
2   pork tenderloins (about 1 pound each), trimmed
3   tablespoons all-purpose flour
1   teaspoon salt
1   teaspoon ground cumin
1   teaspoon ground coriander
½   teaspoon ground cinnamon
½   teaspoon ground ginger

1. Prepare Mango-Kiwi Salsa; cover and refrigerate. Prepare outdoor grill for direct grilling over medium heat.

2. Cut each pork tenderloin lengthwise almost in half, being careful not to cut all the way through. Open and spread flat. Place each tenderloin between two sheets of plastic wrap; with meat mallet or rolling pin, pound to ¼-inch thickness. Cut each tenderloin into 4 pieces. On waxed paper, mix flour, salt, cumin, coriander, cinnamon, and ginger; evenly coat pork cutlets.

3. Place pork on hot grill rack over medium heat and grill until lightly browned on both sides and pork just loses its pink color throughout, 6 to 7 minutes, turning over once. Serve with Mango-Kiwi Salsa.

EACH SERVING: About 215 calories, 23g protein, 15g carbohydrate, 6g total fat (2g saturated), 71mg cholesterol, 455mg sodium

Pork Chops, Sausage Style

Flavored with the licorice punch of fennel seeds, these chops are like a sausage and pepper sandwich without the bread. Crushing the seeds just before using them helps retain their flavor and fragrance.

PREP: 15 minutes   GRILL: 8 to 10 minutes
MAKES: 4 main-dish servings

1	tablespoon fennel seeds
1	garlic clove, crushed with garlic press
1	tablespoon olive oil
3/4	teaspoon salt
3/4	teaspoon coarsely ground black pepper
4	bone-in pork rib or loin chops, 3/4 inch thick (about 6 ounces each), trimmed
2	red and/or yellow peppers, stems and seeds removed, each cut into quarters
4	plum tomatoes, each cut lengthwise in half

1. Prepare outdoor grill for covered direct grilling over medium heat.

2. In mortar with pestle or in zip-tight plastic bag with rolling pin, crush fennel seeds. In cup, mix fennel with garlic, olive oil, and 1/2 teaspoon each salt and pepper; use to rub both sides of pork chops. Sprinkle cut sides of peppers and tomatoes with remaining 1/4 teaspoon each salt and pepper.

3. Arrange chops and peppers on hot grill rack; cover and cook 5 minutes. Turn chops and peppers over; add tomatoes, cut sides down. Cover and cook until chops are browned outside and still slightly pink in center and vegetables are tender, 3 to 5 minutes.

EACH SERVING: About 315 calories, 25g protein, 10g carbohydrate, 19g total fat (6g saturated), 70mg cholesterol, 490mg sodium

Cuban Pork and Plantains with Black-Bean Salsa

Rub the meat with a peppery garlic coating and grill with plantains for a savory splurge. Make sure the plantains are very ripe: The skin should be black, and the fruit should yield to gentle pressure. (To aid ripening, place in a brown paper bag with a lime.)

PREP: 45 minutes GRILL: 15 to 20 minutes
MAKES: 6 main-dish servings

BLACK-BEAN SALSA

2	limes
1	orange
1	can (15 to 19 ounces) black beans, rinsed and drained
½	small sweet onion, diced
¼	cup loosely packed fresh cilantro leaves, chopped
1	medium jalapeño chile, seeded and minced
¾	teaspoon salt

PORK AND PLANTAINS

2	large garlic cloves, crushed with garlic press
1	teaspoon salt
1½	teaspoons coarsely ground black pepper
2	tablespoons olive oil
2	pork tenderloins (about 12 ounces each), trimmed
3	ripe medium plantains (about 1½ pounds total), each peeled and cut lengthwise in half

1. Prepare salsa: From limes, grate ½ teaspoon peel and squeeze 3 tablespoons juice. From orange, grate ½ teaspoon peel. With knife, remove remaining peel and white pith from orange and cut sections into ½-inch chunks. In medium bowl, combine lime peel and juice, orange peel and chunks, beans, onion, cilantro, jalapeño, and salt. Cover and refrigerate salsa up to 2 days if desired. Makes about 3 cups.

2. Prepare outdoor grill for direct grilling over medium heat.

3. Prepare pork and plantains: In cup, mix garlic, salt, pepper, and 1 tablespoon oil. Rub on pork. Brush plantains with remaining oil.

4. Place tenderloins on hot grill rack and grill 15 to 20 minutes, turning over once, until browned outside and slightly pink in center; an instant-read meat thermometer inserted in thickest part of meat should read 150°F. Place plantains on grill rack and cook, turning once, until tender and browned, 7 to 8 minutes.

5. Transfer plantains to platter. Transfer tenderloins to cutting board; let stand 5 minutes to allow juices to set for easier slicing, then thinly slice. Serve with Black-Bean Salsa.

EACH SERVING PORK AND PLANTAINS: About 315 calories, 28g protein, 29g carbohydrate, 11g total fat (3g saturated), 78mg cholesterol, 440mg sodium

EACH ½ CUP SALSA: About 70 calories, 4g protein, 17g carbohydrate, 0g total fat, 0mg cholesterol, 475mg sodium

Chipotle Pork Chops with Corn Salad

Chipotle pepper sauce is made with chipotle chiles, which are smoked jalapeños. If you don't like the smokiness, you can use your favorite hot pepper sauce.

PREP: 15 minutes   **GRILL:** 8 to 10 minutes
MAKES: 4 main-dish servings

1	tablespoon chipotle pepper sauce
1	teaspoon ground cumin
1	teaspoon olive oil
1	clove garlic, crushed with garlic press
½	teaspoon salt
4	bone-in pork loin or rib chops, ¾ inch thick (8 ounces each), trimmed
3	medium ears corn, husks and silk removed
2	ripe medium tomatoes (6 to 8 ounces each), chopped
½	ripe avocado, peeled, pitted, and cut into ¼-inch pieces
¼	cup loosely packed fresh cilantro leaves, chopped
2	tablespoons fresh lime juice

1. Prepare outdoor grill for covered direct grilling over medium heat.

2. In cup, combine chipotle sauce, cumin, oil, garlic, and ¼ teaspoon salt. Rub an even coating of spice mixture on both sides of pork chops.

3. Place pork chops on hot grill rack. Cover grill and cook until nicely browned on outside and still slightly pink in center, 8 to 10 minutes, turning over once.

4. Meanwhile, cut kernels from corn and transfer to medium bowl. Add tomatoes, avocado, cilantro, lime juice, and remaining ¼ teaspoon salt; stir to combine. Makes about 3 cups.

5. Serve corn salad with grilled pork chops.

EACH SERVING PORK: About 455 calories, 35g protein, 1g carbohydrate, 32g total fat (11g saturated), 106mg cholesterol, 235mg sodium

EACH ¼ CUP CORN SALAD: about 35 calories, 1g protein, 6g carbohydrate, 2g total fat (0g saturated), 0mg cholesterol, 55mg sodium

Pan-Grilled Pork Cutlets

Pork cutlets are rubbed with aromatic spices before being quickly browned in a grill pan.

PREP: 15 minutes   GRILL: 6 to 8 minutes
MAKES: 6 main-dish servings

1	tablespoon fennel seeds
1	tablespoon coriander seeds
1	tablespoon cumin seeds
2	garlic cloves, crushed with garlic press
1	tablespoon olive oil
1	teaspoon salt
½	teaspoon coarsely ground black pepper
2	pork tenderloins (about 12 ounces each), trimmed
1	orange, cut into wedges

1. In small zip-tight plastic bag, place fennel, coriander, and cumin seeds. With meat mallet or rolling pin, crush seeds. Transfer to small bowl; stir in garlic, oil, salt, and pepper.

2. Cut each pork tenderloin lengthwise almost in half, being careful not to cut all the way through. Open and spread flat. Place each between two sheets plastic wrap; with meat mallet or rolling pin, pound to about ¹/₂-inch thickness. Cut each into 3 cutlets. Rub both sides of cutlets with spice mixture.

3. Grease large ridged grill pan and heat over medium heat until very hot but not smoking. Add cutlets and cook until lightly browned outside and slightly pink inside, 6 to 8 minutes, turning over once. Serve with orange wedges.

EACH SERVING: About 185 calories, 25g protein, 5g carbohydrate, 7g total fat (2g saturated), 67mg cholesterol, 440mg sodium

Pork Chops with Glazed Peaches

Pork chops and peaches caramelized with a glaze of brown sugar—what a winning combination.

PREP: 15 minutes   GRILL: 8 to 10 minutes
MAKES: 4 main-dish servings

¹/₃	cup Dijon mustard
¼	cup packed brown sugar
1	tablespoon bottled steak sauce
4	pork loin chops, each ¾ inch thick (about 5 ounces each), trimmed
2	tablespoons brown sugar
1	tablespoon water
4	ripe medium peaches, each cut in half and pitted

1. In medium bowl, mix mustard, brown sugar, and steak sauce. Add pork chops, turning to coat chops with mustard mixture.

2. In small bowl, mix brown sugar and water.

3. Prepare outdoor grill for direct grilling over medium heat. When it is ready, place pork chops on hot grill rack and cook until lightly browned on both sides and chops just lose their pink color throughout, 8 to 10 minutes, brushing with mustard sauce remaining in bowl and turning occasionally. Place peach halves on grill rack with pork chops and cook, brushing peaches with brown-sugar mixture and turning peaches occasionally, until hot and lightly browned, 5 to 8 minutes.

EACH SERVING: About 345 calories, 27g protein, 31g carbohydrate, 12g total fat (4g saturated), 54mg cholesterol, 635mg sodium

Rosemary Pork Chops with Grilled Tomato Salad

This is a wonderfully aromatic dish. The pork chops are perfumed with fresh rosemary and partnered with charred grilled tomatoes tossed with grated lemon zest and crushed garlic.

PREP: 15 minutes   GRILL: 10 to 12 minutes
MAKES: 4 main-dish servings

1	tablespoon chopped fresh rosemary leaves
2	teaspoons fennel seeds, crushed
¾	teaspoon salt
⅛	teaspoon ground black pepper
4	bone-in pork loin or rib chops, ¾ inch thick (about 6 ounces each), trimmed
1	pound plum tomatoes, each cut lengthwise in half
1	tablespoon extra-virgin olive oil
2	tablespoons chopped fresh parsley
1	teaspoon freshly grated lemon peel
1	garlic clove, crushed with garlic press

1. Prepare outdoor grill for covered direct grilling over medium heat.

2. In cup, combine rosemary, fennel seeds, ½ teaspoon salt, and pepper. Use to rub on pork chops.

3. In medium bowl, combine tomatoes, oil, and remaining ¼ teaspoon salt; set aside.

4. Place pork chops on hot grill rack, cover, and cook chops 5 minutes. Turn chops and arrange on one side of grill. Place tomatoes, cut sides down, on other side of grill; set bowl aside. Cover grill and cook chops until browned on outside and still slightly pink in center, 3 to 5 minutes; cook tomatoes until evenly charred on both sides, 6 to 7 minutes.

5. Transfer chops to platter and tomatoes to cutting board. Cool tomatoes slightly, then cut into large pieces. Return tomatoes and their juices to bowl; stir in parsley, lemon peel, and garlic. Serve chops with tomato salad.

EACH SERVING: About 315 calories, 28g protein, 6g carbohydrate, 19g total fat (6g saturated), 88mg cholesterol, 520mg sodium

Fennel-Orange Pork Chops with Grilled Vegetables

The combination of fennel, thyme, and orange peel marries well with the richness of pork. Radicchio and Belgian endive, with their slightly bitter taste, also serve as a counterbalance.

PREP: **15 minutes** GRILL: **10 to 12 minutes**
MAKES: **4 main-dish servings**

1	teaspoon fennel seeds
½	teaspoon dried thyme
¼	teaspoon coarsely ground black pepper
¾	teaspoon salt
1	teaspoon freshly grated orange peel
4	pork rib or loin chops, 1 inch thick (about 6 ounces each), trimmed
1	tablespoon olive oil
1	tablespoon balsamic vinegar
2	heads radicchio di Treviso (about 4 ounces each), each cut lengthwise in half, or 1 large round head radicchio (about 8 ounces), cut into 8 wedges
2	large heads Belgian endive (about 5 ounces each), each cut lengthwise into quarters

1. Prepare outdoor grill for direct grilling over medium heat.

2. In mortar with pestle or in zip-tight plastic bag with rolling pin, crush fennel seeds with thyme, pepper, and ½ teaspoon salt. Stir orange peel into fennel-seed mixture. With hand, rub both sides of pork chops with spice mixture.

3. In medium bowl, mix oil, vinegar, and remaining ¼ teaspoon salt. Add radicchio and endive to bowl and gently toss to coat.

4. Place pork chops on hot grill rack and grill 5 minutes. Turn chops and add vegetables to grill. Grill until chops have just a hint of pink color in center and vegetables are browned, 5 to 7 minutes longer.

5. Serve pork chops with grilled vegetables.

EACH SERVING: About 690 calories, 37g protein, 38g carbohydrate, 43g total fat (16g saturated), 172mg cholesterol, 860mg sodium

Cuban Mojo Pork Chops

Mojo (pronounced MO-ho) comes from the Spanish verb mojar, *"to wet." The seasoning mix is an integral component of Latin cuisine, used either as a condiment or as a base for a marinade. It traditionally was made with citrus juice, garlic, salt, and lard (now vegetable oil), but ingredients such as spices, herbs, onions, chiles, and other fruit make it versatile.*

PREP: **15 minutes plus marinating**
GRILL: **8 to 10 minutes**
MAKES: **4 main-dish servings**

2   medium oranges (see Tip)
¼   cup chopped onion
¼   cup red wine vinegar
1   chipotle chile in adobo plus 1 tablespoon adobo
4   garlic cloves, peeled
2   tablespoons fresh lime juice
¼   teaspoon salt
4   bone-in pork loin chops, ¾ inch thick (about 6 ounces each), trimmed

1. From oranges, grate ½ teaspoon peel and squeeze ½ cup juice.

2. In blender or food processor with knife blade attached, puree orange peel, onion, vinegar, chile, adobo, and garlic until smooth.

3. Pour puree into large zip-tight plastic bag; stir in orange and lime juices and salt. Add pork chops to marinade, turning to coat. Seal bag, pressing out excess air. Place bag on plate; let stand 15 minutes at room temperature or 1 hour in the refrigerator, turning several times.

4. Prepare outdoor grill for covered direct grilling over medium heat.

5. Remove chops from bag; pour marinade into 1-quart saucepan and reserve. Place chops on hot grill rack. Cover grill and cook chops until browned outside and still slightly pink in center, 8 to 10 minutes, turning over once.

6. Meanwhile, heat reserved marinade to boiling over high heat; boil 1 minute.

7. Serve pork chops drizzled with marinade.

EACH SERVING: About 395 calories, 42g protein, 10g carbohydrate, 19g total fat (7g saturated), 116mg cholesterol, 410mg sodium

> **TIP:** Need to grate orange or lemon peel for a recipe? Choose pebbly-textured (not smooth), thick-skinned fruit.

Barbecued Pork Spareribs with a Trio of Sauces

It's the sauces that make spareribs special. Here are three of our favorites. The ribs must be precooked so plan ahead.

PREP: 1 hour 20 minutes   GRILL: about 20 minutes
MAKES: 8 main-dish servings

4   pounds pork spareribs, cut into 1- or 2-rib portions
1   recipe sauce of choice (see below)

1. Early in day or one day ahead, precook spareribs: In 8-quart Dutch oven, place ribs. Add enough *water to cover* and heat to boiling over high heat. Reduce heat; cover and simmer until spareribs are tender, about 1 hour. Transfer spareribs to platter; cover and refrigerate.

2. Prepare outdoor grill for direct grilling over medium heat. Meanwhile, prepare desired barbecue sauce.

3. Place cooked spareribs on hot grill rack. Cook, turning ribs frequently and brushing with barbecue sauce often, until heated through, about 20 minutes.

ORANGE-DIJON SAUCE: In cup, combine *1 cup sweet orange marmalade, 1/4 cup Dijon mustard, 1/4 cup packed brown sugar, 1 teaspoon freshly grated orange peel,* and *1 1/2 teaspoons salt.*

EACH SERVING BARBECUED PORK SPARERIBS WITH ORANGE-DIJON SAUCE: About 483 calories, 26g protein, 33g carbohydrate, 27g total fat (10g saturated), 107mg cholesterol, 723mg sodium

BALSAMIC-ROSEMARY SAUCE: Combine *2/3 cup balsamic vinegar, 2 tablespoons brown sugar, 1 teaspoon salt,* and *1/2 teaspoon ground black pepper* in 1-quart saucepan and heat to boiling over medium heat. Cook until sauce has reduced to 1/3 cup, about 15 minutes. Stir in *1 teaspoon dried rosemary,* crumbled.

EACH SERVING BARBECUED PORK SPARERIBS WITH BALSAMIC-ROSEMARY SAUCE: About 368 calories, 26g protein, 4g carbohydrate, 27g total fat (10g saturated), 107mg cholesterol, 376mg sodium

ASIAN BARBECUE SAUCE: In 1-quart saucepan, heat *1 tablespoon vegetable oil* over medium heat; add *2 green onions,* finely chopped, and cook until tender, about 5 minutes. Add *2 teaspoons grated, peeled fresh ginger* and *1 garlic clove,* crushed with garlic press; cook, stirring frequently, 1 minute longer. Stir in *2/3 cup packed brown sugar, 1/4 cup soy sauce, 1/4 cup dry sherry, 1 tablespoon cornstarch,* and *1/2 teaspoon salt.* Heat to boiling over medium-high heat, stirring, until mixture has thickened and boils. Remove from heat; stir in *1 teaspoon Asian sesame oil.*

EACH SERVING BARBECUED PORK SPARERIBS WITH ASIAN BARBECUE SAUCE: About 453 calories, 26g protein, 20g carbohydrate, 29g total fat (10g saturated), 107mg cholesterol, 750mg sodium

Plum-Good Baby Back Ribs

Licorice-flavored star anise—one of the spices in Chinese five-spice powder—gives these ribs their distinctive appeal. The ribs can be cooked in the seasoned liquid up to two days ahead, then cooled, covered, and refrigerated. Remove the ribs from the refrigerator while the grill heats, then proceed with the recipe.

PREP: 1 hour   GRILL: 15 to 20 minutes
MAKES: 8 main-dish servings

4	racks pork baby back ribs (about 1 pound each)
12	whole black peppercorns
2	bay leaves
10	whole star anise
2	cinnamon sticks (each 3 inches long)
¼	cup soy sauce
1	jar (12 ounces) plum jam (1 cup)
1	tablespoon grated, peeled fresh ginger
1	garlic clove, crushed with garlic press

1. In 8-quart saucepot, place ribs, peppercorns, bay leaves, 4 star anise, and 1 cinnamon stick. Add enough *water to cover*; heat to boiling over high heat. Reduce heat to low; cover and simmer until ribs are fork-tender, 50 minutes to 1 hour. Transfer ribs to platter. If not serving right away, cover and refrigerate until ready to serve.

2. In 1-quart saucepan, heat soy sauce and remaining 6 star anise and 1 cinnamon stick to boiling over high heat. Reduce heat to low; cover and simmer 5 minutes. Remove from heat; let stand, covered, 5 minutes. Strain mixture into bowl; discard star anise and cinnamon. Stir in plum jam, ginger, and garlic.

3. Prepare outdoor grill for direct grilling over medium heat.

4. Place ribs on hot grill rack; grill until browned, about 10 minutes, turning over once. Brush ribs with some glaze and grill, brushing with remaining glaze and turning frequently, 5 to 10 minutes longer.

EACH SERVING: About 520 calories, 28g protein, 29g carbohydrate, 32g total fat (12g saturated), 129mg cholesterol, 645mg sodium

RIB RULES

Ribs are the quintessential grill food—part splurge, part fun, all finger-licking flavor. The different kinds are interchangeable (what rib doesn't taste good brushed with BBQ sauce and grilled?), but here's a guide to the basics:

■ **Spareribs**, cut from the underbelly, are most widely available. They're the least meaty and most fatty of all pork ribs, containing long rib bones with a thin covering of meat on the outside and between the ribs.

■ **Back ribs**, also known as loin back ribs and baby back ribs (when small) are short, easy to hold, and meatier than spareribs because they contain loin meat. We love baby back ribs on the grill.

■ **Country-style ribs** are cut from the shoulder end of the loin and have the highest meat-to-bone ratio, with the least fat. They're sometimes mistaken for pork chops—because you usually need a knife and fork to eat them.

Kansas City Ribs

Baby back ribs with a gooey tomato-based sauce are a summer tradition.

PREP: **1 hour 15 minutes**   GRILL: **13 to 20 minutes**
MAKES: **6 main-dish servings**

BABY BACK RIBS

3	racks pork baby back ribs (about 1 pound each)
1	onion, cut into quarters
1	orange, cut into quarters
1	tablespoon whole black peppercorns
1	tablespoon coriander seeds

BARBECUE SAUCE

3	tablespoons butter or margarine
1	medium onion, chopped
4	garlic cloves, chopped
1	can (15 ounces) tomato sauce
¼	cup cider vinegar
¼	cup packed brown sugar
1	teaspoon salt
¼	teaspoon coarsely ground black pepper

1. Prepare ribs: In 8-quart saucepot, place ribs, onion, orange, peppercorns, and coriander seeds. Add enough *water* to cover; heat to boiling over high heat. Reduce heat to low; partially cover and cook until ribs are fork-tender, 50 minutes to 1 hour. Transfer ribs to platter. If not serving right away, cover ribs and refrigerate until ready to serve.

2. Meanwhile, prepare barbecue sauce: In 2-quart saucepan, heat butter over medium heat until melted. Add onion and garlic and cook, stirring occasionally, until softened, about 8 minutes. Add tomato sauce, vinegar, sugar, salt, and pepper; heat to boiling over high heat. Reduce heat to low; simmer, stirring occasionally, until sauce thickens, about 40 minutes. Makes about 2 ⅔ cups.

3. Prepare outdoor grill for covered direct grilling over medium heat.

4. Place ribs on hot grill rack. Cover grill and cook ribs, turning once, until browned, 8 to 10 minutes. Brush ribs with sauce and cook, brushing with remaining sauce and turning frequently, 5 to 10 minutes longer.

5. To serve, cut racks into individual ribs and arrange on platter.

EACH SERVING: About 380 calories, 24g protein, 9g carbohydrate, 27g total fat (12g saturated), 74mg cholesterol, 520mg sodium

Baby Back Ribs Supreme

Only fifteen minutes of grilling time! The trick? Steam the seasoned ribs for an hour in the oven up to two days before barbecuing. With both the ribs and the BBQ sauce prepared in advance, this could easily become a part of your summer weeknight repertoire.

PREP: 1 hour 15 minutes   **GRILL: 15 minutes**
MAKES: 8 main-dish servings

4	teaspoons grated, peeled fresh ginger
2	teaspoons freshly grated lemon peel
¾	teaspoon salt
2	garlic cloves, crushed with garlic press
4	racks pork baby back ribs (about 1 pound each; see Tip)
2	cups boiling water
2	cups Secret-Recipe BBQ Sauce (page 274)

1. Preheat oven to 350°F. In cup, mix ginger, lemon peel, salt, and garlic until combined. Rub ginger mixture on ribs.

2. Place ribs in large roasting pan (15 ½" by 11 ½"), overlapping slightly. Pour *boiling water* into roasting pan. Cover pan tightly with foil and place in oven. Steam ribs 1 hour.

3. Meanwhile, prepare Secret-Recipe BBQ Sauce.

4. Carefully remove foil from roasting pan (escaping steam is very hot). Remove ribs from pan; discard water. Ribs may be grilled immediately or refrigerated, covered, up to 2 days before grilling.

5. Prepare outdoor grill for direct grilling over medium heat.

6. Place ribs, meat side up, on hot grill rack; grill 5 minutes, turning over once. Turn ribs again; brush with BBQ sauce and grill 5 minutes. Repeat turning and brushing once more. Cut racks into 2-rib portions; serve with remaining BBQ sauce.

EACH SERVING: About 460 calories, 27g protein, 12g carbohydrate, 33g total fat (12g saturated), 129mg cholesterol, 570mg sodium

> **TIP:** When buying baby backs, look for ribs that are meaty, with a minimum of visible fat.

Baby Back Ribs with Sweet and Hot Rub

Try this innovative approach to ribs—grill them in cooking bags, along with a few ice cubes. This yields extraordinarily tender results.

PREP: 30 minutes   GRILL: about 1 hour 15 minutes
MAKES: 8 main-dish servings

2	tablespoons paprika
3	tablespoons brown sugar
2 1/2	teaspoons salt
2	teaspoons chili powder
2 1/2	teaspoons coarsely ground black pepper
1	teaspoon ground cumin
1/2	teaspoon ground red pepper (cayenne)
4	racks pork baby back ribs (1 pound each)
	heavy-duty foil
6	ice cubes
2	cups ketchup
1	cup apple cider or apple juice
2	tablespoons Worcestershire sauce
2	tablespoons molasses
2	tablespoons cider vinegar
2	tablespoons yellow mustard

1. Prepare outdoor grill for covered direct grilling over medium heat.

2. In small bowl, combine paprika, 1 tablespoon brown sugar, 2 teaspoons salt, chili powder, 1 1/2 teaspoons black pepper, cumin, and 1/4 teaspoon ground red pepper. Pat ribs dry with paper towels. Rub mixture all over ribs.

3. Place two 30" by 18" sheets heavy-duty foil on work surface to make a double thickness. Place ribs on center of foil with ice cubes underneath. Bring long sides of foil up and over; fold several times, then fold ends to seal tightly. Repeat with more foil, ribs, and ice cubes.

4. Place packets on hot grill rack. Cover and cook 1 hour, carefully turning packets with tongs once halfway through.

5. In 4-quart saucepan, combine ketchup, cider, Worcestershire, molasses, vinegar, mustard, and remaining 1/2 teaspoon salt, 2 tablespoons brown sugar, 1/2 teaspoon black pepper, and 1/4 teaspoon ground red pepper. Heat to boiling. Reduce heat to low and simmer, uncovered, until sauce thickens slightly, 30 to 40 minutes, stirring occasionally. Makes about 2 1/2 cups. Set aside 1 cup for serving.

6. When ribs are done, with kitchen shears, cut X in top of each packet to let steam escape, then carefully pull foil open. Transfer ribs directly to grill rack. Cover and grill ribs until browned, 7 to 10 minutes, turning once. Brush ribs with sauce and cook 7 to 10 minutes longer, brushing with more sauce and turning frequently.

7. Cut into individual ribs and arrange on platter. Pass remaining sauce with ribs.

EACH SERVING: About 340 calories, 19g protein, 22g carbohydrate, 20g total fat (7g saturated), 44mg cholesterol, 1,136mg sodium

Russian Pork and Plum Kabobs

These are perfect with grilled pita pockets.

PREP: **15 minutes plus marinating**
GRILL: **15 to 20 minutes**
MAKES: **6 main-dish servings**

¼ cup raspberry vinegar
1 tablespoon ground coriander
1 tablespoon dark brown sugar
1 tablespoon olive oil
1 tablespoon grated onion
1½ teaspoons salt
½ teaspoon coarsely ground black pepper
⅛ teaspoon ground cloves
2 pounds boneless pork loin, trimmed and cut into 1½-inch chunks
6 (12-inch) metal skewers
5 medium plums, each cut into quarters
¼ cup plum jelly
2 tablespoons chopped fresh cilantro (optional)

1. In zip-tight plastic bag, combine vinegar, coriander, brown sugar, oil, onion, salt, pepper, and cloves. Add pork chunks, turning to coat. Seal bag, pressing out as much air as possible. Place bag on plate; refrigerate 1 hour to marinate, turning once.

2. Prepare outdoor grill for direct grilling over medium heat.

3. Onto skewers, alternately thread pork chunks and plum quarters. Place skewers on hot grill rack; cook until pork just loses its pink color throughout, 15 to 20 minutes, turning occasionally and brushing pork and plums with plum jelly during last 3 minutes of cooking.

4. To serve, arrange kabobs on large platter; sprinkle with cilantro, if you like.

EACH SERVING: About 425 calories, 32g protein, 18g carbohydrate, 25g total fat (9g saturated), 76mg cholesterol, 350mg sodium

Jambalaya Sausage Kabobs

Kielbasa is a great choice for a weekday meal on the grill. Already cooked, it just needs a turn over the coals to develop a tasty brown crust.

PREP: 25 minutes　**GRILL: 10 to 12 minutes**
MAKES: 4 main-dish servings

8　(12-inch) wooden skewers or 4 long metal skewers

2　small zucchini (about 6 ounces each), cut diagonally into ¾-inch-thick slices

1　red pepper, stem and seeds removed, cut into 1¼-inch pieces

½　small Vidalia onion, cut into 4 wedges, each wedge held together with toothpick

1　tablespoon plus 1 teaspoon olive oil

2　teaspoons Cajun seasoning

1　package (16 ounces) light kielbasa or other fully cooked smoked sausage, cut diagonally into 1-inch chunks

1　large stalk celery, chopped

1　package (8.8 ounces) white rice, fully cooked

1　ripe medium tomato (6 to 8 ounces), chopped

2　tablespoons water

1. Prepare outdoor grill for covered direct grilling over medium heat. Meanwhile, if using wooden skewers, soak in water 20 minutes.

2. In large bowl, toss zucchini, red pepper, onion, 1 tablespoon oil, and 1 teaspoon Cajun seasoning. Alternately thread vegetables and kielbasa onto skewers.

3. Place skewers on hot grill rack. Cover grill and cook until kielbasa browns and vegetables are tender-crisp, 10 to 12 minutes, turning skewers occasionally. Remove skewers to platter; keep warm.

4. In nonstick 10-inch skillet, heat remaining 1 teaspoon oil over medium heat. Add celery and remaining 1 teaspoon Cajun seasoning. Cook, covered, until celery softens, about 5 minutes, stirring occasionally. Stir in rice, tomato, and water. Cover and cook until rice is hot, about 3 minutes. Serve rice with kabobs.

EACH SERVING WITHOUT RICE: About 320 calories, 18g protein, 9g carbohydrate, 26g total fat (8g saturated), 76mg cholesterol, 1,160mg sodium

EACH SERVING RICE: About 85 calories, 2g protein, 17g carbohydrate, 1g total fat (0g saturated), 0mg cholesterol, 150mg sodium

Sausage and Pepper Grill

Grill Italian hard rolls and serve the sausage and peppers on top for a hearty open-faced sandwich reminiscent of those found at street fairs. If you'd prefer, toss the grilled sausages and vegetables with a bowl of cooked ziti, add grated Parmesan cheese, and serve.

PREP: 15 minutes   GRILL: 15 to 20 minutes
MAKES: 4 main-dish servings

⅓   cup balsamic vinegar
1   teaspoon brown sugar
½   teaspoon salt
¼   teaspoon coarsely ground black pepper
2   medium red peppers, stems and seeds removed, cut into 1½-inch-wide strips
2   medium green peppers, stems and seeds removed, cut into 1½-inch-wide strips
2   large red onions (12 ounces each), each cut into 6 wedges
1   tablespoon olive oil
¾   pound sweet Italian sausage links
¾   pound hot Italian sausage links

1. Prepare outdoor grill for direct grilling over medium heat.

2. In cup, with fork, mix balsamic vinegar, brown sugar, salt, and black pepper (see Tip). In large bowl, toss red and green peppers and onions with oil to coat.

3. Place sausages on hot grill rack and grill until golden brown and cooked through, 15 to 20 minutes, turning occasionally. Place vegetables on grill at same time as sausages, turning occasionally and brushing with balsamic mixture during last 3 minutes of cooking, until tender, about 15 minutes. Transfer vegetables and sausages to platter as they finish cooking.

4. To serve, cut sausages diagonally into 2-inch slices. Drizzle remaining balsamic mixture over vegetables.

EACH SERVING: About 500 calories, 27g protein, 19g carbohydrate, 36g total fat (12g saturated), 97mg cholesterol, 1,450mg sodium

> **TIP:** Adding a small amount of brown sugar to ordinary balsamic vinegar gives it a smooth, mellow flavor similar to that of an aged vinegar. Try this trick the next time you make a balsamic vinegar dressing.

Spiced Kielbasa and Summer Fruit Kabobs

Smoky sausage and sweet fruit are a delicious combination. To keep grill time short, check out the fully-cooked sausages now available. Flavors range from Chicken & Apple to Sweet Basil and Roasted Garlic. You can also use nectarines or pears in place of the other fruit.

PREP: 10 minutes   GRILL: 6 to 7 minutes
MAKES: 4 main-dish servings

1	package (16 ounces) light kielbasa or other fully cooked smoked sausage, cut into 1-inch chunks
3	apricots, each pitted and cut into quarters
2	ripe plums or peaches, pitted and cut into 1-inch chunks
4 to 6	(12-inch) metal skewers
3	tablespoons sweet orange marmalade
1	tablespoon Chinese five-spice powder

1. Prepare outdoor grill for covered direct grilling over medium heat.

2. Meanwhile, alternately thread kielbasa, apricots, and plums onto skewers. In cup, combine marmalade and five-spice powder.

3. Place skewers on hot grill rack. Cover grill and cook until kielbasa browns and fruit chars slightly, about 5 minutes, turning skewers occasionally. Uncover grill. Brush marmalade mixture all over kielbasa and fruit. Cook 1 to 2 minutes longer, turning occasionally.

EACH SERVING: About 340 calories, 17g protein, 22g carbohydrate, 22g total fat (8g saturated), 76mg cholesterol, 1,032mg sodium

Chile-Rubbed Ham with Peach-Cilantro Salsa

It's a quick grill—a fully cooked ham steak patted with paprika and smoky chiles before searing. Our soothing salsa tames the spice.

PREP: 30 minutes   **GRILL:** 6 to 8 minutes
MAKES: 4 main-dish servings

PEACH-CILANTRO SALSA

4   ripe peaches (about 1¼ pounds total), pitted and cut into ¼-inch chunks
1   cup loosely packed fresh cilantro leaves, chopped
1   jalapeño chile, seeded and minced
2   tablespoons peach jam
2   tablespoons fresh lime juice
¼   teaspoon salt

CHILE-RUBBED HAM

1   tablespoon paprika
1   tablespoon olive oil
2   teaspoons minced canned chipotle chile in adobo (see Tip) or 2 teaspoons adobo sauce
1   fully cooked center-cut ham steak, ½ inch thick (about 1¼ pounds)

1. Prepare outdoor grill for direct grilling over medium heat, or lightly spray a ridged grill pan with nonstick cooking spray, then heat on medium until hot.

2. Prepare salsa: In medium bowl, toss together peaches, cilantro, jalapeño, jam, lime juice, and salt. Cover and refrigerate salsa up to 1 day if not serving right away. Makes about 4 cups.

3. Prepare ham: In cup, mix paprika, oil, and chipotle. Spread mixture on both sides of ham.

4. Place ham on hot grill rack or pan; grill, 6 to 8 minutes, turning ham once, until lightly browned and heated through. Serve ham with salsa.

EACH SERVING HAM: About 180 calories, 24g protein, 1g carbohydrate, 8g total fat (2g saturated), 72mg cholesterol, 1,820mg sodium

EACH ½ CUP SALSA: About 40 calories, 0g protein, 10g carbohydrate, 0g total fat, 0mg cholesterol, 80mg sodium

> **TIP:** Canned chipotle chiles are smoked jalapeño chiles packed in a thick, vinegary sauce called adobo. Look for them in the Hispanic section of your supermarket.

Southwestern Ham Steak

Serve with one of our fresh salsas (pages 276–281).

PREP: 5 minutes   **GRILL:** 6 to 8 minutes
MAKES: 4 main-dish servings

2	teaspoons chili powder
½	teaspoon ground cumin
¼	teaspoon ground coriander
¼	teaspoon ground red pepper (cayenne)
¼	teaspoon sugar
1	fully cooked center-cut ham slice, ½ inch thick (1¼ pounds)

1. Prepare outdoor grill for direct grilling over medium heat, or lightly spray a ridged grill pan with nonstick cooking spray, then heat on medium until hot.

2. In small bowl, combine chili powder, cumin, coriander, ground red pepper, and sugar. Use to rub on ham steak.

3. Place ham steak on hot grill rack or pan and cook until heated through and lightly browned, 6 to 8 minutes per side.

EACH SERVING: About 171 calories, 27g protein, 1g carbohydrate, 6g total fat (2g saturated), 61mg cholesterol, 1,727mg sodium

Cajun Ham Steak

For a down-home supper, pair this sweet-and-spicy ham with cheese grits and sautéed greens.

PREP: 5 minutes   **GRILL:** about 8 minutes
MAKES: 4 main-dish servings

2	teaspoons Cajun seasoning
½	teaspoon sugar
1	fully cooked smoked ham steak, ½ inch thick (about 1¼ pounds)
1	lime, cut into wedges
	cilantro sprigs for garnish

1. Prepare outdoor grill for direct grilling over medium heat, or heat ridged grill pan over medium-high heat until very hot but not smoking. In small bowl, combine Cajun seasoning and sugar. Rub seasoning mixture on both sides of ham steak.

2. Place ham steak on hot grill rack or pan and cook until heated through and lightly browned, 6 to 8 minutes, turning over once.

3. Serve ham steak with lime wedges and garnish with cilantro sprigs.

EACH SERVING: About 135 calories, 25g protein, 1g carbohydrate, 5g total fat (2g saturated), 68mg cholesterol, 1,980mg sodium

Fish and Shellfish

Eating fish is a good way of adding heart-healthy omega-3 fatty acids to your diet, and grilling fish (outside or in a grill pan) is a fantastic way to enjoy this good-for-you protein. Lots of different types of fish work well on the grill including halibut, catfish, salmon, snapper, tuna, and swordfish. Our recipe selection shows a wide range of flavor possibilities, from Thai Snapper to Pepper-Rubbed Party Salmon with Melon Salsa to Swordfish with Balsamic Glaze.

Shrimp seem to be made for the grill, perfect mouthfuls with smoky crisped edges, served up on easy-to-cook skewers. We've got a tasty sextet of recipes to choose from, including Shrimp Saté with Cucumber Salad and Cajun Shrimp with Remoulade Sauce, as well as shrimp and scallop combinations. And for something a little different, try our Garlicky Grilled Clams and Mussels or Grilled Squid and Peppers with Arugula.

Shrimp with Asian Barbecue Sauce, page 229

Grilled Halibut with Fresh Dill

If halibut is not available, substitute swordfish or tuna steaks. White-wine Worcestershire sauce is particularly good with seafood and poultry. If you can't find it, use 2 tablespoons original Worcestershire mixed with 2 tablespoons water.

PREP: **5 minutes plus marinating**
GRILL: **about 10 minutes**

MAKES: **4 main-dish servings**

¼ cup white-wine Worcestershire sauce
2 tablespoons fresh lemon juice
1 tablespoon olive oil
1 tablespoon minced fresh dill
¼ teaspoon coarsely ground black pepper
2 large halibut steaks, 1 inch thick (about 12 ounces each)

1. In medium bowl, stir Worcestershire, lemon juice, oil, dill, and pepper. Place halibut in large zip-tight plastic bag. Add marinade. Seal bag, pressing out excess air, and place on plate; refrigerate up to 2 hours, turning once.

2. Prepare outdoor grill for direct grilling over low heat.

3. Place halibut on hot grill rack, reserving marinade. Grill halibut, turning occasionally and basting frequently with reserved marinade, until opaque throughout, about 10 minutes.

EACH SERVING: About 195 calories, 29g protein, 3g carbohydrate, 7g total fat (1g saturated), 45mg cholesterol, 200mg sodium

Greek-Style Grilled Halibut

Greek cooks have long favored the clean, simple flavors of fresh lemon and oregano with fish. One bite of this, and you'll understand why.

PREP: **10 minutes plus marinating**
GRILL: **6 to 8 minutes**

MAKES: **4 main-dish servings**

1 lemon
3 tablespoons olive oil
2 garlic cloves, finely chopped
2 teaspoons chopped fresh oregano
½ teaspoon salt
4 small halibut steaks, ¾ inch thick (about 6 ounces each)

1. From lemon, grate 1 teaspoon peel and squeeze 2 tablespoons juice. In large bowl, with wire whisk, whisk lemon peel and juice, oil, garlic, oregano, and salt until mixed. Add halibut steaks, turning each to coat. Cover and refrigerate 1 hour to marinate, turning once or twice.

2. Meanwhile, prepare outdoor grill for covered direct grilling over medium heat.

3. Remove halibut from bowl, reserving marinade. Place halibut on hot grill rack and cook, brushing with marinade during first half of grilling, until halibut is just opaque throughout, 6 to 8 minutes, turning over once.

EACH SERVING: About 199 calories, 29g protein, 1g carbohydrate, 8g total fat (1g saturated), 44mg cholesterol, 218mg sodium

Jerk Halibut Steaks with Sweet Potato Wedges

Halibut, a firm-fleshed fish, is often sold as fillets, but it's one of the few flat fish thick enough to be cut into steaks—which are usually a better buy.

PREP: 15 minutes   **GRILL:** 8 to 10 minutes
MAKES: 4 main-dish servings

2	pounds sweet potatoes (about 2 large)
2	green onions, chopped
1	jalapeño chile, seeded and chopped
2	tablespoons fresh lime juice
2	tablespoons Worcestershire sauce
1	tablespoon peeled, grated fresh ginger
1	teaspoon dried thyme
1	teaspoon ground allspice
2	tablespoons olive oil
¼	teaspoon plus ⅛ teaspoon ground red pepper (cayenne)
½	teaspoon salt
4	small halibut steaks, 1 inch thick (about 6 ounces each)

lime wedges for garnish

1. Lightly grease grill rack. Prepare outdoor grill for covered direct grilling over medium heat.

2. Cut each unpeeled sweet potato lengthwise in half. Place sweet potato halves on microwave-safe plate and cook in microwave oven on High 8 minutes or until almost fork-tender, rearranging sweet potatoes halfway through cooking.

3. Meanwhile, in bowl, combine green onions, jalapeño, lime juice, Worcestershire, ginger, thyme, allspice, 1 tablespoon oil, ¼ teaspoon ground red pepper, and ¼ teaspoon salt. Add halibut, turning to coat. Let stand 5 minutes.

4. Cut each sweet potato half into 4 wedges. In another medium bowl, toss sweet potatoes with remaining ¼ teaspoon salt, 1 tablespoon oil, and ⅛ teaspoon ground red pepper until coated.

5. Place halibut and sweet potatoes on hot grill rack. Spoon half of jerk sauce remaining in marinating bowl on halibut; discard remainder. Grill halibut steaks until opaque throughout, 8 to 10 minutes, turning over once. Grill sweet potato wedges until tender and lightly charred, 6 to 7 minutes, turning over once. Transfer to platter as they are done. Garnish with lime wedges.

EACH SERVING: About 410 calories, 38g protein, 42g carbohydrate, 9g total fat (1g saturated), 54mg cholesterol, 390mg sodium

Jamaican Jerk Catfish with Grilled Pineapple

Other fish fillets like sole, flounder, snapper, and bluefish work well with these zesty flavors too. A versatile seasoning, jerk also does wonders for grilled chicken and pork. Add another jalapeño or some crushed red peppers if you'd like it to be even spicier.

PREP: 15 minutes   **GRILL:** 10 to 12 minutes
MAKES: 4 main-dish servings

2	green onions, chopped
1	jalapeño chile, seeded and chopped (see Tip)
2	tablespoons white wine vinegar
2	tablespoons Worcestershire sauce
1	tablespoon minced, peeled fresh ginger
1	tablespoon vegetable oil
1¼	teaspoons dried thyme
1	teaspoon ground allspice
¼	teaspoon salt
4	catfish fillets (about 5 ounces each)
1	small pineapple, cut lengthwise into 4 wedges or crosswise into ½-inch-thick slices
2	tablespoons brown sugar

1. Prepare outdoor grill for direct grilling over medium-high heat.

2. In medium bowl, mix green onions, jalapeño, vinegar, Worcestershire, ginger, oil, thyme, allspice, and salt until combined. Add catfish fillets to bowl, turning to coat; let stand 5 minutes at room temperature.

3. Meanwhile, rub pineapple wedges or slices with brown sugar.

4. Place pineapple and catfish on hot grill rack. Brush half of jerk mixture remaining in bowl on catfish; grill 5 minutes. Turn pineapple and catfish. Brush remaining jerk mixture on fish and grill until fish is just opaque throughout and pineapple is golden brown, 5 to 7 minutes longer.

EACH SERVING: About 350 calories, 23g protein, 35g carbohydrate, 14g total fat (3g saturated), 47mg cholesterol, 280mg sodium

> **TIP:** Fresh jalapeño peppers vary in their degree of heat, while pickled jalapeños from a jar are always hot. Feel free to substitute jarred for fresh in most recipes.

Pan-Grilled Catfish with Tomato-Chipotle Salsa over Polenta

Polenta is made from finely ground yellow cornmeal. We make this side dish with low-fat milk and chicken broth to keep it light.

PREP: 30 minutes **GRILL:** 20 minutes
MAKES: 4 main-dish servings

4	large plum tomatoes (about 1 pound total), each cut lengthwise in half
1	small red onion, cut crosswise into 1/2-inch-thick slices
	nonstick cooking spray
4	catfish fillets (6 ounces each)
3/4	teaspoon chipotle chile powder
3/4	teaspoon salt
3	cups low-fat (1%) milk
1	can (14 to 14 1/2 ounces) reduced-sodium chicken broth (1 3/4 cups)
3/4	cup instant polenta
1	cup fresh corn kernels (from 2 ears corn) or 1 cup frozen (thawed) corn kernels
2	teaspoons fresh lime juice

1. Preheat large ridged grill pan over medium-high heat. On sheet of waxed paper, place tomato halves and onion slices. Spray on both sides with cooking spray, place on grill pan, and cook until lightly browned and softened, 10 minutes, turning once. Transfer to cutting board.

2. While tomatoes and onion are cooking, place catfish fillets on same waxed paper. Sprinkle with 1/2 teaspoon chipotle chile powder and 1/4 teaspoon salt to season both sides, then spray both sides with cooking spray.

3. Place catfish on grill pan; cook just until it turns opaque throughout, 7 to 8 minutes, turning over once.

4. Meanwhile, prepare polenta: In 3-quart saucepan, combine milk, broth, and 1/4 teaspoon salt; cover and heat to boiling over high heat. Remove cover; slowly whisk in polenta and cook, stirring, until mixture begins to thicken. Reduce heat to low; cover and simmer 5 minutes, stirring occasionally. Stir in corn. Remove from heat.

5. Coarsely chop grilled tomatoes and onion; transfer, with any juices, to medium bowl. Stir in lime juice and remaining 1/4 teaspoon chipotle chile powder and 1/4 teaspoon salt. Makes about 1 3/4 cups.

6. To serve, divide polenta among 4 dinner plates; top with grilled catfish and tomato-chipotle salsa.

EACH SERVING: About 480 calories, 38g protein, 46g carbohydrate, 16g total fat (4g saturated), 87mg cholesterol, 980mg sodium

Thai Snapper

Tender fillets are seasoned with lime and ginger and cooked in a foil packet. Don't be tempted to assemble the packets too far ahead of time; the lime juice will start to "cook" the fillets, giving them a mushy texture. Instead, cut the vegetables and prepare the lime juice mixture several hours early and assemble the packets just before cooking.

PREP: **30 minutes**   GRILL: **8 minutes**
MAKES: **4 main-dish servings**

3	tablespoons fresh lime juice
1	tablespoon Asian fish sauce
1	tablespoon olive oil
1	teaspoon grated, peeled fresh ginger (see Tip)
½	teaspoon sugar
½	teaspoon minced garlic
4	(16" by 12") heavy-duty foil sheets
4	red snapper fillets (about 6 ounces each)
1	large carrot, peeled and cut into 2¼-inch-long matchstick strips
1	large green onion, thinly sliced
¼	cup loosely packed fresh cilantro leaves

1. Prepare outdoor grill for direct grilling over medium heat.

2. In small bowl, mix lime juice, fish sauce, oil, ginger, sugar, and garlic.

3. Fold each foil sheet crosswise in half and open up again. Place 1 fillet, skin side down, on one half of each foil sheet. Top each with carrot strips, green onion, and cilantro. Spoon lime juice mixture over snapper and vegetables. Fold unfilled half of foil over fish. To seal packets, beginning at a corner where foil is folded, make small ¹/₂-inch folds, with each new fold overlapping previous one, until packet is completely sealed. Packet will resemble half-circle.

4. Place packets on hot grill rack and cook 8 minutes.

5. To serve, with kitchen shears, cut an X in top of each packet to allow steam to escape before carefully opening foil.

EACH SERVING: About 230 calories, 36g protein, 5g carbohydrate, 6g total fat (1g saturated), 63mg cholesterol, 270mg sodium

> **TIP:** Use a spoon, not a vegetable peeler, next time you need peeled ginger. Use its edge or tip to scrape away the skin. You'll find that a spoon maneuvers better than a peeler around the rhizome's knobby ends. It also removes a thinner layer of skin, keeping more of the ginger for you to use.

Everything You Need to Know about Buying and Storing Fish

BUYING

■ Shop in a clean, reputable market. Don't buy fish that has a distinct "fishy" odor (fresh fish smells like a sea breeze).

■ Buying frozen fish? Select a brand that's well wrapped and rock hard, without any freezer burn.

■ When buying a whole fish, plan on 1/2 to 3/4 pound per person; purchase 1/3 to 1/2 pound per person for fillets and steaks.

■ Make sure fillets and steaks have a shiny, moist, translucent appearance; the flesh should be firm with no gaps between the flakes. There should be no browning or drying around the edges and no evidence of extra liquid.

■ If you're purchasing a whole fish, check to see if it has bright, shiny eyes and scales; the scales should cling tightly to the skin.

STORING

■ Make the fish market your last stop before heading home. To be extra safe on extended rides or on hot days, store fish in a small cooler with a couple of ice packs.

■ Store fish in the coldest part of the fridge—either at the back of the bottom shelf or in the meat drawer.

■ Always keep raw seafood away from other foods to avoid cross-contamination, and wash hands and surfaces thoroughly with hot soapy water after handling.

■ Plan to use fresh fish right away or, at the very latest, within a day or two. Frozen fish can be kept up to six months.

■ If you need to keep fish overnight, remove it from the packaging and pat dry. Then cover it loosely with plastic wrap and layer the wrapped fish with ice in a colander placed over a bowl to catch drips.

Mediterranean Grilled Sea Bass

Grilled whole fish is a summer favorite in the Mediterranean. Sea bass is lovely on the grill; its firm white flesh holds up very well. If you can't get sea bass, substitute red snapper or striped bass.

PREP: **10 minutes plus marinating**
GRILL: **12 to 14 minutes**
MAKES: **4 main-dish servings**

2	lemons
3	tablespoons olive oil
1	tablespoon chopped fresh oregano
1	teaspoon ground coriander
1¼	teaspoons salt
2	whole sea bass, cleaned and scaled (about 1½ pounds each)
¼	teaspoon ground black pepper
2	large oregano sprigs

1. Prepare outdoor grill for covered direct grilling over medium heat.

2. Meanwhile, from 1 lemon, grate 1 tablespoon peel and squeeze 2 tablespoons juice. Cut one half of remaining lemon into slices; cut the remaining half into wedges to use for serving. In small bowl, stir lemon juice and peel, oil, chopped oregano, coriander, and ¼ teaspoon salt.

3. Rinse fish and pat dry with paper towels. Make 3 diagonal slashes in both sides of each fish. Sprinkle inside and out with pepper and remaining 1 teaspoon salt. Place lemon slices and oregano sprigs inside fish cavities. Place fish in 13" by 9" glass baking dish. Set aside half of oil mixture. Rub remaining half of oil mixture on outside of both fish. Let stand 15 minutes at room temperature.

4. Place fish on hot grill rack. Cover grill and cook fish until just opaque throughout, 12 to 14 minutes, turning over once.

5. To serve, place fish on cutting board. Working with one fish at a time, with knife, cut along backbone from head to tail. Slide wide metal spatula or cake server under front section of top fillet and lift off from backbone; transfer to platter. Gently pull out backbone and rib bones from bottom fillet and discard. Transfer bottom fillet to platter. Repeat with second fish. Drizzle fillets with remaining oil mixture. Serve with reserved lemon wedges.

EACH SERVING: About 305 calories, 40g protein, 1g carbohydrate, 15g total fat (3g saturated), 90mg cholesterol, 730mg sodium

Salmon Teriyaki

For an easy accompaniment, throw some whole green onions on the grill alongside the salmon. They'll cook in a few minutes; turn often.

PREP: 10 minutes   GRILL: about 8 minutes
MAKES: 4 main-dish servings

6   tablespoons teriyaki sauce
1   tablespoon brown sugar
1   teaspoon Asian sesame oil
4   salmon steaks, ¾ inch thick
     (about 6 ounces each)
1   green onion, thinly sliced on diagonal

1. Prepare outdoor grill for covered direct grilling over medium heat.

2. Meanwhile, in 2-quart saucepan, heat teriyaki sauce, brown sugar, and sesame oil to boiling over medium-high heat. Boil until slightly thickened, about 3 minutes.

3. With tweezers, remove any pin bones from salmon. Place salmon on hot grill rack. Cover grill and cook salmon, turning once and brushing frequently with teriyaki mixture, until just opaque throughout, about 8 minutes.

4. Transfer salmon steaks to platter; sprinkle with green onion.

EACH SERVING: About 320 calories, 36g protein, 8g carbohydrate, 15g total fat (3g saturated), 110mg cholesterol, 1,120mg sodium

Everything You Need to Know about Preparing Fish

■ **Defrosting:** To ensure the best texture and minimize the growth of bacteria, defrost frozen fish as slowly as possible, preferably in the refrigerator on a plate for approximately 24 hours. If you're in a hurry, place well-wrapped fish in a bowl of cold water. Change the water every 30 minutes until the fish is defrosted (1 to 2 hours per pound of seafood). Be sure to cook immediately.

■ **Removing pin bones:** Although often sold as boneless, some fillets may still have tiny bones near the head end as well as a row of bones down the center of a fillet. You can feel for these small bones by running your fingers along the fillet. They are easily removed with tweezers or needle-nose pliers.

■ **Skinning:** The skin of most fish is edible (and delicious when cooked to a crisp!), but you can easily skin a fillet if necessary. Place the fillet skin side down with the narrow end near you. At the edge of the narrow end, make a small cut through flesh to skin. Grab the skin and slip the knife blade between it and the fillet and, holding the blade amost parallel to work surface, use a gentle sawing motion to separate the skin from the flesh all the way to the head end.

Spiced Salmon Steaks

Juicy summer-ripe red and yellow tomatoes are a cool and easy go-along for this entrée. Dress the tomatoes with a fruity olive oil and a sprinkling of finely shredded basil. Try this preparation with thick bluefish fillets, too; the spice mixture is a delicious complement to the richness of the fish.

PREP: **10 minutes**   GRILL: **about 8 minutes**
MAKES: **4 main-dish servings**

1	tablespoon chili powder
2	teaspoons light brown sugar
1	teaspoon ground cumin
1	teaspoon dried thyme
1	teaspoon salt
2	teaspoons olive oil
4	large salmon steaks, ¾ inch thick (about 8 ounces each)

lemon wedges (optional)

1. Prepare outdoor grill for direct grilling over medium heat.

2. In cup, mix chili powder, brown sugar, cumin, thyme, salt, and oil.

3. With tweezers, remove any pin bones from salmon. With hands, rub spice mixture on both sides of salmon steaks.

4. Place salmon on hot grill rack. Grill, turning once, until just opaque throughout, about 8 minutes. Serve with lemon wedges, if you like.

EACH SERVING: About 405 calories, 40g protein, 4g carbohydrate, 24g total fat (5g saturated), 118mg cholesterol, 720mg sodium

> **TIP:** This recipe doubles easily. Prepare a double batch, serve half, and refrigerate the remainder. Serve the salmon chilled or at room temperature the next day.

STEAK OR FILLET?

A steak is a cross-section cut containing a portion of the fish's backbone and possibly a few rib bones; a fillet is a boneless section of flesh cut from either side of the fish. Salmon steaks and fillets are equally tasty and are interchangeable in most recipes. However, diners afraid of bones may prefer fillets.

Miso-Glazed Salmon with Edamame Salad

Spread a mixture of miso, ginger, and cayenne pepper on a salmon fillet. Enjoy with our healthy soybean salad for a Japanese-inspired meal.

PREP: 30 minutes   **GRILL:** 10 to 12 minutes
MAKES: 4 main-dish servings

EDAMAME SALAD

1	bag (16 ounces) frozen shelled edamame (green soybeans) or frozen baby lima beans
¼	cup seasoned rice vinegar
1	tablespoon vegetable oil
1	teaspoon sugar
¾	teaspoon salt
⅛	teaspoon ground black pepper
1	bunch radishes (8 ounces), each cut in half and thinly sliced
1	cup loosely packed fresh cilantro leaves, chopped

MISO-GLAZED SALMON

2	tablespoons red miso
1	green onion, minced
1	tablespoon grated, peeled fresh ginger
1	teaspoon brown sugar
⅛	teaspoon ground red pepper (cayenne)
1½	pounds salmon fillet in one piece with skin on

1. Prepare salad: Cook edamame as label directs; drain. Rinse edamame with cold running water to stop cooking and drain again.

2. In medium bowl, whisk vinegar, oil, sugar, salt, and pepper until blended. Add edamame, radishes, and cilantro and toss until evenly coated. Cover and refrigerate salad up to 1 day if not serving right away. Makes about 4 cups.

3. Prepare outdoor grill for direct grilling over medium-low heat.

4. Prepare salmon: With tweezers, remove any pin bones from salmon. In small bowl, with spoon, mix miso, green onion, ginger, brown sugar, and ground red pepper. Rub miso mixture on flesh side of salmon.

5. Place salmon, skin side down, on hot grill rack. Grill salmon until just opaque throughout, 10 to 12 minutes, turning over once. Serve with Edamame Salad.

EACH SERVING SALMON: About 280 calories, 29g protein, 3g carbohydrate, 16g total fat (3g saturated), 80mg cholesterol, 450mg sodium

EACH 1 CUP SALAD: About 220 calories, 16g protein, 23g carbohydrate, 8g total fat (0g saturated), 0mg cholesterol, 1,020mg sodium

Grilled Salmon with Succotash

If you have time, buy 1 ½ pounds fresh lima beans or 1 pound fresh edamame from a farmers' market. Shell, then cook in boiling water until tender. Add along with the other ingredients in step 3. You'll love the fresh taste.

PREP: 20 minutes   **GRILL:** about 8 minutes
MAKES: 4 main-dish servings

- 1   package (10 ounces) frozen baby lima beans or 2 cups frozen shelled edamame
- 2   slices bacon, cut crosswise into ¼-inch pieces
- 1   medium onion, chopped
- 1   stalk celery, cut into ¼-inch dice
- 2   cups fresh corn kernels (from about 4 ears)
- ¼   cup chicken broth or water
- 1   teaspoon salt
- ¼   teaspoon ground black pepper
- 4   salmon steaks, ¾ inch thick (about 6 ounces each)
- 2   tablespoons snipped fresh chives or sliced green onions

1. Lightly grease grill rack. Prepare outdoor grill for covered direct grilling over medium heat.

2. Meanwhile, rinse beans under hot running water until beginning to thaw; drain. In 12-inch skillet, cook bacon over medium heat until browned. With slotted spoon, transfer bacon to paper towels to drain.

3. Add onion and celery to bacon fat in skillet. Cook over medium-high heat until vegetables are tender and golden, about 5 minutes, stirring frequently. Stir in lima beans, corn, broth, $1/2$ teaspoon salt, and $1/8$ teaspoon pepper. Reduce heat to low; cover and simmer until heated through, about 2 minutes. Remove from heat; keep warm. Makes about 4 cups.

4. Sprinkle salmon with remaining $1/2$ teaspoon salt and remaining $1/8$ teaspoon pepper to season both sides. Place salmon on hot grill rack. Cover grill and cook salmon until just opaque throughout, about 8 minutes, turning over once. Transfer salmon to platter.

5. When salmon is cooked, stir chives and bacon into succotash. Serve succotash with salmon.

EACH SERVING SALMON: About 240 calories, 34g protein, 0g carbohydrate, 11g total fat (2g saturated), 93mg cholesterol, 365mg sodium

EACH 1-CUP SERVING SUCCOTASH: About 285 calories, 10g protein, 36g carbohydrate, 12g total fat (4g saturated), 13mg cholesterol, 550mg sodium

Provençal Salmon with Tomato-Olive Relish

Lightly season salmon steaks with herbes de Provence, a store-bought mix of dried herbs—often a combination of lavender, basil, thyme, and sage—that originated in southern France.

PREP: 25 minutes   **GRILL:** about 8 minutes
MAKES: 4 main-dish servings

TOMATO-OLIVE RELISH

1	lemon
$1/2$	cup green olives, pitted and coarsely chopped
1	ripe medium tomato (6 to 8 ounces), cut into $1/4$-inch chunks
1	tablespoon minced red onion

PROVENÇAL SALMON

1	tablespoon fennel seeds, crushed
2	teaspoons herbes de Provence
1	teaspoon freshly grated orange peel
$3/4$	teaspoon salt
4	salmon steaks, $3/4$ inch thick (about 6 ounces each)

1. Prepare relish: From lemon, grate $1/2$ teaspoon peel and squeeze 1 tablespoon juice. In medium bowl, toss lemon peel and juice with olives, tomato, and onion. Cover and refrigerate relish up to 1 day if not serving right away. Makes about $1 1/4$ cups.

2. Prepare outdoor grill for covered direct grilling over medium heat.

3. Prepare salmon: In cup, mix fennel seeds, herbes de Provence, orange peel, and salt. Rub herb mixture on both sides of salmon.

4. Place salmon on hot grill rack. Grill until just opaque throughout, about 8 minutes, turning over once. Serve salmon with relish.

EACH SERVING SALMON: About 270 calories, 29g protein, 1g carbohydrate, 16g total fat (3g saturated), 80mg cholesterol, 515mg sodium

EACH $1/4$ CUP RELISH: About 25 calories, 0g protein, 3g carbohydrate, 2g total fat (0g saturated), 0mg cholesterol, 330mg sodium

ANOTHER GOOD REASON TO EAT FISH

Despite a reputation for clogging arteries and packing on unwanted pounds, all fats are not villainous. Indeed, one type of polyunsaturated fat, omega-3, is thought to combat heart disease. Omega-3s help inhibit the formation of blood clots and reduce the incidence of heartbeat abnormalities. Preliminary studies also suggest that these fats possibly have a beneficial effect in the treatment of other disorders, ranging from asthma to rheumatoid arthritis. Where do you find omega-3s? In fish. And the oilier the fish (think salmon, mackerel, and sardines) the more omega-3 it contains.

Grilled Salmon with Herb-Caper Cream

A grill pan cooks simply seasoned salmon steaks perfectly. All you need is our light yet flavorful sauce, made in a mini food processor, to top it off. Add a few whole green onions to the pan and grill them alongside the salmon for a delicious edible garnish.

PREP: 5 minutes   **GRILL:** about 8 minutes
MAKES: 4 main-dish servings

4	salmon steaks, ¾ inch thick (about 6 ounces each)
½	teaspoon salt
½	teaspoon coarsely ground black pepper
½	cup loosely packed fresh parsley leaves
2	tablespoons capers, drained
1	green onion, cut into 4 pieces
⅓	cup reduced-fat sour cream
¼	cup light mayonnaise
1	tablespoon fresh lemon juice

1. Grease ridged grill pan; heat over medium heat until very hot but not smoking. Sprinkle salmon with salt and ¼ teaspoon pepper, and place in grill pan. Cook until salmon flakes easily when tested with a fork, about 8 minutes, turning once; transfer to platter.

2. Meanwhile, in mini food processor, with sharp side of blade facing up, process parsley, capers, and green onion until finely chopped. Transfer mixture to small bowl and stir in sour cream, mayonnaise, lemon juice, and remaining ¼ teaspoon pepper until blended. Makes about ¾ cup sauce.

3. Serve sauce with salmon.

EACH SERVING SALMON: About 230 calories, 32g protein, 0g carbohydrate, 10g total fat (2g saturated), 91mg cholesterol, 360mg sodium

EACH TABLESPOON SAUCE: About 30 calories, 0g protein, 1g carbohydrate, 3g total fat (1g saturated), 4mg cholesterol, 85mg sodium

FARM-RAISED VERSUS WILD SALMON

Farm-raised (usually Atlantic) salmon, with a rich, almost buttery texture and a milder flavor than its wilder sister, is mainly bred along the northeast coast of the United States or off the coast of Chile, first in freshwater hatcheries and then in pens submerged in cold saltwater off the coastline, where the fish have a chance to swim against currents and changing tides. Since it's available all year, we generally use it in our recipes.

Wild salmon, with a lean, firm texture and a more pronounced fish flavor, comes mostly from Alaska and is available only in summer months unless purchased frozen or canned. Alaska salmon is called "wild" because the fish swim freely in the Bering Sea, the Gulf of Alaska, and the waters of the northern Pacific. The five commercially sold varieties of wild Alaskan salmon are King (or Chinook), Sockeye (or Red or Blueback), Silver (or Coho), Chum, and Pink (which is primarily canned).

Salmon with Summer Squash Ribbons and Olives

Cooked in a foil packet on the grill, this dish couldn't be easier and it delivers spectacular results, with the salmon served on beautiful yellow and green ribbons of squash.

PREP: 20 minutes   **GRILL:** 12 minutes
MAKES: 4 main-dish servings

1	medium yellow summer squash (about 6 ounces)
1	medium zucchini (about 6 ounces)
	heavy-duty foil
2	plum tomatoes, cut into ½-inch dice
¾	cup Kalamata olives, pitted and coarsely chopped
½	cup loosely packed fresh parsley leaves, chopped
2	tablespoons extra-virgin olive oil
¾	teaspoon salt
1	teaspoon freshly grated lemon peel
1	piece skinless salmon fillet (about 1 pound), cut into 4 pieces

1. Prepare outdoor grill for covered direct grilling over medium heat.

2. Place two 30" by 18" sheets heavy-duty foil on work surface to make a double thickness. Trim ends from yellow squash and zucchini. With vegetable peeler, peel squash and zucchini lengthwise into long, thin ribbons. Arrange ribbons down center of foil in a 12-inch area. Sprinkle tomatoes, olives, parsley, oil, and ½ teaspoon salt over squash and zucchini ribbons. Sprinkle lemon peel and remaining ¼ teaspoon salt over salmon.

3. With tweezers, remove any pin bones from salmon. Place salmon on top of squash mixture; bring long sides of foil up and over salmon; fold several times to seal well, then fold in ends to seal tightly.

4. Place foil packet on hot grill rack. Cover grill and cook 12 minutes.

5. When salmon is done, cut an X in top of foil packet to let steam escape, then carefully pull back foil to open. Slide vegetables and salmon onto 4 dinner plates to serve.

EACH SERVING: About 325 calories, 33g protein, 8g carbohydrate, 18g total fat (3g saturated), 65mg cholesterol, 725mg sodium

Tarragon-Rubbed Salmon with Nectarine Salsa

We love the ease of salmon fillets, but if you find it easier to cook and turn salmon steaks, simply use the ten-minutes-per-inch-of-thickness rule as a guide for your cooking time.

PREP: 10 minutes plus standing
GRILL: 8 to 10 minutes

MAKES: 4 main-dish servings

2	tablespoons chopped red onion
2	large ripe nectarines, pitted and chopped
1	small red pepper, stem and seeds removed, chopped
1	jalapeño chile, finely chopped
2	tablespoons fresh lime juice
1	tablespoon chopped fresh cilantro
½	teaspoon salt
1	tablespoon dried tarragon
¼	teaspoon coarsely ground black pepper
4	pieces salmon fillet (about 6 ounces each), skin removed
1	teaspoon olive oil

1. Grease clean grill rack. Prepare outdoor grill for covered direct grilling over medium heat.

2. In cup, place onion; cover with *cold water* and let sit 10 minutes. (This will reduce sharpness of raw onion.) In medium bowl, stir together nectarines, red pepper, jalapeño, lime juice, cilantro, and ¼ teaspoon salt; set aside.

3. In small bowl, mix together tarragon, pepper, and remaining ¼ teaspoon salt. With tweezers, remove any pin bones from salmon. Brush salmon with oil and rub with tarragon mixture to coat both sides.

4. Place salmon on hot grill rack. Cover grill and cook salmon until it turns opaque throughout, 8 to 10 minutes, turning over once with large spatula. Transfer to platter.

5. Drain onion well. Stir onion into nectarine mixture. Serve nectarine salsa with grilled salmon.

EACH SERVING: About 305 calories, 35g protein, 14g carbohydrate, 12g total fat (2g saturated), 93mg cholesterol, 365mg sodium

Honey-Lime Salmon

You can rub and refrigerate the salmon up to eight hours before grilling.

PREP: 10 minutes   GRILL: about 8 minutes
MAKES: 4 main-dish servings

4	pieces salmon fillet, ¾ inch thick (about 6 ounces each), skin removed
3	tablespoons honey
1	teaspoon ground cumin
1	teaspoon ground coriander
¾	teaspoon salt
¾	teaspoon freshly grated lime peel
¼	teaspoon coarsely ground black pepper
1	teaspoon very hot water
3	tablespoons chopped fresh cilantro

lime wedges

1. Prepare outdoor grill for direct grilling over medium heat.

2. With tweezers, remove any pin bones from salmon. In cup, mix honey, cumin, coriander, salt, lime peel, pepper, and water until blended. With hands, rub mixture on salmon pieces.

3. Place salmon on hot grill rack. Grill just until salmon turns opaque throughout, about 8 minutes, turning over once.

4. Sprinkle salmon with cilantro and serve with lime wedges.

EACH SERVING: About 350 calories, 32g protein, 14g carbohydrate, 18g total fat (4g saturated), 95mg cholesterol, 535mg sodium

> **TIP:** You can substitute red snapper or bluefish fillets for the salmon; cook 6 to 8 minutes.

Sweet and Smoky Salmon Kabobs

These easy-prep kabobs feature a delectable spice rub.

PREP: 10 minutes   GRILL: 20 minutes
MAKES: 8 main-dish servings

12	(10-inch) metal or bamboo skewers
2	tablespoons packed dark brown sugar
1½	teaspoon smoked paprika
1	teaspoon chili powder
½	teaspoon ground red pepper (cayenne)
¾	teaspoon salt
½	teaspoon freshly ground black pepper
2¼	pounds skinless salmon fillet, cut into 1½-inch chunks
2	medium (8 ounce each) zucchini, cut into ¼-inch-thick slices

1. If using bamboo skewers, soak in hot water at least 20 minutes. Prepare outdoor grill for direct grilling over medium heat.

2. In large bowl, combine sugar, paprika, chili powder, red pepper, salt, and pepper. Rub mixture between fingers to break up any lumps of sugar. Add salmon and zucchini and toss to evenly coat with spice mixture.

3. Thread zucchini slices, 2 at a time and alternating with salmon, onto skewers. Place on hot grill grate and cook 9 to 11 minutes or until salmon turns opaque throughout, turning occasionally.

EACH SERVING: About 205 calories, 26g protein, 6g carbohydrate, 8g total fat (1g saturated), 70mg cholesterol, 280mg sodium

Swordfish with Balsamic Glaze

Balsamic vinegar, blended with brown sugar and reduced to a syrup, makes a rich, winelike glaze that is perfect with meaty swordfish. For a delicious variation, serve the fish atop a salad.

PREP: 15 minutes   **GRILL: 8 to 9 minutes**
MAKES: 4 servings

2	teaspoons olive oil
¼	cup finely chopped shallots
½	cup balsamic vinegar
2	teaspoons brown sugar
2	teaspoons tomato paste
¼	teaspoon dried thyme
¼	teaspoon salt
¼	teaspoon ground black pepper
4	swordfish steaks, 1 inch thick (about 6 ounces each)

1. Prepare outdoor grill for direct grilling over medium-high heat.

2. In 10-inch skillet, heat oil over medium-low heat. Add shallots and cook, stirring occasionally, until tender, about 4 minutes. Add vinegar and brown sugar; heat to boiling over high heat. Boil until liquid has thickened and is syrupy, about 5 minutes. Remove from heat and stir in tomato paste until blended.

3. Sprinkle thyme, salt, and pepper on swordfish. Place fish on hot grill rack and cook 4 minutes. Turn and brush each swordfish steak with glaze; cook until just opaque throughout, 4 to 5 minutes longer.

EACH SERVING: About 226 calories, 30g protein, 5g carbohydrate, 8g total fat (2g saturated), 59mg cholesterol, 305mg sodium

BALSAMIC-GLAZED SWORDFISH WITH GREENS: Prepare fish as directed above. In large bowl, whisk together *2 tablespoons balsamic vinegar, 2 tablespoons extra-virgin olive oil,* and *1/8 teaspoon salt*. Add *2 cups each washed, dried, and torn Bibb and Boston lettuce,* and *2 cups sliced Belgian endive*; toss to coat. Arrange greens on dinner plates; top with fish.

EACH SERVING BALSAMIC-GLAZED SWORDFISH WITH GREENS: About 299 calories, 31g protein, 8g carbohydrate, 16g total fat (3g saturated), 59mg cholesterol, 388mg sodium

Sicilian-Style Swordfish with Pasta

Chunks of grilled fish are tossed with pasta in a light vinaigrette made with fresh mint and tomato. If you don't have mint, substitute fresh basil or parsley.

PREP: 15 minutes plus standing
GRILL: 8 to 10 minutes
MAKES: 6 main-dish servings

3	ripe medium tomatoes (6 to 8 ounces each), cut into ½-inch chunks (about 2½ cups)
¼	cup chopped fresh mint
1	tablespoon red wine vinegar
1	small garlic clove, minced
3	tablespoons olive oil
¾	teaspoon salt
½	teaspoon coarsely ground black pepper
1	teaspoon freshly grated orange peel
1	swordfish steak, 1 inch thick (about 1 pound)
1	pound penne or bow-tie pasta

1. In large bowl, combine tomatoes, mint, vinegar, garlic, 2 tablespoons oil, ½ teaspoon salt, and ¼ teaspoon pepper. Cover and let stand at room temperature 30 minutes.

2. Prepare outdoor grill for direct grilling over medium heat.

3. In cup, combine orange peel, remaining 1 tablespoon oil, remaining ¼ teaspoon salt, and remaining ¼ teaspoon pepper. Brush mixture on both sides of swordfish.

4. Place swordfish on hot grill rack. Grill until just opaque throughout, 8 to 10 minutes, turning over once. Transfer to cutting board and cut into 1-inch pieces.

5. Meanwhile, cook pasta in boiling salted water as label directs. Drain.

6. Add swordfish and pasta to tomato mixture; toss to combine.

EACH SERVING: About 440 calories, 24g protein, 61g carbohydrate, 11g total fat (2g saturated), 26mg cholesterol, 430mg sodium

Swordfish Kabobs

This is the method of choice for preparing swordfish along the coasts of Turkey. Serve it with steamed rice.

PREP: **25 minutes plus marinating**
GRILL: **5 to 8 minutes**
MAKES: **4 main-dish servings**

1	swordfish steak, 1 inch thick (about 1 pound)
½	cup chicken or vegetable broth
3	tablespoons fresh lemon juice
1	tablespoon olive oil
1	very small onion, thinly sliced
2	garlic cloves, thinly sliced
14	large bay leaves
½	teaspoon salt
½	teaspoon paprika
¼	teaspoon ground coriander
⅛	teaspoon ground black pepper
12	(7-inch) bamboo skewers
12	thin lemon slices, each seeded and cut in half
1	tablespoon chopped fresh parsley

1. Remove skin from swordfish and discard. Cut fish into 1-inch cubes.

2. In medium bowl, combine broth, lemon juice, oil, onion, garlic, 2 bay leaves, salt, paprika, coriander, and pepper. Add swordfish and toss to coat. Cover and refrigerate 3 hours to marinate, tossing occasionally.

3. Meanwhile, soak remaining 12 bay leaves and bamboo skewers in enough *boiling water* to cover 1 hour. Drain. With kitchen shears, snip each bay leaf crosswise in half.

4. Prepare outdoor grill for covered direct grilling over medium-high heat.

5. Remove swordfish from marinade, reserving marinade. Thread each skewer as follows: ½ bay leaf, 1 swordfish cube, ½ lemon slice, 1 swordfish cube; then repeat once, gently pressing bay leaves, lemon slices, and fish together.

6. Place kabobs on hot grill rack, cover, and cook, turning kabobs and brushing with marinade during first half of cooking, until fish is just opaque throughout, 5 to 8 minutes.

7. Meanwhile, strain remaining marinade into small saucepan and heat to boiling; boil 3 minutes. Arrange kabobs on platter, drizzle with hot marinade, and sprinkle with parsley.

EACH SERVING: About 189 calories, 22g protein, 7g carbohydrate, 8g total fat (2g saturated), 42mg cholesterol, 514mg sodium

Spiced Grilled Tuna on Spinach Salad

A blend of aromatic spices rubbed on tuna steaks before pan-grilling adds great flavor.

PREP: 25 minutes   **GRILL:** 8 to 10 minutes
MAKES: 4 main-dish servings

TUNA WITH SPICE RUB

1	tablespoon olive oil
1	teaspoon ground cumin
1	teaspoon ground coriander
1	teaspoon paprika
1	teaspoon freshly grated lime peel
3/4	teaspoon salt
1/2	teaspoon coarsely ground black pepper
4	tuna steaks, 1 inch thick (about 6 ounces each)

SPINACH SALAD

2	tablespoons olive oil
2	tablespoons fresh lime juice
1	teaspoon sugar
1/4	teaspoon ground cumin
1/4	teaspoon salt
1/8	teaspoon coarsely ground black pepper
1	bag (6 ounces) baby spinach
1/2	English (seedless) cucumber (about 8 ounces), unpeeled, cut lengthwise in half, then thinly sliced crosswise
1	bunch radishes, each cut in half, then thinly sliced
4	radishes with tops for garnish

1. Prepare spice rub: In small bowl, with spoon, combine oil, cumin, coriander, paprika, lime peel, salt, and pepper until well blended. Rub spice mixture on both sides of tuna steaks.

2. Heat ridged grill pan over medium heat until hot but not smoking. Add tuna to pan and cook 8 to 10 minutes, until fish turns opaque throughout, turning over once. (If you prefer seared tuna, grill about 2 minutes per side.) Transfer to cutting board.

3. Meanwhile, prepare salad: In large bowl, with wire whisk or fork, mix oil, lime juice, sugar, cumin, salt, and pepper. Add cucumber, spinach, and sliced radishes; toss to coat.

4. Cut tuna steaks into 1/2-inch-thick slices. Arrange salad on dinner plates or large platter; top with steak. Garnish with radishes.

EACH SERVING: About 300 calories, 42g protein, 5g carbohydrate, 12g total fat (2g saturated), 76mg cholesterol, 700 mg sodium

Shrimp with Asian Barbecue Sauce

Fresh ginger and five spice powder create a delicious sauce for these succulent shrimp kabobs. Serve on a bed of romaine with extra sauce for dipping. For photo, see page 204.

PREP: 15 minutes   **GRILL:** 3 to 4 minutes
MAKES: 4 main-dish servings

romaine lettuce leaves
1¼ pounds large shrimp
4   (10- to 12-inch) skewers
⅓   cup hoisin sauce
3   tablespoons ketchup
1½ teaspoons grated, peeled fresh ginger
¼   teaspoon Chinese five-spice powder
2   tablespoons rice vinegar
2   tablespoons water

1. Soak skewers in hot water at least 20 minutes. Lightly grease grill rack. Prepare outdoor grill for direct grilling over medium heat.

2. Arrange romaine on platter and set aside. Shell and devein shrimp, leaving tail shell on, if you like. Thread shrimp on skewers.

3. In small bowl, stir hoisin sauce, ketchup, ginger, five-spice powder, and 1 tablespoon vinegar. Transfer ¼ cup sauce to ramekin; stir in water and remaining 1 tablespoon vinegar and reserve to use as dipping sauce.

4. Brush shrimp with some barbecue sauce remaining in bowl. Place shrimp on hot grill rack and cook 2 minutes. Brush with more sauce; turn, brush with remaining sauce, and grill until shrimp turn opaque throughout, 1 to 2 minutes longer.

5. Arrange shrimp skewers on romaine and serve with reserved dipping sauce.

EACH SERVING: About 185 calories, 25g protein, 13g carbohydrate, 3g total fat (1g saturated), 175mg cholesterol, 540mg sodium

---

SHELLING AND DEVEINING SHRIMP

Deveining small and medium shrimp is optional. However, do remove the vein of large shrimp; it can contain grit.

1. With kitchen shears or small knife, cut the shrimp shell along the outer curve, just deep enough into the flesh to expose the dark vein.

2. Peel back the shell from the cut and gently separate the shell from the shrimp. Discard the shell (or use it to make stock).

3. Hold the shrimp under cold running water; remove the vein with the tip of the knife.

Five-Spice Shrimp and Scallops

An intriguing mix of sweet and spicy flavors. Great with our Cucumber Relish (page 283).

PREP: 20 minutes   GRILL: 4 to 5 minutes
MAKES: 6 main-dish servings

1	pound large shrimp
¾	pound sea scallops
1	tablespoon light brown sugar
1	tablespoon soy sauce
1	tablespoon vegetable oil
2	teaspoons Chinese five-spice powder
1¼	teaspoons salt
¼	teaspoon coarsely ground black pepper
6	(12-inch) metal skewers

1. Prepare outdoor grill for direct grilling over medium heat. Shell and devein shrimp, leaving tail shell on, if you like; rinse with cold water. Pull off and discard tough crescent-shaped muscle, if any, from each scallop. Rinse well to remove sand from crevices. Pat shrimp and scallops dry with paper towels.

2. In large bowl, mix brown sugar, soy sauce, oil, five-spice powder, salt, and pepper; add shrimp and scallops, tossing to coat.

3. Onto skewers, alternately thread shrimp and scallops. Place on hot grill rack; cook until shrimp and scallops turn opaque throughout, 4 to 5 minutes, turning occasionally and dabbing with any remaining spice mixture halfway through cooking.

EACH SERVING: About 155 calories, 26g protein, 4g carbohydrate, 4g total fat (0g saturated), 150mg cholesterol, 905mg sodium

Scallop and Cherry Tomato Skewers

These skewers make for a memorable contrast in flavor and texture—the smooth creaminess of the scallops against the burst of juice from the sweet and slightly tart grilled tomatoes.

PREP: 10 minutes   GRILL: 12 to 14 minutes
MAKES: 4 main-dish servings

8	(8-inch) bamboo skewers
1	lemon
2	tablespoons olive oil
2	tablespoons Dijon mustard
⅛	teaspoon salt
24	cherry tomatoes
16	large sea scallops (1¼ pounds)

1. Soak skewers in hot water at least 20 minutes. Prepare outdoor grill for direct grilling over medium heat.

2. Meanwhile, from lemon, grate 1½ teaspoons peel and squeeze 1 tablespoon juice. In small bowl, whisk lemon peel and juice, oil, Dijon, and salt until blended; set aside.

3. Thread 3 tomatoes and 2 scallops alternately on each skewer, beginning and ending with tomatoes.

4. Brush scallops and tomatoes with half of Dijon mixture; place on hot grill rack. Cook 7 to 9 minutes, turning several times. Brush with remaining Dijon mixture, and cook until scallops just turn opaque throughout, about 5 minutes longer.

EACH SERVING: About 215 calories, 25g protein, 9g carbohydrate, 9g total fat (1g saturated), 47mg cholesterol, 355mg sodium

Shrimp and Scallop Kabobs

Shrimp and scallops cook in a flash and require no marinating. If the scallops are very large, halve them horizontally. Don't substitute bay scallops; they're small and will cook too quickly. If you like, serve with Pineapple Salsa (page 278) and a bowl of rice.

**PREP: 20 minutes   GRILL: 4 to 5 minutes
MAKES: 6 main-dish servings**

1	pound large shrimp
1	pound large sea scallops
3	tablespoons soy sauce
3	tablespoons seasoned rice vinegar
2	tablespoons grated, peeled fresh ginger
1	tablespoon brown sugar
1	tablespoon Asian sesame oil
2	garlic cloves, crushed with garlic press
1	bunch green onions, cut diagonally into 3-inch-long pieces
12	cherry tomatoes
6	(12-inch) metal skewers

1. Prepare outdoor grill for direct grilling over medium heat.

2. Shell and devein shrimp, leaving tail shell on, if you like; rinse with cold water. Pull off and discard tough crescent-shaped muscle, if any, from each scallop. Rinse scallops well to remove sand from crevices. Pat shrimp and scallops dry with paper towels.

3. In large bowl, mix soy sauce, vinegar, ginger, brown sugar, sesame oil, and garlic (see Tip). Add shrimp and scallops; toss until evenly coated.

4. Alternately thread shrimp, scallops, green onions, and tomatoes onto skewers. Place on hot grill rack; grill, turning occasionally and basting with any remaining soy-sauce mixture halfway through cooking, until just opaque throughout, 4 to 5 minutes.

EACH SERVING: About 185 calories, 26g protein, 10g carbohydrate, 4g total fat (1g saturated), 118mg cholesterol, 880mg sodium

TIP: The soy mixture can be made several hours in advance, covered, and refrigerated. Whisk to combine before adding the shrimp and scallops.

BUYING SHRIMP

When purchasing shrimp by the pound, remember that the number you'll get depends on the size you select. Here, the quantity per pound for the different sizes available:

SHRIMP SIZE	NUMBER PER POUND
Small	36–45
Medium	31–35
Large	21–30
Extra large	16–20
Jumbo	11–15

Shrimp Sonoma

Some of the sweetest dried tomatoes come from the Sonoma Valley in California. Look for dried tomatoes that are plump rather than dry and leathery. Make a batch of Balsamic-Glazed Veggie Kabobs (page 246) and grill them alongside the shrimp. Serve on a bed of couscous seasoned with extra-virgin olive oil.

PREP: 25 minutes   **GRILL: 8 to 10 minutes**
MAKES: 6 main-dish servings

1	ounce dried tomatoes without salt
1	cup boiling water
1½	pounds large shrimp
2	tablespoons fresh lemon juice
2	tablespoons olive oil
½	teaspoon salt
½	teaspoon crushed red pepper
4	(12-inch) metal skewers

1. Place dried tomatoes in small bowl. Pour boiling water over tomatoes; let stand while preparing shrimp.

2. Meanwhile, pull off legs from shrimp. Insert tip of kitchen shears under shell of each shrimp and snip along back to tail, cutting about ¼ inch deep to expose dark vein. Leaving shell on, rinse shrimp to remove vein; pat dry with paper towels. Place shrimp in bowl.

3. Prepare outdoor grill for direct grilling over medium heat.

4. Drain tomatoes, reserving ¼ cup liquid.

5. In blender or in food processor with knife blade attached, puree tomatoes, reserved liquid, lemon juice, oil, salt, and crushed red pepper until smooth. Pour over shrimp.

6. Thread shrimp onto skewers. Place skewers on hot grill rack. Grill shrimp, turning skewers occasionally and basting with any remaining tomato puree, until just opaque throughout, 8 to 10 minutes.

EACH SERVING: About 140 calories, 20g protein, 3g carbohydrate, 5g total fat (1g saturated), 140mg cholesterol, 290mg sodium

SHRIMP SAVVY

■ **You can buy shrimp all year-round— 95 percent of what's sold in the United States has been previously frozen.**

■ **Depending on variety, shrimp shells can be light gray, brownish pink, or red, but when cooked, all will turn reddish.**

■ **Select raw shrimp with firm-looking meat and shiny shells that feel full.**

■ **Avoid black spots, which are a sign of aging. The heads are usually removed before shrimp are sold; if not, gently pull the head away from the body before shelling. Cooked, shelled shrimp should be plump with white flesh.**

■ **Allow about ¼ pound of shelled shrimp per serving.**

Shrimp Saté with Cucumber Salad

An aromatic rice such as jasmine or basmati makes a delicious accompaniment to this Indonesian-inspired dish.

PREP: 45 minutes plus marinating
GRILL: 4 to 5 minutes
MAKES: 4 main-dish servings

8	(7-inch) bamboo skewers
1	tablespoon vegetable oil
6	tablespoons fresh lime juice (from 3 to 4 limes)
3	tablespoons minced fresh cilantro
½	teaspoon salt
½	teaspoon crushed red pepper
1	pound large shrimp
2	small cucumbers (about 8 ounces each)
2	tablespoons sugar
1	tablespoon snipped fresh chives
2	tablespoons slivered fresh basil
3	tablespoons chopped dry-roasted salted peanuts

1. Prepare outdoor grill for direct grilling over medium heat.

2. Soak skewers in water to cover for 30 minutes. Drain before using.

3. While skewers soak, in medium bowl, whisk together oil, 3 tablespoons lime juice, 2 tablespoons cilantro, ¼ teaspoon salt, and ¼ teaspoon crushed red pepper. Stir in shrimp and marinate at room temperature 15 minutes.

4. Shell and devein shrimp, leaving tail shell on, if you like; rinse with cold water.

5. Cut each unpeeled cucumber lengthwise in half. With spoon, scoop out seeds. Thinly slice cucumber halves crosswise. In another medium bowl, stir cucumbers, sugar, chives, 1 tablespoon basil, and remaining 3 tablespoons lime juice, 1 tablespoon cilantro, ¼ teaspoon salt, and ¼ teaspoon crushed red pepper. Set salad aside. Makes about 3 cups.

6. Thread about 4 shrimp on each skewer. With long-handled basting brush, lightly oil grill rack. Place skewers on hot grill rack. Cook shrimp just until opaque throughout, turning over once, 4 to 5 minutes.

7. Spoon cucumber salad onto dinner plates; sprinkle with peanuts. Arrange skewers with shrimp over salad. Sprinkle with remaining 1 tablespoon basil.

EACH SERVING: About 205 calories, 22g protein, 13g carbohydrate, 8g total fat (1g saturated), 180mg cholesterol, 555mg sodium

Cajun Shrimp with Rémoulade Sauce

This takes only four minutes on the fire! We added fresh lemon peel to jarred Cajun seasoning (a blend of garlic, onion, chiles, peppers, and herbs). Seasoning mixes vary among manufacturers, especially with regard to salt content. Add salt to taste if necessary.

**PREP: 25 minutes   GRILL: 4 to 5 minutes
MAKES: 4 main-dish servings**

RÉMOULADE SAUCE

½   cup light mayonnaise
2   tablespoons ketchup
2   tablespoons minced celery
1   tablespoon coarse-ground Dijon mustard
1   tablespoon minced fresh parsley
2   teaspoons fresh lemon juice
½   teaspoon Cajun seasoning
1   green onion, minced

CAJUN SHRIMP

1¼   pounds large shrimp
1   tablespoon Cajun seasoning
1   tablespoon olive oil
2   teaspoons freshly grated lemon peel
lemon, cut into wedges

1. Prepare outdoor grill for direct grilling over medium-high heat.

2. Prepare sauce: In small bowl, mix mayonnaise, ketchup, celery, mustard, parsley, lemon juice, Cajun seasoning, and green onion. Cover and refrigerate up to 3 days if not serving right away. Makes about 1 cup.

3. Prepare shrimp: Shell and devein shrimp, leaving tail shell on, if you like; rinse with cold water. In medium bowl, mix Cajun seasoning, oil, and lemon peel. Add shrimp and toss until evenly coated.

4. Place shrimp on hot grill rack (or hot flat grill topper) and grill, turning once, just until opaque throughout, 4 to 5 minutes.

5. Transfer shrimp to platter; serve with Rémoulade Sauce and lemon wedges.

EACH SERVING SHRIMP: About 155 calories, 24g protein, 2g carbohydrate, 5g total fat (1g saturated), 175mg cholesterol, 575mg sodium

EACH 1 TABLESPOON SAUCE: About 30 calories, 0g protein, 2g carbohydrate, 3g total fat (1g saturated), 3mg cholesterol, 95mg sodium

Garlicky Grilled Clams and Mussels

Buy your shellfish from a reputable purveyor and plan to serve them the day of purchase. If you're not cooking right away, store them in a large bowl covered with a wet towel in the refrigerator, not on ice, until the grill is ready.

PREP: 20 minutes **GRILL:** about 10 minutes
MAKES: 4 main-dish or 8 appetizer servings

4	tablespoons butter or margarine, cut into pieces
2	tablespoons olive oil
3	garlic cloves, minced
1	large shallot, minced (¼ cup)
½	cup dry white wine
¼	teaspoon crushed red pepper
2	pounds mussels, scrubbed, with beards removed
2	dozen littleneck clams, scrubbed
⅔	cup loosely packed fresh parsley leaves, coarsely chopped

lemon and/or lime wedges

French bread slices

1. Prepare outdoor grill for covered direct grilling over medium-high heat.

2. Place butter and oil in large disposable foil roasting pan (about 16″ by 12 ½″). Place pan on hot grill rack and heat until butter has melted. Remove pan from grill. Add garlic, shallot, wine, and crushed red pepper; stir to combine. Add mussels and clams, spreading out to an even layer. Cover pan tightly with foil.

3. Return pan to grill rack. Cover grill and cook until mussels and clams open, 8 to 10 minutes.

4. Discard any mussels or clams that have not opened. Sprinkle with parsley and serve with lemon and/or lime wedges and French bread.

EACH SERVING: About 360 calories, 28g protein, 10g carbohydrate, 22g total fat (14g saturated), 130mg cholesterol, 408mg sodium

Grilled Squid and Peppers with Arugula

Squid can turn chewy if it's not cooked properly. To ensure a tender result, remove each piece from the grill just as it becomes opaque.

PREP: 15 minutes **GRILL: 11 to 17 minutes**
MAKES: 4 main-dish servings

1½ pounds cleaned squid

1 garlic clove, crushed with garlic press

2 tablespoons plus 2 teaspoons extra-virgin olive oil

½ teaspoon salt

¼ teaspoon coarsely ground black pepper

4 medium peppers (red, orange, and/or yellow)

2 lemons, each cut in half

1 bag (5 ounces) baby arugula

1. With kitchen shears, cut each squid body lengthwise down 1 side and open flat. Cut large tentacles in half. Rinse squid with cold water and pat dry with paper towels. Transfer squid to bowl; add garlic, 1 tablespoon oil, ¼ teaspoon salt, and pepper, and toss to coat; set aside. Cut each pepper lengthwise into quarters; discard seeds and stems.

2. Heat large ridged grill pan over medium-high heat (or prepare outdoor grill for direct grilling over medium-high heat).

3. In large bowl, toss peppers with 2 teaspoons oil. Place on grill pan and cook until charred and tender, 10 to 15 minutes, turning once. Place lemon halves, cut sides down, on grill with peppers and cook until marks appear and lemons soften, about 5 minutes. Transfer peppers to large bowl. Set lemon halves aside.

4. Place squid on grill pan and cook just until opaque throughout, 1 to 2 minutes, turning over once. Add squid to peppers in bowl and toss with remaining 1 tablespoon oil and ¼ teaspoon salt.

5. Arrange arugula on platter; top with squid mixture. Serve with grilled lemons to squeeze over servings.

EACH SERVING: About 300 calories, 30g protein, 23g carbohydrate, 12g total fat (2g saturated), 396mg cholesterol, 380mg sodium

Vegetables and Side Dishes

If you've got the grill going, why not stay out of the kitchen entirely and grill the whole meal? We've provided you with a handy Guide to Grilling Vegetables, with basic directions for grilling everything from corn on the cob to portobello mushrooms and vine-ripe tomatoes to perfection. If you've never thought of cooking potatoes on the grill, try our potato "packets," with eight different flavor variations, including Jalapeno-Cilantro and Lemon-Garlic. We've also got recipes for polenta and garlic bread on the grill.

In addition to a host of tasty side dishes, we've included recipes for grilled vegetarian main courses. No one will miss the meat with dishes like Flame-Roasted Chiles Relleños, Grilled Eggplant with Fresh Oregano and Ricotta Salata, and Grilled Vegetarian Burritos.

Grilled Eggplant with Feta and Fresh Mint, page 260

Grilled Vegetables with Bagna Cauda

Classic bagna cauda is a sauce made with olive oil, butter, anchovies, and garlic, served warm, as an appetizer, with raw vegetables for dipping. Our version, poured over a platter of grilled vegetables, is hearty enough for a main dish.

PREP: 30 minutes   **GRILL:** 5 to 15 minutes
MAKES: 10 side-dish servings

BAGNA CAUDA

¼	cup olive oil
5	canned anchovy fillets, minced
2	garlic cloves, minced
½	teaspoon freshly grated lemon peel
½	teaspoon salt
¼	teaspoon coarsely ground black pepper

VEGETABLES

3	large all-purpose potatoes (about 1½ pounds total), unpeeled, cut lengthwise into ½-inch-thick slices
2	tablespoons fresh lemon juice
1	tablespoon olive oil
4	small zucchini (about 6 ounces each), each cut lengthwise into 3 pieces
3	medium heads Belgian endive, each cut lengthwise in half
2	large red peppers, each cut lengthwise in half, stems and seeds removed
1	large yellow pepper, cut lengthwise in half, stem and seeds removed
2	bunches green onions
2	tablespoons chopped fresh parsley for garnish

1. Prepare Bagna Cauda: In small bowl, with wire whisk, combine oil, anchovies, garlic, lemon peel, salt, and pepper; set aside. Makes ½ cup.

2. In deep 12-inch skillet, heat potato slices and enough water to cover to boiling. Reduce heat to low; cover and simmer until tender, 8 to 12 minutes. With slotted spoon, remove potatoes to paper towels to drain; pat dry.

3. Prepare outdoor grill for direct grilling over medium heat.

4. In small bowl, mix lemon juice and oil. Brush cooked potato slices and other vegetables with lemon-juice mixture on 1 side. Grill vegetables in batches, turning over once and brushing with remaining lemon-juice mixture, until browned and tender, 5 to 15 minutes, depending on the vegetable.

5. Transfer vegetables to large platter as they are done. Stir Bagna Cauda and pour over vegetables. Sprinkle with parsley for garnish.

EACH SERVING: About 200 calories, 4g protein, 18g carbohydrate, 7g total fat (1 saturated), 2mg cholesterol, 195mg sodium

Grilled Vegetable Stacks

These colorful vegetable "napoleons" can be served hot, warm, or at room temperature. If you like, grate Parmesan cheese over each stack before serving or set out in a bowl for self-serve.

PREP: 20 minutes   **GRILL: 8 to 13 minutes**
MAKES: 4 main-dish servings

wooden toothpicks or bamboo skewers

1	medium red onion, cut into ½-inch-thick slices
2	medium zucchini and/or yellow summer squashes, cut diagonally into ½-inch-thick slices
1	large yellow or red pepper, stems and seeds removed, cut lengthwise into quarters
1	medium eggplant (1½ to 2 pounds), cut diagonally into eight ½-inch-thick slices
3	tablespoons olive oil
½	cup balsamic vinegar
½	teaspoon crushed red pepper
½	teaspoon salt
4	plum tomatoes, each cut lengthwise in half
8	large fresh basil leaves
¾	pound fresh mozzarella cheese, thinly sliced

basil sprigs for garnish

1. Prepare outdoor grill for covered direct grilling over medium heat.

2. Soak toothpicks in water for 10 minutes. Insert two toothpicks horizontally through center of each onion slice to hold rings together.

3. In large bowl, toss onion, zucchini, yellow pepper, and eggplant with oil; set aside.

4. In microwave-safe 2-cup liquid measuring cup, combine vinegar, crushed red pepper, and salt. Heat vinegar mixture in microwave oven on High 2 to 3 minutes or until reduced to ¼ cup.

5. Place onion, zucchini, yellow pepper, and eggplant on hot grill rack. Place tomatoes, cut sides down, on same rack. Cover grill and cook all vegetables until grill marks appear on vegetables and they begin to soften, 4 to 5 minutes. Turn over; brush with vinegar mixture. Cook, covered, until tender, 4 to 8 minutes longer, transferring vegetables to platter as they are done.

6. Assemble vegetable stacks: Remove toothpicks from onion slices. In center of each of 4 dinner plates, place 1 eggplant slice. Top each with one-fourth of onion, zucchini, yellow pepper, tomatoes, basil leaves, and mozzarella to make 4 equal stacks. Top each stack with another eggplant slice. Drizzle any juices over and around stacks. Garnish with basil sprigs.

EACH SERVING: About 445 calories, 19g protein, 29g carbohydrate, 29g total fat (13g saturated), 66mg cholesterol, 370mg sodium

Mexican Veggie Stacks

These veggie stacks feature onions, cheese, and corn on a tomato half and turn up the heat with grilled poblano peppers. Pop a foil packet of tortillas on the grill for ten minutes to make it a full meal.

PREP: 25 minutes   GRILL: 20 to 25 minutes
MAKES: 4 main-dish servings

4	(10-inch) wooden skewers
2	teaspoons hot Mexican-style chili powder or 1 tablespoon regular chili powder
3	tablespoons olive oil
¾	teaspoon salt
¼	cup chopped fresh cilantro
2	tablespoons fresh lime juice
1	large poblano chile (6 ounces)
2	ears corn, husks and silk removed
1	jumbo red onion (1 pound), cut crosswise into 4 slices
1	medium zucchini (10 ounces), cut diagonally into ½-inch-thick slices
2	ripe large tomatoes (10 to 12 ounces each), each cut horizontally in half
4	ounces Monterey Jack cheese with jalapeño chiles, shredded

1. Prepare outdoor grill for direct grilling over medium-high heat. Soak skewers 20 minutes.

2. In cup, combine chili powder, 2 tablespoons oil, and ½ teaspoon salt; set chili oil aside. In small bowl, combine cilantro, lime juice, and remaining ¼ teaspoon salt and 1 tablespoon oil; set aside.

3. Place poblano and corn on hot grill rack. Grill until poblano is blistered on all sides and corn is charred in a few spots, 10 to 15 minutes, turning occasionally. Remove poblano from grill; wrap in foil and set aside 15 minutes. Transfer corn to cutting board.

4. Push each skewer horizontally through large center onion slice to hold slice together. Brush both sides of onion and zucchini slices and cut sides of tomatoes with chili oil; place on hot grill rack. Grill onion and zucchini until tender, about 10 minutes, turning over once. Grill tomatoes until slightly softened, 6 to 8 minutes, turning over once. As vegetables are done, remove to platter and keep warm.

5. Unwrap poblano; cut off stem. Cut poblano lengthwise in half; peel off skin and discard seeds, then cut into ¼-inch-wide strips. Cut corn kernels from cobs; add to cilantro mixture.

6. Assemble stacks: Remove skewers from onion slices. On each of 4 dinner plates, place a tomato half, cut side up; top with all of zucchini, then half of cheese. Arrange onion slice on top, separating it into rings; sprinkle with remaining cheese, then poblano strips. Top with corn mixture.

EACH SERVING: About 340 calories, 13g protein, 31g carbohydrate, 21g total fat (8g saturated), 30mg cholesterol, 670mg sodium

Grilled Vegetarian Burritos

To make this all-in-one entrée, roll grilled onion, peppers, and zucchini in tortillas with shredded cheeses. If you prefer your burritos mild, substitute Monterey Jack without jalapeño chiles or use all Cheddar cheese. Serve with your favorite bottled salsa and a dollop of sour cream. Burritos may be cut into bite-size portions and served as appetizers.

PREP: 25 minutes   GRILL: 16 to 21 minutes
MAKES: 4 main-dish servings

4	teaspoons vegetable oil
1	teaspoon chili powder
1	teaspoon ground cumin
½	teaspoon salt
¼	teaspoon coarsely ground black pepper
2	medium zucchini (about 10 ounces each), cut lengthwise into ¼-inch-thick slices
1	large onion (12 ounces), cut into ½-inch-thick slices
1	medium red pepper, stem and seeds removed, cut into quarters
1	medium green pepper, stem and seeds removed, cut into quarters
4	(10-inch) flour tortillas
2	ounces sharp Cheddar cheese, shredded (½ cup)
2	ounces Monterey Jack cheese with jalapeño chiles, shredded (½ cup)
½	cup loosely packed fresh cilantro leaves

bottled salsa (optional)

1. Prepare outdoor grill for covered direct grilling over medium heat.

2. In small bowl, mix oil, chili powder, cumin, salt, and black pepper. Brush one side of zucchini slices, onion slices, and pepper pieces with oil mixture.

3. Place vegetables, oiled side down, on hot grill rack and grill, turning over once and transferring vegetables to plate as they are done, until tender and golden, 15 to 20 minutes.

4. Arrange one-fourth of grilled vegetables down center of each tortilla; sprinkle with Cheddar and Monterey Jack cheeses. Place open burritos on grill rack. Cover grill and cook until cheeses melt, about 1 minute.

5. Transfer burritos to plates. Sprinkle cilantro over cheese, then fold sides of tortillas over filling. Serve with salsa, if you like.

EACH SERVING: About 330 calories, 11g protein, 43g carbohydrate, 14g total fat (4g saturated), 15mg cholesterol, 655mg sodium

GUIDE TO GRILLING VEGETABLES

Preheat grill to medium-high.

VEGETABLE (4 SERVINGS)	PREPARATION	SEASONING	GRILLING TIME
8 ears corn	Soak 15 minutes, then remove silk from tops only or remove husks and silk	Brush with 1 tablespoon oil	20 to 30 minutes, with husks 12 to 15 minutes, turning occasionally, without husks
1½-pound eggplant	Cut crosswise into ½-inch-thick slices	Brush with ¼ cup oil	11–13 minutes per side
4 heads Belgian endive	Cut lengthwise in half	Brush with 1 tablespoon oil	10–12 minutes per side
2 medium fennel bulbs (1 pound each)	Cut lengthwise into ¼-inch-thick slices	Brush with 4 teaspoons oil	6–8 minutes per side
6 medium leeks	Remove dark green tops; blanch 1 minute and cut lengthwise in half	Toss with 1 tablespoon oil	11–13 minutes per side
8 ounces large white mushrooms	Trim and thread onto skewers	Brush with 2 teaspoons oil	20 minutes per side, turning several times
4 large portobello mushrooms (about 1 pound)	Remove stems	Brush with 4 teaspoons oil	15 minutes per side
4 medium red or white onions	Cut crosswise into ½-inch-thick slices; secure with toothpicks	Brush with 4 teaspoons oil	12–14 minutes per side
2 bunches small green onions	Trim root ends and tops	Toss with 4 teaspoons oil	2–4 minutes, turning several times
4 red, green, or yellow peppers	Cut lengthwise into quarters; discard stems and seeds.	No oil necessary	10–12 minutes per side
2 heads radicchio (12 ounces each)	Cut lengthwise into quarters	Brush with 2 tablespoons oil	5 minutes per side
4 medium yellow squash or zucchini (8 ounces each)	Cut lengthwise into ¼-inch-thick slices	Brush with 4 teaspoons oil	5 minutes per side
4 medium tomatoes (6 to 8 ounces each)	Cut crosswise in half	Brush cut sides with 2 tablespoons oil	14–17 minutes per side
1 pint cherry tomatoes	Thread onto skewers	Brush with 2 teaspoons oil	5–7 minutes per side

Balsamic-Glazed Veggie Kabobs

A slightly sweet balsamic vinaigrette adds zip to an assortment of colorful vegetables. For variety, thread large mushroom caps and wedges of red onion onto the skewers with the other vegetables; just prepare extra vinaigrette and additional skewers.

PREP: 15 minutes   GRILL: 15 to 20 minutes
MAKES: 6 side-dish servings

3   small zucchini (about 6 ounces each),
     cut diagonally into 1-inch chunks

3   small yellow summer squash
     (about 6 ounces each), cut diagonally into
     1-inch chunks

6   plum tomatoes (about 1¼ pounds total),
     each cut lengthwise in half

6   (12-inch) metal skewers

1   tablespoon brown sugar

1   tablespoon balsamic vinegar

½   teaspoon salt

⅛   teaspoon coarsely ground black pepper

⅛   teaspoon ground cinnamon

3   tablespoons olive oil

¾   cup loosely packed fresh basil leaves,
     thinly sliced

1. Prepare outdoor grill for direct grilling over medium heat.

2. Alternately thread zucchini chunks, yellow squash chunks, and tomato halves onto metal skewers, leaving about ⅛-inch space between each vegetable piece. (Threading zucchini and squash through skin side gives vegetables more stability on skewers.)

3. In cup, combine brown sugar, vinegar, salt, pepper, cinnamon, and 2 tablespoons oil. Brush kabobs with remaining 1 tablespoon oil.

4. Place kabobs on hot grill rack and grill, turning kabobs occasionally and brushing vegetables with some vinaigrette during last 3 minutes of cooking, until vegetables are browned and tender, 15 to 20 minutes.

5. To serve, arrange kabobs on large platter; drizzle with any remaining vinaigrette and sprinkle with basil.

EACH SERVING: About 120 calories, 3g protein, 13g carbohydrate, 7g total fat (1g saturated), 0mg cholesterol, 210mg sodium

Grilled Vegetables Vinaigrette

Serve these vegetables as an accompaniment to any grilled meat, poultry, or seafood. For a delightful summer salad, cut the grilled vegetables into bite-size pieces and toss them with potatoes from Lemon-Garlic Potato Packets (page 253) or from one of the other grilled potato packets.

PREP: **15 minutes**   GRILL: **10 to 15 minutes**
MAKES: **8 side-dish servings**

½	cup olive oil
½	cup white wine vinegar
8	teaspoons chopped fresh tarragon
1½	teaspoons salt
1½	teaspoons coarsely ground black pepper
1	teaspoon sugar
2	medium yellow peppers, stems and seeds removed, each cut lengthwise in half
2	medium red peppers, stems and seeds removed, each cut lengthwise in half
4	small zucchini (about 6 ounces each), each cut lengthwise in half
4	baby eggplants (about 4 ounces each), each cut in half lengthwise
2	medium portobello mushrooms (about 4 ounces each), stems removed

1. Prepare outdoor grill for direct grilling over medium heat.

2. In large bowl, with wire whisk, mix oil, vinegar, tarragon, salt, black pepper, and sugar. Add yellow and red peppers, zucchini, eggplants, and mushrooms to bowl; toss to coat.

3. Place vegetables on hot grill rack and grill, turning occasionally and brushing with some remaining vinaigrette, until they are browned and tender when pierced with a fork, 10 to 15 minutes.

4. Once vegetables are cooked, cut each portobello into quarters. Serve vegetables with remaining vinaigrette.

EACH SERVING: About 170 calories, 3g protein, 11g carbohydrate, 14g total fat (2g saturated), 0mg cholesterol, 445mg sodium

> **TIP:** Going to a picnic? You can grill the vegetables, toss them with the vinaigrette, and carry them along.

Hot Buttered Chili-Lime Corn

Serve sweet corn hot off the grill already buttered and seasoned.

PREP: **15 minutes**   GRILL: **12 minutes**
MAKES: **4 side-dish servings**

4	ears corn, husks and silk removed, and each ear cut crosswise in half

heavy-duty foil

2	tablespoons butter or margarine, softened
1	teaspoon chili powder
½	teaspoon salt
½	teaspoon freshly grated lime peel

lime wedges (optional)

1. Prepare outdoor grill for direct grilling over medium heat.

2. Layer two 20″ by 18″ sheets heavy-duty foil to make a double thickness. Place corn on center of foil. In cup, stir butter, chili powder, salt, and lime peel until blended. Dot mixture on corn and bring short ends of foil up and over ingredients; fold two times to seal well. Fold remaining sides of foil two times to seal in juices.

3. Place foil packet on hot grill rack. Cook corn, turning once halfway through, 12 minutes.

4. Before serving, with kitchen shears, cut an X in top of packet to let steam escape, then carefully pull back foil to open. Serve with lime wedges, if you like.

EACH SERVING: About 115 calories, 3g protein, 17g carbohydrate, 5g total fat (4g saturated), 31mg cholesterol, 242mg sodium

Corn on the Cob with Molasses Butter

Cayenne pepper and coriander add kick to this molasses-sweetened butter.

PREP: **10 minutes**   GRILL: **12 to 15 minutes**
MAKES: **8 side-dish servings**

2	tablespoons butter or margarine, softened
1	teaspoon light (mild) molasses
½	teaspoon ground coriander
½	teaspoon salt

pinch ground red pepper (cayenne)

8	ears corn, husks and silk removed

1. Prepare outdoor grill for covered direct grilling over medium-high heat.

2. In small bowl, with fork, stir butter, molasses, coriander, salt, and ground red pepper until well combined.

3. Place corn on hot grill rack. Cover grill and cook corn, turning frequently, until brown in spots, 12 to 15 minutes.

4. Transfer corn to platter; spread each ear with molasses butter.

EACH SERVING: About 105 calories, 3g protein, 18g carbohydrate, 4g total fat (2g saturated), 8mg cholesterol, 186mg sodium

Campfire Corn with Herb Butter

Roasting brings out the nutty flavor of fresh corn on the cob, and leaving the husks on prevents the delicate kernels from drying out. For an added taste treat, serve the corn with wedges of lemon or lime; the tart citrus flavor complements the sweetness of the corn.

PREP: 15 minutes plus soaking
GRILL: 20 to 30 minutes
MAKES: 6 side-dish servings

6	medium ears corn, with husks and silk
6	(8-inch) pieces kitchen twine
1	medium shallot, minced
3	tablespoons butter or margarine, softened
2	tablespoons minced fresh parsley
1	teaspoon minced fresh tarragon
1	teaspoon freshly grated lemon peel
½	teaspoon salt
1⅛	teaspoons ground black pepper

1. Prepare outdoor grill for direct grilling over medium heat.

2. Gently pull husks three-fourths of way down on each ear of corn; remove silk. In large saucepot, place corn with husks and kitchen twine. Add *water* to cover; soak for at least 15 minutes. (This helps keep husks from burning on grill.)

3. Meanwhile, in small bowl, stir shallot, butter, parsley, tarragon, lemon peel, salt, and pepper. Let stand at room temperature up to 20 minutes or refrigerate overnight, if you like.

4. Drain corn well. With pastry brush, brush each ear with butter mixture. Pull husks up and, with twine, tie at top of ears.

5. Place corn on hot grill rack. Grill, turning occasionally, until husks are brown and dry and kernels are tender, 20 to 30 minutes.

EACH SERVING: About 140 calories, 3g protein, 20g carbohydrate, 7g total fat (4g saturated), 16mg cholesterol, 252mg sodium

---

THE SWEETNESS OF SUMMER CORN

Fresh local corn hits its stride from July through September in most regions. But Florida ships its Supersweets nationwide all year. These have a longer shelf life than other varieties and are better able to withstand travel because their sugar takes longer to turn to starch (approximately ten days from harvest time, as long as the ears are kept well chilled). The Southern Supersweet Corn Council recommends husking and rinsing ears, then storing them in an airtight container or plastic bag in the fridge if you're not eating them right away.

No matter which variety you buy, look for tightly wrapped, bright-green husks and plentiful, golden-brown tassels at the top that are not dried out. It's not necessary to pull a husk all the way down to examine the kernels—you can feel for plumpness through the inner husk, or peek under it near the top to make sure there are full rows of kernels. They should be glossy, with no spaces in between.

Flame-Roasted Chiles Relleños

If you prefer hotter flavor, after grilling and before filling the chiles, remove the seeds and veins but don't rinse the insides. Serve the chiles with salsa, if you like, but be aware that poblanos can sometimes be very hot; choose your salsa accordingly. If you have access to a Latin American market, look for queso blanco and use it in place of the Monterey Jack.

PREP: **20 minutes plus steaming**
GRILL: **20 to 25 minutes**
MAKES: **6 side-dish servings**

6   medium poblano chiles (about 4 ounces each)

6   ounces Monterey Jack cheese, shredded (1½ cups)

1   cup corn kernels cut from cobs (about 2 medium ears)

½   cup loosely packed fresh cilantro leaves, chopped

1. Prepare outdoor grill for direct grilling over medium heat.

2. Place whole chiles on hot grill rack over medium heat and cook, turning occasionally, until blistered and blackened on all sides, 10 to 15 minutes.

3. Transfer chiles to large sheet of foil. Wrap chiles in foil, seal tightly, and allow to steam at room temperature until cool enough to handle, about 15 minutes.

4. Meanwhile, in medium bowl, combine cheese, corn, and cilantro.

5. Cut 2-inch lengthwise slit in side of each chile, being careful not to cut through top or bottom. Under cold running water, gently peel off skin. Remove seeds and veins from opening; rinse with running water. Pat chiles dry with paper towels.

6. With spoon, fill each chile with about ½ cup cheese mixture. Gently reshape chiles to close opening. Place 3 filled chiles in single layer on each of two 18-inch square sheets of heavy-duty foil. Bring two sides of foil up and fold several times to seal. Fold over ends to seal in juices. (Chiles can be prepared to this point and refrigerated up to 6 hours before grilling.)

7. Place foil packet on hot grill rack and cook until heated through and cheese has melted, about 10 minutes.

EACH SERVING: About 160 calories, 9g protein, 13g carbohydrate, 9g total fat (5g saturated), 30mg cholesterol, 160mg sodium

Grilled Polenta with Fontina

Precooked polenta comes in a log shape and may be found in the dairy section of your supermarket.

PREP: **10 minutes** GRILL: **about 10 minutes**
MAKES: **6 side-dish servings**

2 ripe medium tomatoes (6 to 8 ounces each), chopped
2 tablespoons chopped fresh parsley
¼ teaspoon salt
⅛ teaspoon coarsely ground black pepper
1 package (24 ounces) precooked polenta, cut into 12 slices
1 tablespoon olive oil
2 ounces Fontina cheese, shredded (½ cup; see Tip)

1. Prepare outdoor grill for direct grilling over medium heat.

2. In small bowl, combine tomatoes, parsley, salt, and pepper; set aside.

3. Brush both sides of polenta slices with oil. Place slices on hot grill rack and grill until undersides are golden, about 5 minutes. Turn slices and top with cheese. Grill polenta just until cheese melts, about 5 minutes longer. Transfer to platter and top with tomato mixture.

EACH SERVING: About 150 calories, 5g protein, 19g carbohydrate, 5g total fat (2g saturated), 11mg cholesterol, 380mg sodium

> **TIP: Can't find Fontina?** Substitute Monterey Jack or Muenster cheese. To save time, top the grilled polenta with store-bought pesto or salsa instead of our fresh tomato topping.

Grilled Sweet Potatoes

You can steam the potatoes the day before and refrigerate them until ready to grill.

PREP: **5 minutes plus steaming**
GRILL: **10 to 12 minutes**
MAKES: **4 side-dish servings**

2½ pounds sweet potatoes (5 medium), cut into ½-inch-thick slices on diagonal (peeling optional)
1 tablespoon olive oil
¼ teaspoon salt
¼ teaspoon coarsely ground black pepper
   parsley sprigs for garnish

1. Prepare outdoor grill for covered, direct grilling over medium heat.

2. In 5- to 6-quart saucepot or Dutch oven, place collapsible steamer basket and *1 inch water*. Cover saucepot; heat water to boiling over high heat on range top. Place potato slices in steamer basket; reduce heat to low. Cover saucepot and simmer until potatoes are just fork-tender, 12 to 15 minutes; do not overcook.

3. Transfer potato slices to jelly-roll pan; brush with oil and sprinkle on both sides with salt and pepper. Place slices on hot grill rack. Cover grill and cook potatoes until lightly charred and tender, 10 to 12 minutes, turning over once with large metal spatula. Transfer potatoes to serving bowl; garnish with parsley.

EACH SERVING: About 245 calories, 3g protein, 50g carbohydrate, 4g total fat (1g saturated), 0mg cholesterol, 170mg sodium

Chili Potato Packet

We've included ground red pepper, onion, and chili powder for Tex-Mex appeal. To jazz these potatoes up even further, toss them after grilling with cooked corn kernels, fresh lime juice, chopped cilantro, and shredded Monterey Jack cheese.

PREP: 15 minutes   **GRILL:** 30 minutes
MAKES: 8 side-dish servings

2½ pounds red potatoes, unpeeled, cut into 1-inch chunks
1   large red pepper, stem and seeds removed, cut into 1-inch pieces
1   medium onion, coarsely chopped
2   tablespoons olive oil
1   tablespoon chili powder
1   teaspoon salt
¼   teaspoon ground red pepper (cayenne)
heavy-duty foil

1. Prepare outdoor grill for covered direct grilling over medium heat.

2. In large bowl, toss potatoes, red pepper, onion, oil, chili powder, salt, and ground red pepper until potatoes are evenly coated.

3. Lay out two 30" by 18" sheets foil on work surface to make double thickness. Place potato mixture on center of stacked foil. Bring short sides up and over mixture; fold several times to seal well, then fold in ends to seal tightly.

4. Place packet on hot grill rack and cook, turning once halfway through grilling, until potatoes are fork-tender, about 30 minutes.

5. Before serving, with kitchen shears, cut an X in top of foil packet to let steam escape, then carefully pull back foil to open.

EACH SERVING: About 145 calories, 4g protein, 26g carbohydrate, 4g total fat (1g saturated), 0mg cholesterol, 285mg sodium

ROSEMARY POTATO PACKET: Follow the directions left but combine potatoes with *1 tablespoon olive oil; 1 tablespoon fresh rosemary leaves, chopped; 1 teaspoon freshly grated orange peel; 1 teaspoon salt*; and *¼ teaspoon coarsely ground black pepper.*

EACH SERVING ROSEMARY POTATO PACKET: About 135 calories, 3g protein, 28g carbohydrate, 2g total fat (0g saturated), 0mg cholesterol, 300mg sodium

LEMON-GARLIC POTATO PACKET: Follow the directions left but combine potatoes with *12 garlic cloves*, peeled; *2 tablespoons olive oil; 1½ teaspoons grated lemon peel; 1 teaspoon salt*; and *¼ teaspoon coarsely ground black pepper.*

EACH SERVING LEMON-GARLIC POTATO PACKET: About 140 calories, 3g protein, 25g carbohydrate, 4g total fat (1g saturated), 0mg cholesterol, 275mg sodium

SHALLOT AND HERB POTATO PACKET: Follow the directions left but combine potatoes with *2 medium shallots*, thinly sliced; *2 tablespoons olive oil*; and *2 teaspoons minced fresh thyme or ½ teaspoon dried thyme.* Sprinkle with *⅓ cup chopped fresh parsley* before serving.

EACH SERVING SHALLOT AND HERB POTATO PACKET: About 140 calories, 3g protein, 25g carbohydrate, 4g total fat (1g saturated), 0mg cholesterol, 280mg sodium

Grilled Potato Packet

Aluminum foil pouches seal in seasoning so you won't have to stand over the coals, basting and glazing. Potatoes are a wonderful choice, but squash and peppers work equally well.

PREP: 10 minutes   **GRILL: 30 minutes**
MAKES: 4 side-dish servings

4   large red potatoes (about 1½ pounds total), unpeeled, cut into 1½-inch chunks
2   tablespoons vegetable oil
¾   teaspoon salt
½   teaspoon ground black pepper
heavy-duty foil

1. Prepare outdoor grill for covered direct grilling over medium heat.

2. Place two 30″ by 18″ sheets foil on work surface to make double thickness. Place potatoes, oil, salt, and pepper on center part of stacked foil. Bring short sides of foil up and over; fold several times to seal well, then fold in ends to seal tightly. Gently shake to combine ingredients.

3. Place packet on hot grill rack. Cover grill and cook 30 minutes, turning bag over once halfway through grilling.

4. With kitchen shears, cut an X in top of foil packet to let steam escape, then carefully pull back foil to open. Transfer potato mixture to platter.

EACH SERVING: About 205 calories, 3g protein, 34g carbohydrate, 7g total fat (1g saturated), 0mg cholesterol, 445mg sodium

POTATOES O'BRIEN: Prepare potato packet as in step 1. In step 2, before sealing foil, also add *1 large green pepper*, stem and seeds removed, cut into 1-inch pieces, and *1 large onion (12 ounces)*, cut into 1-inch pieces. Gently shake sealed packet to combine. Complete recipe as in steps 3 and 4.

EACH SERVING POTATOES O'BRIEN: About 250 calories, 5g protein, 44g carbohydrate, 7g total fat (1g saturated), 0mg cholesterol, 450mg sodium

JALAPEÑO-CILANTRO POTATOES: Prepare potato packet as in step 1. In step 2, before sealing foil, also add *1 bunch green onions*, cut into 1-inch pieces; *1 medium jalapeño chile*, thinly sliced crosswise (discard seeds for milder flavor); and *½ cup loosely packed fresh cilantro leaves*. Gently shake sealed packet to combine. Complete recipe as in steps 3 and 4. Sprinkle potatoes with *1 tablespoon chopped fresh cilantro* to serve.

EACH SERVING JALAPEÑO-CILANTRO POTATOES: About 220 calories, 4g protein, 37g carbohydrate, 7g total fat (1g saturated), 0mg cholesterol, 455mg sodium

LEMON-MINT POTATOES: Prepare potato packet as in step 1. In step 2, before sealing foil, also add *2 teaspoons freshly grated lemon peel, 2 tablespoons fresh lemon juice, 2 slices lemon*, and *¼ cup chopped fresh mint*. Gently shake sealed packet to combine. Complete recipe as in steps 3 and 4. Sprinkle potatoes with *1 tablespoon chopped fresh mint* to serve.

EACH SERVING LEMON-MINT POTATOES: About 215 calories, 4g protein, 36g carbohydrate, 7g total fat (1g saturated), 0mg cholesterol, 450mg sodium

Glazed Japanese Eggplant

Make sure you buy Japanese eggplants for this recipe—they're purple and usually long and slender. These glazed eggplants are delicious hot off the grill, chilled, or at room temperature. For an added flavor punch, sprinkle them with toasted sesame seeds just before serving.

PREP: 15 minutes   **GRILL:** about 10 minutes
MAKES: 6 side-dish servings

6   medium Japanese eggplants (about 5 ounces each), each cut lengthwise in half
1   tablespoon dark brown sugar
1   tablespoon minced, peeled fresh ginger
3   tablespoons soy sauce
1   tablespoon seasoned rice vinegar
½   teaspoon Asian sesame oil
¼   teaspoon cornstarch
3   garlic cloves, crushed with garlic press
3   tablespoons water
4   teaspoons vegetable oil

1. Prepare outdoor grill for direct grilling over medium heat.

2. With knife, score cut side of each eggplant half with several ¼-inch-deep parallel diagonal slits, being careful not to cut through to skin. Repeat with second set of slits perpendicular to first to form diamond pattern.

3. In small bowl, with fork, mix brown sugar, ginger, soy sauce, vinegar, sesame oil, cornstarch, garlic, and water.

4. Brush cut side of eggplant halves with vegetable oil. With tongs, place eggplant halves, cut side down, on hot grill rack over medium heat and grill until lightly browned, about 5 minutes.

5. Fold one 30" by 18" sheet of heavy-duty foil crosswise in half. Place grilled eggplant halves on double thickness of foil. Pour soy-sauce mixture over eggplant halves, bring long sides of foil up, and fold several times to seal. Fold over ends to seal in juices.

6. Place foil packet on hot grill rack and cook until eggplant is soft, about 5 minutes.

7. Before serving, with kitchen shears, cut an X in top of foil packet to let steam escape, then carefully pull back foil to open. To serve, lift out eggplant and spoon any juices over.

EACH SERVING: About 85 calories, 2g protein, 13g carbohydrate, 4g total fat (0g saturated), 0mg cholesterol, 570mg sodium

Grilled Eggplant with Fresh Oregano and Ricotta Salata

Fresh oregano, plum tomatoes, and crumbled ricotta salata cheese play off of the smoky flavors of grilled eggplant. Serve as a side with grilled chicken or fish or as a satisfying vegetarian main entrée.

PREP: 15 minutes   GRILL: 7 to 10 minutes
MAKES: 8 side-dish or 4 main-dish servings

2   tablespoons extra-virgin olive oil

2   teaspoons fresh oregano leaves

2   medium-large eggplants (about 1½ pounds each), cut lengthwise into ½-inch-thick slices

nonstick cooking spray

½   teaspoon salt

¼   teaspoon coarsely ground pepper

1   ounce ricotta salata or feta cheese, crumbled (¼ cup)

2   plum tomatoes, cut into ½-inch dice

lemon wedges

oregano sprigs for garnish

1. Prepare outdoor grill for covered direct grilling over medium-high heat.

2. Meanwhile, in small saucepan, heat oil over medium heat until hot but not smoking. Remove saucepan from heat; add oregano leaves. Let steep until ready to serve.

3. Lightly spray both sides of eggplant slices with cooking spray; sprinkle with salt and pepper. Place eggplant on hot grill rack. Cover grill and cook until tender and browned, 7 to 10 minutes, turning over once.

4. Transfer eggplant to platter; drizzle with oregano oil and top with ricotta salata and tomatoes. Serve with lemon wedges. Garnish with oregano sprigs.

EACH SERVING: About 85 calories, 2g protein, 10g carbohydrate, 5g total fat (1g saturated), 3mg cholesterol, 210mg sodium

THE INCREDIBLE, EDIBLE EGGPLANT

Late summer is peak season for this vegetable, which can show up in a variety of shapes and sizes. With its mild flavor and meaty texture, eggplant is great for use in vegetarian dishes. Here are some tips for getting the most out of this vegetable:

- Look for eggplant that feels heavy for its size with smooth skin and no cuts or bruises.

- Use within several days of purchase, and store in your refrigerator's crisper drawer.

- Often recipes call for salting to remove excess moisture, reduce bitterness, or prevent eggplant from absorbing too much oil when frying, but it's not always necessary.

- The flesh will discolor quickly, so make sure to cut it just before cooking.

Grilled Eggplant Parmesan

Grilling gives eggplant a smoky flavor, and eliminating frying makes this outdoor version of Eggplant Parmesan light and fresh tasting. Use the ripest summer tomatoes you can find for this flavorful twist on the traditional.

PREP: 25 minutes   GRILL: 11 to 13 minutes
MAKES: 4 side-dish or main-dish servings

1	medium-large eggplant (about 1½ pounds), cut lengthwise into 4 slices
4	teaspoons olive oil
½	teaspoon salt
¼	teaspoon coarsely ground black pepper
4	ounces mozzarella cheese, shredded (1 cup)
¼	cup freshly grated Parmesan cheese
½	cup loosely packed fresh basil leaves, thinly sliced
2	ripe medium tomatoes (6 to 8 ounces each), each cut into 4 slices

1. Prepare outdoor grill for covered direct grilling over medium heat.

2. Lightly brush eggplant with oil and sprinkle with salt and pepper. In small bowl, mix mozzarella, Parmesan, and basil; set aside.

3. Place eggplant on hot grill rack and grill, turning once, until tender and lightly browned, 10 to 12 minutes. Top with tomato slices and cheese mixture. Cover grill and cook until cheese melts and tomato slices are warm, 1 to 2 minutes.

EACH SERVING: About 205 calories, 10g protein, 15g carbohydrate, 13g total fat (5g saturated), 26mg cholesterol, 500mg sodium

Grilled Eggplant, Peppers, and Zucchini

Great served hot or at room temperature.

PREP: 15 minutes   GRILL: 7 to 10 minutes
MAKES: 8 side-dish servings

3	tablespoons olive oil
2	tablespoons red wine vinegar
¼	teaspoon salt
¼	teaspoon coarsely ground black pepper
¼	cup loosely packed fresh basil leaves, coarsely chopped
1	medium red pepper, stem and seeds removed, cut lengthwise into quarters
1	medium yellow pepper, stem and seeds removed, cut lengthwise into quarters
4	baby eggplants (about 5 ounces each), each cut lengthwise in half
4	small zucchini and/or yellow summer squash (about 6 ounces each), each cut lengthwise in half

1. Prepare outdoor grill for covered direct grilling over medium-high heat. Mix oil, vinegar, salt, pepper, and basil.

2. Place peppers, eggplant, and zucchini on hot grill rack. Cover grill and cook, turning and brushing with herb mixture occasionally and transferring vegetables to platter as they become tender and browned, 7 to 10 minutes.

3. Drizzle vegetables with any remaining herb mixture and serve hot or at room temperature.

EACH SERVING: About 80 calories, 2g protein, 8g carbohydrate, 5g total fat (1g saturated), 0mg cholesterol, 75mg sodium

Grilled Eggplant with Feta and Fresh Mint

We love the combination of smoky grilled eggplant and tangy feta cheese. Serve with grilled lamb chops for a zesty, Mediterranean-inspired meal. For photo, see page 238.

PREP: 10 minutes   GRILL: 8 to 10 minutes
MAKES: 6 side-dish servings

1   large eggplant (about 1½ pounds),
     cut into ½-inch-thick slices
2   tablespoons olive oil
¼   cup crumbled feta cheese
2   tablespoons chopped fresh mint
     orange wedges

1. Heat a ridged grill pan over medium-high until hot. Brush each eggplant slice with oil.

2. Place eggplant slices on hot pan; cook until tender, 8 to 10 minutes, turning over once. Transfer to platter.

3. Sprinkle with feta and mint, and drizzle with juice from 1 orange wedge. Garnish with remaining orange wedges.

EACH SERVING: About 105 calories, 3g protein, 9g carbohydrate, 7g total fat (2g saturated), 8mg cholesterol, 110mg sodium

Grilled Fennel

Fennel is an interesting change from the usual grilled vegetables. Its anise flavor pairs well with steak and pork.

PREP: 5 minutes   GRILL: about 10 minutes
MAKES: 4 side-dish servings

2   large fennel bulbs (1¼ pounds each)
1   tablespoon olive oil
¼   teaspoon salt
¼   teaspoon coarsely ground black pepper

1. Prepare outdoor grill for covered, direct grilling over medium heat. Trim tops from bulbs and cut each bulb into 8 wedges. Place in microwave-safe large bowl. Cover with vented plastic wrap. Microwave on High 5 minutes. Drain liquid from bowl. (Fennel can be microwaved up to 1 day ahead and refrigerated.)

2. In same bowl, toss fennel with oil and sprinkle with salt and pepper. Place fennel on hot grill rack. Cover grill and cook fennel until lightly charred and tender, about 10 minutes, turning over once.

EACH SERVING: About 95 calories, 3g protein, 15g carbohydrate, 4g total fat (1g saturated), 0mg cholesterol, 250mg sodium

Grilled Plum Tomatoes

Be sure to use plum tomatoes. They are firm, with low moisture content, and hold up well when grilled.

PREP: 10 minutes   **GRILL:** 8 to 10 minutes
MAKES: 8 side-dish servings

8   large plum tomatoes (about 2 pounds), cored and each cut lengthwise in half
2   tablespoons olive oil
½   teaspoon salt
¼   teaspoon ground black pepper

1. Prepare outdoor grill for covered direct grilling over medium-high heat.

2. In large bowl, toss tomatoes with oil, salt, and pepper.

3. Place tomatoes on hot grill rack. Cover grill and cook tomatoes until they begin to char and soften, 8 to 10 minutes, turning over once.

EACH SERVING: About 50 calories, 1g protein, 5g carbohydrate, 4g total fat (1g saturated), 0mg cholesterol, 155mg sodium

Crumb-Topped Tomatoes

You can't get the bread crumbs crusty on the grill, so brown them ahead of time in a skillet. The crumbs may be prepared up to a day ahead and refrigerated. These would make the perfect accompaniment to Grilled Halibut with Fresh Dill (page 206) or Red-Wine and Rosemary Porterhouse (page 143).

PREP: 15 minutes   **GRILL:** 8 to 10 minutes
MAKES: 8 side-dish servings

2   tablespoons butter or margarine
1   cup fresh bread crumbs (about 2 slices firm white bread)
1   garlic clove, crushed with garlic press
2   tablespoons chopped fresh parsley
½   teaspoon salt
½   teaspoon coarsely ground black pepper
8   ripe large plum tomatoes

1. Prepare outdoor grill for direct grilling over medium heat.

2. In 10-inch skillet, melt butter over low heat. Add crumbs and cook, stirring, until lightly browned. Stir in garlic; cook 30 seconds. Remove from heat; stir in parsley, salt, and pepper.

3. Cut each tomato horizontally in half. Top each half with crumb mixture. Place tomatoes on hot grill rack and grill until hot but not mushy, 8 to 10 minutes.

EACH SERVING: About 40 calories, 1g protein, 3g carbohydrate, 3g total fat (2g saturated), 8mg cholesterol, 191mg sodium

Charbroiled Portobellos

If you can't find portobellos, substitute large cremini or white mushrooms. Steaming them first speeds up the grill time and requires less olive oil. Serve straight from the coals, or grill the mushrooms ahead and enjoy at room temperature. They're wonderful paired with a juicy grilled steak.

PREP: **7 minutes plus steaming and marinating**
GRILL: **8 minutes**

MAKES: **8 side-dish servings**

8	large portobello mushrooms (about 2½ pounds total), stems removed
¼	cup olive oil
¼	cup balsamic vinegar
1	teaspoon sugar
½	teaspoon salt
½	teaspoon dried rosemary
¼	teaspoon ground black pepper

1. Preheat oven to 400°F. Place rack in large roasting pan (17″ by 11½″). Pour in enough *boiling water to cover* bottom of pan without touching top of rack. Place mushrooms, stemmed side down, on rack; cover with foil and steam in oven 20 minutes.

2. Meanwhile, in large zip-tight plastic bag, combine oil, vinegar, sugar, salt, rosemary, and pepper.

3. Pat mushrooms dry with paper towels. Place in bag with oil mixture, turning to coat. Seal bag, pressing out excess air. Place bag on plate; marinate 2 hours at room temperature, turning bag occasionally.

4. Meanwhile, prepare outdoor grill for direct grilling over medium heat.

5. Remove mushrooms from marinade; reserve marinade. Place mushrooms, stemmed side down, on hot grill rack. Grill, turning once and basting frequently with marinade, until browned, about 8 minutes.

EACH SERVING: About 90 calories, 2g protein, 6g carbohydrate, 7g total fat (1g saturated), 0mg cholesterol, 140mg sodium

> **TIP:** Grilled portobellos make great "pizzas." Once the mushrooms have been turned and grilled, top them with shredded mozzarella and continue grilling just until the cheese has melted. Top each with a sprinkling of finely chopped tomato and a sprig of fresh basil.

Grilled Garlic and Herb Bread

There is something about bread grilled over fire that just can't be replicated in the oven. Here are three versions to enjoy.

PREP: 10 minutes   GRILL: about 10 minutes
MAKES: 6 side-dish servings

5   tablespoons soft spreadable cheese with garlic and herbs
½   long loaf (16 ounces) French or Italian bread, split horizontally in half
1   plum tomato, seeded and chopped

1. Prepare outdoor grill for covered direct grilling over medium heat.

2. Evenly spread garlic-and-herb cheese on cut sides of bread. Sprinkle bottom half of bread with tomato. Replace top half of bread. Wrap bread tightly in heavy-duty foil.

3. Place foil-wrapped bread on hot grill rack. Cover grill and cook 10 minutes, turning over once halfway through grilling.

4. Transfer bread to cutting board. To serve, carefully remove foil. With serrated knife, cut bread crosswise into slices.

EACH SERVING: About 155 calories, 4g protein, 20g carbohydrate, 7g total fat (4g saturated), 15mg cholesterol, 305mg sodium

BASIL-ROMANO BREAD: Prepare grill as in step 1 above. In step 2, brush cut sides of bread with *2 tablespoons bottled Italian salad dressing.* Sprinkle bottom half of bread with *⅓ cup torn fresh basil leaves* and *¼ cup freshly grated Pecorino Romano cheese.* Replace top half of bread; wrap in foil. Complete recipe as in steps 3 and 4.

EACH SERVING BASIL-ROMANO BREAD: About 140 calories, 5g protein, 20g carbohydrate, 4g total fat (1g saturated), 4mg cholesterol, 310mg sodium

HORSERADISH-CHIVE BREAD: Prepare grill as in step 1 above. In step 2, in small bowl, combine *2 tablespoons light mayonnaise, 1 tablespoon drained prepared white horseradish,* and *1 tablespoon snipped fresh chives.* Spread mayonnaise mixture on cut sides of bread. Replace top half of bread; wrap in foil. Complete recipe as in steps 3 and 4.

EACH SERVING HORSERADISH-CHIVE BREAD: About 120 calories, 3g protein, 21g carbohydrate, 3g total fat (1g saturated), 2mg cholesterol, 265mg sodium

Rubs, Sauces, Glazes, Salsas, and More

Flame and flavor go together, and there are so many ways to add it when you're grilling. Spice rubs massaged into meat, fish, and poultry add a deep extra layer of flavor—we offer a range of combinations (from Sweet Ginger Rub to Spicy Peppercorn Rub) plus two salt-free mixes. Marinades, sauces, and glazes add flavors before and after your protein hits the grill; follow our tips for their use and you'll bask in the glow of your diners' enjoyment.

Adding flavor doesn't end once the food comes off the grill. We've provided you with a spunky selection of salsas that will complement and contrast your grilled food in taste and texture. Fruit is a perfect partner for the flavor of grilling and you'll find fruit in many of our salsas—try our Grapefruit Salsa, Melon Salsa, or Horseradish Salsa. And if you'd like a cooling bit of flavor on the plate, try Guacamole or Cucumber Relish.

Peach Salsa, Fire-Roasted Tomato Salsa, and Tomatillo Salsa, pages 277-280

Sweet Ginger Rub

Use every last bit of this on 1 1/2 to 2 pounds of steak. Serve extra soy sauce on the side.

PREP: 2 minutes
MAKES: about 5 tablespoons

2   tablespoons soy sauce
1   tablespoon Chinese five-spice powder
1   tablespoon brown sugar
1   teaspoon ground ginger
1   teaspoon salt
1/2   teaspoon ground red pepper (cayenne)
1/2   teaspoon Asian sesame oil

In cup, stir all ingredients together. Rub full amount all over steak before grilling. If not using right away, store rub in tightly sealed container in a cool, dry place up to 6 months.

EACH TABLESPOON: About 25 calories, 0.5g protein, 5 carbohydrate, 1g total fat, 0mg cholesterol, 827mg sodium

Spicy Peppercorn Rub

Our simple salt-free blend works well for steak, pork, chicken, or lamb. We like to pat 2 tablespoons on a 1- to 2-pound steak—use more or less, depending on the meat's thickness.

PREP: 10 minutes
MAKES: about 1/2 cup

3   tablespoons coriander seeds
3   tablespoons cumin seeds
3   tablespoons fennel seeds
1   tablespoon whole black peppercorns

Spoon coriander seeds, cumin seeds, fennel seeds, and peppercorns into zip-tight plastic bag. Place kitchen towel over bag and, with meat mallet or rolling pin, coarsely crush spices. Rub desired amount all over meat before grilling. If not using right away, store rub in tightly sealed container in cool, dry place up to 6 months.

EACH TABLESPOON: About 25 calories, 2g protein, 4g carbohydrate, 1g total fat (0g saturated), 0mg cholesterol, 7mg sodium

French Tarragon Rub

This rub has all the luscious flavor but none of the fat of a rich béarnaise sauce.

PREP: 10 minutes
MAKES: about 1/2 cup

2   medium shallots, minced (1/4 cup)
2   tablespoons red wine vinegar
1   tablespoon dried tarragon
1   teaspoon salt
1/2   teaspoon coarsely ground black pepper

In cup, stir together shallots, vinegar, tarragon, salt, and pepper. Rub full amount all over meat or chicken before grilling. If not using right away, store rub in tightly sealed container in a cool, dry place up to 6 months.

EACH TABLESPOON: About 6 calories, 0g protein, 1g carbohydrate, 0g total fat, 0mg cholesterol, 292mg sodium

Cajun Rub

This spicy mix gives the protein of your choice a yummy crust. Use 1 tablespoon per pound of uncooked beef or pork, 2 teaspoons per pound of uncooked fish or chicken.

PREP: **5 minutes**

MAKES: about $^1/_3$ cup

2 tablespoons paprika
1 tablespoon coarsely ground black pepper
1 tablespoon ground cumin
1 tablespoon brown sugar
1 tablespoon salt
2 teaspoons ground coriander
1 teaspoon dried thyme
1 teaspoon ground red pepper (cayenne)
½ teaspoon garlic powder
½ teaspoon ground allspice

In small bowl, mix all ingredients. If not using right away, store rub in tightly sealed container in a cool, dry place up to 6 months.

EACH TABLESPOON: About 26 calories, 1g protein, 5g carbohydrate, 1g total fat (0g saturated), 0mg cholesterol, 1,400mg sodium

Lime-Herb Rub

Try this fragrant Thai-inspired rub under the skin of a whole chicken or turkey breast, over a pork tenderloin, or on salmon or other oily fish.

PREP: **15 minutes**

MAKES: about $^3/_4$ cup

1 lime
1 cup loosely packed fresh cilantro leaves, chopped
1 cup loosely packed fresh mint leaves, chopped
1 tablespoon brown sugar
1 tablespoon minced, peeled fresh ginger
1 garlic clove, crushed with garlic press
1 green onion, thinly sliced
1 teaspoon salt
½ teaspoon crushed red pepper

1. From lime, grate 1 teaspoon peel and squeeze 1 tablespoon juice.

2. In medium bowl, combine lime and juice, cilantro, mint, brown sugar, ginger, garlic, green onions, salt, and crushed red pepper. Use rub right away.

EACH ¼ CUP: About 70 calories, 3g protein, 16g carbohydrate, 1g total fat (0g saturated), 0mg cholesterol, 1,195mg sodium

Salt-Free Red Chile Rub

Use 1 tablespoon per pound of pork or chicken.

PREP: 2 minutes

MAKES: 3 tablespoons

1   tablespoon ground cumin
1   tablespoon paprika
2   teaspoons chipotle chile powder
1   teaspoon dried oregano

In cup, combine all ingredients. Store rub in tightly sealed container in a cool, dry place up to 6 months.

EACH TABLESPOON: About 25 calories, 1g protein, 3.5g carbohydrate, 1g total fat, 0mg cholesterol, 6mg sodium

Salt-Free Herb Rub

Use 1 tablespoon per pound of beef or pork, 2 teaspoons per pound of fish or chicken.

PREP: 5 minutes

MAKES: about ¼ cup

2   tablespoons dried rosemary
2   tablespoons dried thyme
1   tablespoon dried tarragon
1   tablespoon coarsely ground black pepper

In mortar with pestle, or with your fingers, crush together rosemary, thyme, tarragon, and pepper. Store rub in a cool, dry place up to 6 months.

EACH TEASPOON: About 5 calories, 0g protein, 1g carbohydrate, 0g total fat, 0mg cholesterol, 1mg sodium

Balsamic-Soy Glaze

Brush on beef, pork, chicken, or salmon during the last five minutes of grilling.

PREP: 1 minute   COOK: 2 minutes

MAKES: 6 tablespoons

2   tablespoons balsamic vinegar
2   tablespoons dark brown sugar
2   tablespoons soy sauce

In microwave-safe small bowl, stir vinegar, brown sugar, and soy sauce until blended. Cook, uncovered, in microwave oven on High 2 minutes, stirring once.

EACH TABLESPOON: About 25 calories, 0.5g protein, 6g carbohydrate, 0g total fat, 0mg cholesterol, 303mg sodium

Apricot-Ginger Glaze

Brush on poultry or pork during the last five minutes of grilling.

PREP: 1 minute   COOK: 30 seconds

MAKES: about ¼ cup

2   tablespoons apricot jam
2   tablespoons prepared horseradish
½   teaspoon ground ginger

In microwave-safe small bowl, stir together jam, horseradish, and ginger until blended. Cook, uncovered, in microwave oven on High 30 seconds, stirring once.

EACH TABLESPOON: About 30 calories, 0g protein, 7g carbohydrate, 0g total fat, 0mg cholesterol, 28mg sodium

Rubs, Marinades, and Glazes

Here are four ways to leave boring BBQ behind:

PREMADE SEASONING BLENDS

We sampled dozens in our test kitchens; some favorites are Thai, Cajun, jerk, and garam masala seasoning mixes, available in the spice aisle.

HOMEMADE RUBS

Check out the recipes in this chapter or use the ideas that follow as general guidelines, determining how much of which ingredient tastes best to you. Toss with shrimp or scallops or rub into the poultry or meat of your choice.

- Ground red pepper (cayenne), ground cumin, chili powder.

- Black pepper, ground coriander, ground cumin, crushed fennel seeds.

- Ground cinnamon, curry powder, brown sugar.

- Crumbled dried rosemary, dried thyme, dried oregano.

MARINADES

Whisk together in a large bowl; add steak, pork tenderloin, or chicken quarters and let stand fifteen minutes at room temperature before cooking.

- Grated, peeled fresh ginger; fresh lemon juice; soy sauce.

- Crumbled dried rosemary, minced garlic, red wine.

- Ground coriander, ground cumin, minced garlic, plain nonfat yogurt.

- Minced shallot, grainy mustard, red wine vinegar.

GLAZES

Whisk together in a small bowl, then brush over beef, pork, or poultry during the last few minutes the meat is on the grill.

- Crushed red pepper, ground ginger, balsamic vinegar, apricot jam.

- Chinese five-spice powder, fresh lime juice, honey.

- Chopped fresh cilantro leaves, pureed mango chutney.

- Sliced green onion, hoisin sauce, seasoned rice vinegar.

Hoisin and Five-Spice Glaze

Brush this on beef, pork, chicken, or salmon during the last 5 minutes of grilling.

PREP: 1 minute   **COOK:** 30 seconds
MAKES: about 6 tablespoons

¼   cup hoisin sauce
2   tablespoons soy sauce
1   teaspoon Chinese five-spice powder

In microwave-safe small bowl, stir together hoisin and soy sauces and five-spice powder. Cook, uncovered, in microwave oven on High 30 seconds, stirring once.

EACH TABLESPOON: About 28 calories, 1g protein, 5g carbohydrate, 0.5g total fat, 0.5mg cholesterol, 473mg sodium

Moroccan-Spice Glaze

Try this on lamb or chicken.

PREP: 2 minutes   **COOK:** 1 minute
MAKES: about ¼ cup

3   tablespoons honey
1   tablespoon fresh lemon juice
½   teaspoon ground cinnamon
½   teaspoon ground cumin

In microwave-safe small bowl, stir honey, lemon juice, cinnamon, and cumin until blended. Cook, uncovered, in microwave oven on High 1 minute, stirring once.

EACH TABLESPOON: About 50 calories, 0g protein, 14g carbohydrate, 0g total fat, 0mg cholesterol, 1mg sodium

Honey-Mustard Glaze

Perfect on salmon or chicken.

PREP: 1 minute   **COOK:** 30 seconds
MAKES: about ¼ cup

2   tablespoons stone-ground Dijon mustard
2   tablespoons honey
½   teaspoon dried thyme or 2 teaspoons minced fresh thyme

In microwave-safe small bowl, stir mustard, honey, and thyme until blended. Cook, uncovered, in microwave oven on High 30 seconds, stirring once.

EACH TABLESPOON: About 40 calories, 0g protein, 10g carbohydrate, 0g total fat, 0mg cholesterol, 180mg sodium

Soy Marinade

This wonderful combination of Asian flavors turns chicken or pork into a scrumptious supper with no muss, no fuss. Simply let the meat marinate at least one hour and as long as four hours, then grill.

PREP: 10 minutes

MAKES: about 1 cup

⅓	cup soy sauce
3	tablespoons seasoned rice vinegar
2	tablespoons packed brown sugar
2	tablespoons minced, peeled fresh ginger
1	tablespoon vegetable oil
2	garlic cloves, crushed with garlic press
2	green onions, thinly sliced
½	teaspoon Asian sesame oil
¼	teaspoon crushed red pepper

In medium bowl, stir together all ingredients.

EACH TABLESPOON: About 30 calories, 1g protein, 4g carbohydrate, 1g total fat (0g saturated), 0mg cholesterol, 530mg sodium

---

THE BEST WAY TO MARINATE

We love the ease of zip-tight plastic bags. Simply add the marinade ingredients, then the meat or poulty, and zip to seal. Squish the bag all around so the marinade covers the meat. Then put the bag on a plate in the fridge and turn occasionally. If you use a bowl or pan instead of a bag, be sure it's made of a noncorrosive material (glass, ceramic, or stainless steel) that won't be affected by the acid in the marinade.

To avoid contamination, never let marinade in which you've soaked raw meat, fish, or poultry (or the dish it's been in) come in contact with cooked food you'll be eating. Play it safe: Discard marinade after using or boil it for 1 minute to make a sauce; never reuse it for marinating.

■ If a recipe calls for basting with marinade, don't baste during the last ten minutes of grilling, so there's enough time for the marinade to cook through.

■ Don't marinate meat, poultry, or seafood longer than thirty minutes at room temperature. If the recipe calls for longer marinating, place in the refrigerator.

How long to marinate? For the best, fullest flavor, most meat and poultry need one to three hours; seafood, fifteen to thirty minutes. But timing also depends on the marinade ingredients: The more acidic the mixture—the greater the percentage of vinegar, lemon juice, yogurt—the less time needed to marinate. (Leaving meat or seafood in a highly acidic marinade for too long can alter the texture of the food and leave it unpleasantly mushy.) Marinades penetrate about ½ inch (from all sides), so don't expect really thick cuts of meat to pick up flavor in the center.

Trio of Creamy Burger Toppings

Who said ketchup was the only way to top your burger—or grilled chicken sandwich or fire-roasted veggie panini? Here is a trio of creamy, flavor-packed alternatives.

Horseradish-Mustard Mayo

PREP: 5 minutes

MAKES: about ¹/₂ cup

¼	cup light mayonnaise
1	tablespoon undrained prepared white horseradish
2	teaspoons stone-ground Dijon mustard

In small serving bowl, combine mayonnaise, horseradish, and mustard; stir until blended.

EACH TABLESPOON: About 45 calories, 0g protein, 1g carbohydrate, 4g total fat (1g saturated), 4mg cholesterol, 105mg sodium

Bacon-Chipotle Mayo

PREP: about 7 minutes

MAKES: about ¹/₃ cup

2	slices bacon
¼	cup light mayonnaise
1	teaspoon canned chipotle chile puree (adobo)

1. Place bacon between 2 paper towels on microwave-safe plate. Cook bacon in microwave on High 1¹/₂ to 2 minutes, until well browned. Cool bacon until crisp.

2. Crumble bacon; place in small serving bowl. Stir in mayonnaise and chile puree until blended.

EACH TABLESPOON: About 55 calories, 1g protein, 1g carbohydrate, 5g total fat (1g saturated), 6mg cholesterol, 135mg sodium

Grilled Onion–Thyme Mayo

PREP: 5 minutes   GRILL: 8 to 10 minutes

MAKES: about ¹/₂ cup

1	medium onion, cut crosswise into ½-inch-thick slices
¼	cup light mayonnaise
1	teaspoon fresh thyme leaves, chopped

1. Prepare outdoor grill for covered direct grilling over medium heat. Place onion slices on hot grill rack and cook until tender and browned on both sides, 8 to 10 minutes, turning over once.

2. Transfer onion to cutting board; coarsely chop. Place onion in small serving bowl; stir in mayonnaise and thyme until blended.

EACH TABLESPOON: About 30 calories, 0g protein, 2g carbohydrate, 3g total fat (1g saturated), 3mg cholesterol, 60mg sodium

Chimichurri Sauce

This tasty green sauce, thick with fresh herbs, is as common in Argentina as ketchup is in the United States. It can be prepared ahead and refrigerated up to two days. Drizzle it over meat and poultry—or toss with hot cooked pasta. You can even use it as a salad dressing.

PREP: **15 minutes**

MAKES: **about ¹/₂ cup**

1½ cups loosely packed fresh parsley leaves, finely chopped

1½ cups loosely packed fresh cilantro leaves, finely chopped

¼ cup olive oil

3 tablespoons red wine vinegar

1 garlic clove, crushed with garlic press

¼ teaspoon coarsely ground black pepper

¼ teaspoon salt

In small bowl, mix parsley, cilantro, oil, vinegar, garlic, pepper, and salt. Cover and refrigerate if not using right away.

EACH TABLESPOON: About 65 calories, 0g protein, 1g carbohydrate, 7g total fat (0g saturated), 0mg cholesterol, 70mg sodium

Chunky BBQ Sauce

Good on pork or chicken, this will keep in the refrigerator up to one week or in the freezer up to two months.

PREP: **10 minutes**   COOK: **17 to 18 minutes**

MAKES: **about 4 cups**

1 tablespoon vegetable oil

1 large onion, chopped

3 garlic cloves, minced

2 tablespoons minced, peeled fresh ginger

1 teaspoon ground cumin

1 can (14½ ounces) tomatoes in puree, chopped, puree reserved

1 bottle (12 ounces) chili sauce

¹/₃ cup cider vinegar

2 tablespoons brown sugar

2 tablespoons light (mild) molasses

2 teaspoons dry mustard

1 tablespoon cornstarch

2 tablespoons water

1. In 12-inch skillet, heat oil over medium heat. Add onion and cook, stirring occasionally, until tender, about 10 minutes. Add garlic and ginger and cook, stirring, 1 minute. Stir in cumin, tomatoes, puree, chili sauce, vinegar, sugar, molasses, and mustard; heat to boiling over high heat. Reduce heat to medium-high and cook, uncovered, 5 minutes, stirring occasionally.

2. In cup, mix cornstarch and water until blended. Stir mixture into sauce and cook until sauce boils and thickens, 1 to 2 minutes longer. Cover and refrigerate if not using right away.

EACH ¹/₂ CUP: About 120 calories, 2g protein, 25g carbohydrate, 2g total fat (0g saturated), 0mg cholesterol, 655mg sodium

Secret-Recipe BBQ Sauce

Pineapple adds tang to this slow-simmered sauce. Brush it over anything from chicken to hamburgers.

PREP: 15 minutes   COOK: about 37 minutes
MAKES: about 5 cups

1   tablespoon olive oil
1   large onion (12 ounces), chopped
2   tablespoons chopped, peeled fresh ginger
3   tablespoons chili powder
3   garlic cloves, crushed with garlic press
1   can (8 ounces) crushed pineapple in juice
1   can (28 ounces) crushed tomatoes in puree
⅓   cup ketchup
¼   cup cider vinegar
3   tablespoons dark brown sugar
3   tablespoons light (mild) molasses
2   teaspoons dry mustard
1   teaspoon salt

1. In 5- to 6-quart saucepot, heat oil over medium heat until hot. (Do not use a smaller pan; sauce bubbles up and splatters during cooking—the deeper the pan, the better.) Add onion and ginger; cook until onion is tender and golden, about 10 minutes, stirring occasionally. Add chili powder; cook, stirring, 1 minute. Add garlic and pineapple with its juice, and cook 1 minute longer.

2. Remove pot from heat. Stir in tomatoes with their puree, ketchup, vinegar, brown sugar, molasses, mustard, and salt. Spoon one-fourth of sauce into blender. At low speed, puree until smooth. Pour sauce into bowl; repeat with remaining sauce.

3. Return sauce to saucepot; heat to boiling over high heat. Reduce heat to medium-low and cook, partially covered, stirring occasionally, until reduced to about 5 cups, about 25 minutes.

4. Cover and refrigerate if not using right away. Sauce will keep up to 1 week in refrigerator or up to 2 months in freezer.

EACH 1 CUP: About 220 calories, 3g protein, 47g carbohydrate, 3g total fat (0g saturated), 0mg cholesterol, 960mg sodium

Asian Cucumber Salsa

This simple and refreshing salsa, with crisp cucumbers and fragrant mint, goes well with grilled chicken of any kind.

PREP: **15 minutes**

MAKES: **about 3 1/2 cups**

4	medium Kirby cucumbers (about 4 ounces each), unpeeled, each cut lengthwise into quarters, then crosswise into 1/4-inch-thick pieces
1	medium carrot, peeled and grated
1	cup loosely packed fresh mint leaves, chopped
1/4	cup seasoned rice vinegar

In medium bowl, place cucumbers, carrot, mint, and vinegar; toss to combine. If not serving right away, cover and refrigerate up to 1 day.

EACH 1/4 CUP: About 15 calories, 0g protein, 3g carbohydrate, 0g total fat, 0mg cholesterol, 135mg sodium

Horseradish Salsa

For a peppier salsa, add more horseradish.

PREP: **15 minutes**

MAKES: **about 2 cups**

3	ripe medium tomatoes (about 1 pound) cut into 1/2-inch pieces
1	cup loosely packed fresh parsley leaves, chopped
1/2	small red onion, minced
2	tablespoons bottled white horseradish
1	tablespoon balsamic vinegar
1	tablespoon olive oil
1/2	teaspoon salt

In medium bowl, place tomatoes, parsley, red onion, horseradish, vinegar, oil, and salt; toss to combine. Cover and refrigerate up to 2 hours.

EACH 1/4 CUP: About 35 calories, 1g protein, 4g carbohydrate, 2g total fat (0g saturated), 0mg cholesterol, 180mg sodium

Tomatillo Salsa

The tomatillo, sometimes called a Mexican green tomato, is actually related to the gooseberry. It has an acidic fruity flavor that is excellent with grilled meats and fish. For photo, see page 264.

PREP: 25 minutes plus chilling
MAKES: about 2 cups

1   pound fresh tomatillos (about 10 medium), husked, washed well, and cut into quarters

¾   cup loosely packed fresh cilantro leaves, chopped

¼   cup finely chopped onion

1 or 2 serrano or jalapeño chiles, seeded and minced

1   garlic clove, minced

1   tablespoon olive oil

1   teaspoon sugar

½   teaspoon salt

1. In food processor with knife blade attached, coarsely chop tomatillos.

2. In medium bowl, gently stir tomatillos, cilantro, onion, serranos, garlic, oil, sugar, and salt until well mixed. Cover and refrigerate at least 1 hour to blend flavors or up to 3 days.

EACH ¼ CUP: About 34 calories, 1g protein, 3g carbohydrate, 2g total fat (0g saturated), 0mg cholesterol, 146mg sodium

Orange-Chipotle Salsa

The sauce in canned chipotle chiles in adobo sauce adds a nice smoky note to salsas and grill sauces. If you don't have a can open, use chipotle hot sauce.

PREP: about 20 minutes
MAKES: about 1½ cups

3   medium navel oranges

2   plum tomatoes, seeded and chopped, or ¾ cup grape tomatoes, quartered

2   green onions, thinly sliced

1   tablespoon chopped fresh cilantro

½   teaspoon canned chipotle chile sauce or 1 teaspoon chipotle hot sauce

¼   teaspoon salt

1. From 1 orange, grate 1 teaspoon peel; place in medium bowl. Cut peel and white pith from all oranges. Holding oranges, 1 at a time, over bowl, cut on either side of membranes to remove each segment, allowing fruit and juice to drop into bowl. Discard seeds, if any. With kitchen shears, coarsely cut up orange segments.

2. To bowl with fruit, add tomatoes, green onions, cilantro, chipotle puree, and salt; stir to combine. Cover and refrigerate salsa up to 6 hours if not serving right away.

EACH ¼ CUP: About 40 calories, 1g protein, 10g carbohydrate, 0g total fat, 0mg cholesterol, 105mg sodium

Pineapple Salsa

Spiked with jalapeño and cilantro, this spicy-sweet fruit salsa turns simply grilled fish, pork, and chicken into a sensational meal.

PREP: 15 minutes

MAKES: about 4 cups

1	large lime
1	ripe pineapple, rind removed, cored, and coarsely chopped
1	cup loosely packed fresh cilantro leaves, chopped
1	jalapeño chile, seeded and minced
1	green onion, thinly sliced
1	teaspoon sugar
¼	teaspoon salt
⅛	teaspoon coarsely ground black pepper

1. From lime, grate ¹/₂ teaspoon peel and squeeze 2 tablespoons juice.

2. In medium bowl, mix lime peel and juice with pineapple, cilantro, jalapeño, green onion, sugar, salt, and pepper. If not serving right away, cover and refrigerate up to 4 hours.

EACH ¼ CUP: About 20 calories, 0g protein, 5g carbohydrate, 0g total fat, 0mg cholesterol, 35mg sodium

Grapefruit Salsa

The pucker of grapefruit, the sweetness of orange, and heat of hot chile make this a great choice for any rich-tasting protein—try it with grilled pork or turkey.

PREP: about 20 minutes

MAKES: about 3 cups

3	pink grapefruit
1	navel orange
1	serrano or jalapeño chile, seeded and minced
1	green onion, thinly sliced
2	tablespoons chopped fresh basil
¼	teaspoon salt

1. Cut peel and white pith from grapefruit and orange. Holding fruit, 1 at a time, over medium bowl, cut on either side of membranes to remove each segment, allowing fruit and juice to drop into bowl. Discard seeds, if any. With kitchen shears, coarsely cut up grapefruit and orange segments.

2. To bowl with fruit, add chile, green onion, basil, and salt; stir to combine. If not serving right away, cover and refrigerate up to 6 hours.

EACH ¼ CUP: About 25 calories, 1g protein, 6g carbohydrate, 0g total fat, 0mg cholesterol, 55mg sodium

Melon Salsa

Try this with grilled pork or poultry.

PREP: 15 minutes
MAKES: about 4 cups

2   cups diced (¼-inch), peeled cantaloupe
2   cups diced (¼-inch), peeled honeydew melon
2   tablespoons fresh lemon juice
2   tablespoons chopped fresh cilantro
¼   teaspoon salt

In medium bowl, stir together cantaloupe, honeydew, lemon juice, cilantro, and salt until mixed. If not serving right away, cover and refrigerate up to 4 hours.

EACH ¼ CUP: About 15 calories, 0g protein, 4g carbohydrate, 0g total fat, 0mg cholesterol, 40mg sodium

Peach Salsa

Be patient. Wait until it is the height of peach season to make this sweet-hot salsa. Spoon over grilled chicken breasts or pork chops. For photo, see page 264.

PREP: 30 minutes plus chilling
MAKES: about 3 cups

1¾ pounds ripe peaches (5 medium), peeled, pitted, and chopped
2   tablespoons finely chopped red onion
1   tablespoon chopped mint
1   teaspoon seeded, minced jalapeño chile
1   tablespoon fresh lime juice
⅛   teaspoon salt

In medium bowl, gently stir peaches, onion, mint, jalapeño, lime juice, and salt until well mixed. Cover and refrigerate 1 hour to blend flavors or up to 2 days.

EACH ¼ CUP: About 23 calories, 0g protein, 6g carbohydrate, 0g total fat, 0mg cholesterol, 25mg sodium

Fire-Roasted Tomato Salsa

Serve this wonderfully smoky, spicy dip with tortilla chips. For photo, see page 264.

PREP: **15 minutes**　GRILL: **about 8 minutes**
MAKES: **about 3 cups**

1	recipe Grilled Plum Tomatoes (page 261)
1	large jalapeño chile
¼	cup minced red onion
⅓	cup chopped fresh cilantro
¼	cup fresh lime juice
¾	teaspoon salt

1. Prepare Grilled Plum Tomatoes.

2. While tomatoes are grilling, place whole jalapeño on same rack and grill, turning occasionally, until skin is charred and blistered, about 8 minutes. Transfer jalapeño to cutting board; set aside until cool enough to handle.

3. Remove stem, skin, and seeds from jalapeño; discard. Finely chop jalapeño. Chop tomatoes.

4. In large bowl, combine jalapeño, tomatoes with their juices, onion, cilantro, lime juice, and salt. If not serving right away, cover and refrigerate up to 3 hours.

EACH ¼ CUP: About 40 calories, 1g protein, 4g carbohydrate, 3g total fat (0g saturated), 0mg cholesterol, 250mg sodium

Southwest Corn Salsa

Toss fresh summer corn kernels with bold Southwestern flavors and a splash of lime for a delicious accompaniment to grilled chicken.

PREP: **15 minutes**
MAKES: **about 4 cups**

2	limes
4	cups fresh corn kernels (cut from about 8 ears)
⅓	cup finely chopped red pepper
1	jalapeño chile, seeded and minced
1	green onion, thinly sliced
½	cup loosely packed fresh cilantro leaves, chopped
½	teaspoon salt
⅛	teaspoon coarsely ground black pepper
⅛	teaspoon ground cumin

From limes, grate ½ teaspoon peel and squeeze 3 tablespoons juice; place in medium bowl. Add corn, red pepper, jalapeño, green onion, cilantro, salt, pepper, and cumin; toss well to combine. If not serving right away, cover and refrigerate up to 12 hours.

EACH ¼ CUP: About 35 calories, 1g protein, 8g carbohydrate, 0g total fat, 8mg cholesterol, 80mg sodium

Mango-Kiwi Salsa

The combination of mango and kiwifruit gives this salsa its sweet and tangy flavor. Try substituting chopped pitted fresh cherries and a diced yellow pepper for the mango and kiwi.

PREP: 15 minutes

MAKES: about 4 cups

2   ripe mangoes, peeled, pitted, and coarsely chopped
2   medium kiwifruit, peeled and coarsely chopped
3   tablespoons seasoned rice vinegar
1   tablespoon grated, peeled fresh ginger
1   tablespoon minced fresh cilantro

In medium bowl, combine mangoes, kiwifruit, vinegar, ginger, and cilantro. If not serving right away, cover and refrigerate up to 12 hours.

EACH ¼ CUP: About 25 calories, 0g protein, 6g carbohydrate, 0g total fat, 0mg cholesterol, 60mg sodium

MANGOES MADE EASY

1. With a sharp knife, cut a lengthwise slice down each side as close to the long seed as possible; set aside the section containing the seed.

2. Deeply score the flesh of each mango half into a crosshatch without cutting through the skin, then gently push out the skin so that the flesh stands out in rows of cubes. Eat the cubes directly from the skin or cut them off with a paring knife.

3. You can also peel the mango skin from the cut-off halves as if you are cutting a grapefruit: Insert a small, sharp knife between skin and flesh. Pull the cut skin back to expose the flesh, then run the knife along the rounded part of the mango to release it from the skin. Dice or slice as desired.

Guacamole

Great with fajitas, grilled pork, or grilled chicken.

PREP: 20 minutes

MAKES: about 3 cups

2   ripe medium avocados (about 8 ounces each), peeled, pitted, and cut into 1-inch chunks (see Tip)

2   ripe medium tomatoes (6 to 8 ounces each), coarsely chopped

1   jalapeño chile, seeded and minced

1   cup loosely packed fresh cilantro leaves, chopped

1   tablespoon fresh lime juice

½   teaspoon salt

In medium bowl, gently stir avocados, tomatoes, jalapeño, cilantro, lime juice, and salt until mixed. If not serving right away, cover and refrigerate up to 4 hours.

EACH TABLESPOON: About 15 calories, 0g protein, 1g carbohydrate, 1g total fat (0g saturated), 0mg cholesterol, 25mg sodium

> **TIP:** To ripen a hard avocado, place it in a paper bag at room temperature for two days, until it yields to gentle pressure when you squeeze it lightly. (Putting an apple or banana in the bag speeds up the process.) Once ripe, avocados can be stored in the refrigerator for a few days.

Cucumber Relish

This is delicious with saté (pages 31–32) or served alongside grilled fish.

PREP: 10 minutes

MAKES: about 2 ½ cups

4   medium Kirby cucumbers (about 4 ounces each), cut into ¼-inch pieces

¼   cup seasoned rice vinegar

2   tablespoons chopped red onion

1   tablespoon vegetable oil

¼   teaspoon crushed red pepper

In medium bowl, with spoon, combine cucumbers, vinegar, onion, oil, and crushed red pepper. If not serving right away, cover and refrigerate up to 2 hours.

EACH ¼ CUP: about 25 calories, 0g protein, 3g carbohydrate, 1g total fat (0g saturated), 0mg cholesterol, 120mg sodium

Desserts on Fire

Yes, you can grill your dessert. Your guests (and your family) will be surprised and delighted to see you serving dessert hot off the grill. And you'll enjoy the change of routine—instead of baking indoors, you can whip up something sweet and satisfying outdoors, without leaving your guests.

Grilled fruit is the star in most of these desserts, so along with recipes for Grilled Peach Melba, Honeyed Hot Fruit Salad, and Fire-Roasted Nectarines, you'll find tips on selecting juicy ripe pineapples and peaches. With Toasted Angel Cake with Summer Berries, you can have your cake and grill it, too. And finally, there is pizza for dessert—Chocolate, Hazelnut, and Banana Pizza, to be specific. Enjoy it all!

Fire-Roasted Nectarines, page 289

Honeyed Hot Fruit Salad

A few turns on the grill transform fresh fruit into a sumptuous finale.

PREP: **15 minutes**   GRILL: **10 to 15 minutes**
MAKES: **6 servings**

½   cup honey

1   tablespoon fresh lemon juice

¼   cup loosely packed fresh mint leaves, thinly sliced

1   medium pineapple, cut lengthwise into 6 wedges, with leaves attached

2   large bananas, each peeled and cut diagonally into thirds

3   medium plums, each cut in half and pitted

2   medium nectarines or peaches, each cut into quarters and pitted

1. Prepare outdoor grill for direct grilling over medium heat.

2. In cup, stir together honey, lemon juice, and 1 tablespoon sliced mint.

3. With tongs, place fruit pieces on hot grill rack and grill, turning fruit occasionally and brushing it with honey mixture during last 3 minutes of cooking, until browned and tender, 10 to 15 minutes.

4. To serve, arrange grilled fruit on large platter; drizzle with any remaining honey mixture. Sprinkle with remaining mint.

EACH SERVING: About 215 calories, 2g protein, 55g carbohydrate, 1g total fat (0g saturated), 0mg cholesterol, 5mg sodium

---

PINEAPPLE PRIMER

Once you know how to select and cut a pineapple, it graduates from being an intimidating fruit to a great light dessert option. It's fat-free, and 1 cup of fresh chunks contains just 80 calories and 40 percent of your daily vitamin C requirement.

CHOOSING A SWEETIE

Once a pineapple is harvested, it won't get any sweeter. Growers don't pick it until it's juicy and ripe but firm. (If picked when too ripe and soft, it could spoil before distribution.) When you shop, smell the fruit—it should have a sweet floral aroma (less pronounced when the fruit is cold). Choose one that's firm and heavy, with fresh green leaves. Don't buy a pineapple with bruises or soft spots—especially at the base. At home, refrigerate it whole or cut for three to five days; for softer, juicier fruit, store whole at room temperature for up to five days.

GET TO THE HEART OF THE MATTER

1. After cutting off the crown and stem ends with a sharp chef's knife, hold the pineapple upright and cut the skin off in long pieces, slicing from top to base.

2. To remove the "eyes," lay the pineapple on its side. Cut in at an angle on either side of a row of eyes, inserting the knife into fruit about ¼ inch, and lift out the row. Repeat with next row.

3. Cut the pineapple lengthwise into quarters, slicing straight down from the crown to stem end. Hold each quarter upright and cut off the tough core along the center edge, then cut the fruit as directed in the recipe.

Buttermilk Ice Cream with Grilled Peaches

Homemade ice cream and brandied, brown-sugar-glazed, summer-ripe peaches hot off the grill? A match made in heaven!

PREP: 30 minutes   **GRILL:** 5 to 6 minutes
MAKES: 6 servings

BUTTERMILK ICE CREAM

1½ cups heavy or whipping cream
4   large egg yolks
⅛   teaspoon salt
1   cup packed light brown sugar
1   cup buttermilk
6   ounces cream cheese, softened
2   teaspoons red wine vinegar

GRILLED PEACHES

¼   cup packed light brown sugar
2   tablespoons brandy
1   tablespoon fresh lemon juice
1   teaspoon ground cinnamon
3   ripe medium peaches, each cut in half and pitted
1   teaspoon butter
⅓   cup slivered almonds

1. Prepare ice cream: In microwave-safe 2-cup liquid measuring cup, heat cream in microwave oven on High 1 minute or until hot but not boiling, stirring once. In 2-quart saucepan, whisk egg yolks, salt, and ½ cup brown sugar until combined. Gradually whisk in hot cream. Cook over medium-low heat until mixture thickens slightly and coats the back of a spoon, 7 to 8 minutes, stirring constantly (do not boil). Remove from heat; whisk in buttermilk.

2. In large bowl, with mixer at medium speed, beat cream cheese and remaining ½ cup brown sugar until smooth, about 1 minute. Whisk hot cream mixture and vinegar into cream-cheese mixture until blended. Cover and refrigerate until cold, at least 4 hours or overnight.

3. Freeze buttermilk mixture in ice cream maker as manufacturer directs. Scoop into covered container and freeze until firm, at least 2 hours or overnight. Makes about 3⅔ cups.

4. Prepare peaches: In large zip-tight plastic bag, combine brown sugar, brandy, lemon juice, and cinnamon. Seal bag and turn to mix. Add peaches; seal bag, pressing out excess air. Let stand 30 minutes at room temperature or up to 2 hours in refrigerator to blend flavors.

5. In small skillet, melt butter over medium heat. Add almonds and cook until toasted, 3 to 5 minutes, stirring frequently. Set aside.

6. Prepare outdoor grill for covered direct grilling over medium heat. Place peach halves, cut sides down, on hot grill rack. Cover grill and cook until cut sides are browned, 5 to 6 minutes, turning over once. If not serving right away, transfer peaches to plate; let stand at room temperature up to 2 hours.

7. To serve, scoop ⅓ cup ice cream into each of 6 dessert bowls and top each serving with a peach half. Sprinkle with almonds.

EACH SERVING: About 490 calories, 7g protein, 47g carbohydrate, 32g total fat (17g saturated), 196mg cholesterol, 175mg sodium

Fire-Roasted Nectarines

Grilling intensifies the fruit's flavors, creating a sweet-and-smoky succulence. Garnish with a simple salsa of blueberries, strawberries, and raspberries.

PREP: **20 minutes**   GRILL: **5 minutes**
MAKES: **2 servings**

2   cups strawberries (8 to 10 ounces), hulled and coarsely chopped

½   cup raspberries

⅓   cup blueberries

2   tablespoons sugar

2   teaspoons finely chopped crystallized ginger

1   teaspoon fresh lemon juice

pinch salt

4   ripe medium nectarines, each cut in half and pitted

nonstick cooking spray

1. Prepare salsa: In medium bowl, mix strawberries, raspberries, blueberries, sugar, ginger, lemon juice, and salt. Set aside. Makes 2 cups.

2. Prepare outdoor grill for direct grilling over medium heat. Spray cut sides of nectarine halves with nonstick cooking spray. Place on hot grill grate and cook 5 to 6 minutes or until lightly charred and tender, turning over once.

3. To serve, in each of 4 dessert bowls, place 2 nectarine halves, cut sides up, and top with berry salsa.

EACH SERVING: About 130 calories, 2g protein, 32g carbohydrate, 1g total fat (0g saturated), 5g fiber, 0mg cholesterol, 35mg sodium

> **Tip:** No access to an outdoor grill? Nectarines can be cooked indoors on a ridged grill pan. Spray the pan with nonstick cooking spray and heat on medium until hot, then grill nectarines as directed.

Grilled Peach Melba

Try this with nectarines or apricots; top with frozen yogurt and strawberry sauce.

PREP: 5 minutes   GRILL: 5 to 6 minutes
MAKES: 4 servings

2   ripe large peaches, each cut in half and pitted
½   pint raspberries
1   tablespoon sugar
1½   cups vanilla ice cream

1. Prepare outdoor grill for direct grilling over medium heat.

2. Place peach halves on hot grill rack and cook until lightly charred and tender, 5 to 6 minutes, turning over once.

3. Meanwhile, prepare sauce: In bowl, with fork, mash half the raspberries with sugar. Stir in remaining raspberries.

4. To serve, place a peach half in each of 4 dessert bowls; top with ice cream and raspberry sauce.

EACH SERVING: About 160 calories, 2g protein, 22g carbohydrate, 8g total fat (5g saturated), 26mg cholesterol, 25mg sodium

PEACH PRIMER
Tree-ripe peaches are a pure pleasure. These tips will help you get the most out of them:

SELECT THE BEST
■ Buy peaches at their peak. Varieties grown at local orchards may be available from April to October, but are unsurpassed in July and August.

■ The skin and flesh should range from light pinkish white to reddish yellow (the amount of reddish pink skin is determined by the variety and is not an indicator of ripeness). Skip fruit with hints of green; this usually means it was picked too early and won't be sweet.

■ If you are planning to eat your peaches right away, choose soft (not mushy), fragrant ones that aren't bruised. If you want to save them for a few days, select fruit that is fairly firm but yields slightly when pressed along the seam.

■ Guidelines for recipes: 1 pound equals 2 large or 3 medium ones, 2 cups peeled and sliced, 1²/₃ cups peeled and diced, or 1½ cups peeled and pureed.

STORING YOUR RICHES
■ To ripen hard peaches, place them in a closed paper bag at room temperature for a few days; adding an apple or banana will speed up the process.

■ Once your peaches are ripe, they will keep in the refrigerator for up to five days. Just be sure to bring them to room temperature before eating.

■ A cut peach will quickly darken. Preserve its color by squeezing on lemon or lime juice.

Chocolate, Hazelnut, and Banana Pizza

Surprise your guests with the perfect ending to a summer buffet on the patio—a dessert pizza!

PREP: 20 minutes   **GRILL: 5 minutes**
MAKES: 8 servings

1   pound fresh or frozen (thawed) pizza dough
½   cup chocolate-hazelnut spread (like Nutella)
1   ripe large bananas, peeled and thinly sliced

1. Prepare outdoor grill for covered, direct grilling over medium-low heat.

2. Cut dough into 4 equal pieces. On one end of oiled cookie sheet, flatten 1 piece dough to about ¹/₈-inch thickness. (Edge does not need to be even.) On same cookie sheet, repeat with another piece of dough. Repeat with a second oiled cookie sheet and remaining dough.

3. Place all 4 pieces of dough, oiled side down, on hot grill rack. Cook until grill marks appear on underside (dough will stiffen and puff), 2 to 3 minutes.

4. With tongs, turn crusts over and remove to a work surface. Working quickly, spread one-fourth of chocolate-hazelnut spread, leaving ¹/₈-inch border, over each crust. Return to the grill, cover, and cook pizzas until undersides are evenly browned and cooked through, 3 to 4 minutes longer.

5. Transfer to cutting board; arrange the sliced bananas over pizzas. Cut into wedges.

EACH SERVING: About 215 calories, 5g protein, 38g carbohydrate, 7g total fat (0.5g saturated fat), 0mg cholesterol, 204mg sodium

Toasted Angel Cake with Summer Berries

Serve golden wedges of cake with sun-ripened berries and brown-sugar whipped cream. Try with grilled pound cake slices, too!

PREP: 10 minutes   **GRILL:** about 1 minute
MAKES: 6 servings

1	pint strawberries, hulled and cut into quarters
1	cup blueberries
3	tablespoons light brown sugar
½	cup heavy or whipping cream
1	teaspoon vanilla extract
1	store-bought angel food cake (12 ounces)

1. Prepare outdoor grill for direct grilling over medium heat.

2. In medium bowl, toss berries with 1 tablespoon brown sugar; set aside.

3. In small bowl, with mixer at medium speed, beat cream and vanilla until soft peaks form when beaters are lifted. Gradually add remaining 2 tablespoons brown sugar and beat until stiff peaks form. Cover and refrigerate.

4. Cut cake into 6 wedges. Place cake on hot grill rack over medium heat and toast, turning once, until golden on both sides, about 1 minute.

5. To serve, place cake on dessert plates; top each wedge with berry mixture, then a dollop of whipped cream.

EACH SERVING: About 270 calories, 4g protein, 47g carbohydrate, 8g total fat (5g saturated), 27mg cholesterol, 435mg sodium

Metric Equivalents

The recipes in this book use the standard United States method for measuring liquid and dry or solid ingredients (teaspoons, tablespoons, and cups). The information on this chart is provided to help cooks outside the U.S. successfully use these recipes. All equivalents are approximate.

METRIC EQUIVALENTS FOR DIFFERENT TYPES OF INGREDIENTS

A standard cup measure of a dry or solid ingredient will vary in weight depending on the type of ingredient. A standard cup of liquid is the same volume for any type of liquid. Use the following chart when converting standard cup measures to grams (weight) or milliliters (volume).

Standard Cup	Fine Powder (e.g., flour)	Grain (e.g., rice)	Granular (e.g., sugar)	Liquid Solids (e.g., butter)	Liquid (e.g., milk)
1	140 g	150 g	190 g	200 g	240 ml
3/4	105 g	113 g	143 g	150 g	180 ml
2/3	93 g	100 g	125 g	133 g	160 ml
1/2	70 g	75 g	95 g	100 g	120 ml
1/3	47 g	50 g	63 g	67 g	80 ml
1/4	35 g	38 g	48 g	50 g	60 ml
1/8	18 g	19 g	24 g	25 g	30 ml

COOKING / OVEN TEMPERATURES

	Fahrenheit	Celsius	Gas Mark
Freeze water	32° F	0° C	
Room temperature	68° F	20° C	
Boil water	212° F	100° C	
Bake	325° F	160° C	3
	350° F	180° C	4
	375° F	190° C	5
	400° F	200° C	6
	425° F	220° C	7
	450° F	230° C	8
Broil			Grill

LIQUID INGREDIENTS BY VOLUME

1/4 tsp	=			1 ml
1/2 tsp	=			2 ml
1 tsp	=			5 ml
3 tsp	=	1 tblsp	= 1/2 fl oz	= 15 ml
2 tblsp	= 1/8 cup	= 1 fl oz		= 30 ml
4 tblsp	= 1/4 cup	= 2 fl oz		= 60 ml
5 1/3 tblsp	= 1/3 cup	= 3 fl oz		= 80 ml
8 tblsp	= 1/2 cup	= 4 fl oz		= 120 ml
10 2/3 tblsp	= 2/3 cup	= 5 fl oz		= 160 ml
12 tblsp	= 3/4 cup	= 6 fl oz		= 180 ml
16 tblsp	= 1 cup	= 8 fl oz		= 240 ml
1 pt	= 2 cups	= 16 fl oz		= 480 ml
1 qt	= 4 cups	= 32 fl oz		= 960 ml
		33 fl oz		= 1000 ml

DRY INGREDIENTS BY WEIGHT

(To convert ounces to grams, multiply the number of ounces by 30.)

1 oz	=	1/16 lb	=	30 g
4 oz	=	1/4 lb	=	120 g
8 oz	=	1/2 lb	=	240 g
12 oz	=	3/4 lb	=	360 g
16 oz	=	1 lb	=	480 g

LENGTH

(To convert inches to centimeters, multiply the number of inches by 2.5.)

1 in	=		2.5 cm
6 in	= 1/2 ft =		15 cm
12 in	= 1 ft =		30 cm
36 in	= 3 ft	= 1 yd =	90 cm
40 in	=		100 cm = 1 m

Photography Credits

Front Cover: Ian Garlick/Getty Images
Spine: Thomas Barwick/Getty Images
Back Cover: James Baigrie

Antonis Achilleos: 5, 50, 94, 155, 174, 204

James Baigrie: 36, 48, 56, 61, 62, 68, 101, 108, 170, 179, 180, 201, 222, 223, 284, 291, 292

Courtesy of www.barbecue-store.com: 15

Mary Ellen Bartley: 74, 76 (both photos)

Monica Buck: 91

Courtesy of CHEFScatalog.com: 19 bottom

Courtesy of The Coleman Company: 18

Tara Donne: 59, 132, 185, 207, 210, 237

Miki Duisterhof: 147

Getty Images: James Baigrie: 275; Brian Hagiwara: 19 top; Alison Miksch/Food Pix: 282

Brian Hagiwara: 6, 17, 20, 47, 51, 52, 66, 71, 92, 103, 105, 131, 136, 145, 152, 159, 161, 169, 189, 193, 209, 216, 221, 229 (all photos), 232, 238, 255, 264

Lisa Hubbard: 198

iStockphoto: 256

Frances Janisch: 72, 83, 86, 89, 272

Courtesy of Kitchenkaboodle.com: 12 bottom

Rita Maas: 26

Kate Mathis: 25, 79

Alan Richardson: 44, 49, 110, 158, 164, 167, 195, 250, 258, 287, 293

Courtesy of Sears: 14

Kate Sears: 35, 42, 122

Courtesy of The Sharper Image: 16

Shutterstock: 28, 39, 45, 85, 102, 112, 125, 139, 142, 150, 156, 171, 177, 181, 187, 200, 202, 218, 226, 236, 244, 267, 289; Teresa Azevedo: 82, 273; Gualberto Becerra: 12 top; Jacek Chabraszewski: 119; Norman Chan: 65, 134; Dusty Cline: 10; Fribus Ekaterina: 81; Freddy Eliasson: 261; Irina Fischer: 225; Stephen Folkes: 88; Eric Gevaert: 133 left, 173; Insuratelu Gabriela Gianina: 246; Raymond Gregory: 75; Karen Grigoryan: 141 top; Mark Herreid: 107; HLPhoto: 203; Lasse Kristensen: 271; Hao Liang: 262; Robyn Mackenzie: 276; Viktar Malyshchyts: 281 left; Dimitry Melnikov: 118; Olga Miltsova: 270; Elena Moiseeva: 166, 228; Werner Muenzker: 27; Nayashkova Olga: 269; Francesco Ridolfi: 117; Yuliya Rusyayeva: 99; Anna Sedneva: 58; Alex Staroseltsev: 133 right; Valentyn Volkov: 197; Tomasz Wieja: 141 bottom; Feng Yu: 279; Dusan Zidar: 212

Ann Stratton: 22, 183, 243, 281 (right three photos)

Mark Thomas: 2, 115

Veer: Alloy Photography: 11

Courtesy of Weber-Stephen Products Co.: 13

Index

The Good Housekeeping Triple-Test Promise

At Good Housekeeping, we want to make sure that every recipe we print works in any oven, with any brand of ingredient, no matter what. That's why, in our test kitchens at the Good Housekeeping Research Institute, we go all out: We test each recipe at least three times—and, often, several more times after that.

When a recipe is first developed, one member of our team prepares the dish and we judge it on these criteria: It must be delicious, family-friendly, healthy, and easy to make.

1. The recipe is then tested several more times to fine-tune the flavor and ease of preparation, always by the same team member, using the same equipment.

2. Next, another team member follows the recipe as written, varying the brands of ingredients and kinds of equipment. Even the types of stoves we use are changed.

3. A third team member repeats the whole process using yet another set of equipment and alternative ingredients.

By the time the recipes appear on these pages, they are guaranteed to work in any kitchen, including yours. WE PROMISE.